SOCIETY AND CULTURE IN THE
SLAVE SOUTH

0415070554

REWRITING HISTORIES
Series editor: Jack R. Censer

THE INDUSTRIAL REVOLUTION AND WORK IN
NINETEENTH-CENTURY EUROPE
Edited by Lenard R. Berlanstein

GENDER AND AMERICAN HISTORY SINCE 1890
Edited by Barbara Melosh

ATLANTIC AMERICAN SOCIETIES
From Columbus through Abolition
Edited by J. R. McNeill and Alan Karras

NAZISM AND GERMAN SOCIETY 1933–1945
Edited by David Crew

DIVERSITY AND UNITY IN EARLY NORTH AMERICA
Edited by P. Morgan

SOCIETY AND CULTURE IN THE SLAVE SOUTH

Edited by
J. William Harris

London and New York

First published 1992
by Routledge
11 New Fetter Lane, London EC4P 4EE

Simultaneously published in the USA and Canada
by Routledge
a division of Routledge, Chapman and Hall, Inc.
29 West 35th Street, New York, NY 10001

Typeset in 10 on 12 point Palatino by
Intype, London
Printed in Great Britain by
T J Press (Padstow) Ltd, Padstow, Cornwall

British Library Cataloguing in Publication Data
Society and Culture in the Slave South.
(Rewriting History Series)
I. Harris, J. William II. Series
975

Library of Congress Cataloging in Publication Data
Society and culture in the slave South / edited by J. William Harris
p. cm. — (Re-writing histories)
Includes bibliographical references and index.
1. Southern States—Social conditions. 2. Southern States—Economic
conditions. 3. Slavery—Southern States. 4. Slavery—Economic
aspects—Southern States. 5. Women—Southern States—Psychology.
6. Slaves—Southern States—Psychology. I. Harris, J. William,
II. Series.
HN79.A13S36 1993
306′.0975–dc20 92–8841

ISBN 0–415–07054–6 ISBN 0–415–07055–4 (pbk)

Cover illustration reproduced courtesy of the Senate House Library,
University of London.

CONTENTS

CONTENTS

Part III Women and men

vi

EDITOR'S PREFACE

Rewriting history, or revisionism, has always followed closely in the tow of history writing. In their efforts to re-evaluate the past, professional as well as amateur scholars have followed many approaches, most commonly as empiricists, uncovering new information to challenge earlier accounts. Historians have also revised previous versions by adopting new perspectives, usually fortified by new research, which overturn received views.

Even though rewriting is constantly taking place, historians' attitudes towards using new interpretations have been anything but settled. For most, the validity of revisionism lies in providing a stronger, more convincing account that better captures the objective truth of the matter. Although such historians might agree that we never finally arrive at the 'truth', they believe it exists and over time may be better and better approximated. At the other extreme stand scholars who believe that each generation or even each cultural group or subgroup necessarily regards the past differently, each creating for itself a more usable history. Although these latter scholars do not reject the possibility of demonstrating empirically that some contentions are better than other, they focus upon generating new views based upon different life experiences. Different truths exist for different groups. Surely such an understanding, by emphasizing subjectivity, further encourages rewriting history. Between these two groups are those historians who wish to borrow from both sides. This third group, while accepting that every congeries of individuals sees matters differently, still wishes somewhat contradictorily to fashion a broader history that incorporates both of these particular visions.

Revisionists who stress empiricism fall into the first of the three camps, while others spread out across the board.

Today the rewriting of history seems to have accelerated to a blinding speed as a consequence of the evolution of revisionism. A variety of approaches has emerged. A major factor in this process has been the enormous increase in the number of researchers. This explosion has reinforced and enabled the retesting of many assertions. Significant ideological shifts have also played a major part in the growth of revisionism. First, the crisis of Marxism, culminating in the events in eastern Europe in 1989, has given rise to doubts about explicitly Marxist accounts. Such doubts have spilled over into the entire field of social history which has been a dominant subfield of the discipline for several decades. Focusing on society and its class divisions implied that these are the most important elements in historical analysis. Because Marxism was built on the same claim, the whole basis of social history has been questioned, despite the very many studies that had little directly to do with Marxism. Disillusionment with social history simultaneously opened the door to cultural and linguistic approaches largely developed in anthropology and literature. Multiculturalism and feminism further generated revisionism. By claiming that scholars had, wittingly or not, operated from a white European/ American male point of view, newer researchers argued other approaches had been neglected or misunderstood. Not surprisingly, these last historians are the most likely to envision each subgroup rewriting its own usable history, while other scholars incline towards revisionism as part of the search for some stable truth.

Rewriting Histories will make these new approaches available to the student population. Often new scholarly debates take place in the scattered issues of journals which are sometimes difficult to find. Furthermore, in these first interactions, historians tend to address one another, leaving out the evidence that would make their arguments more accessible to the uninitiated. This series of books will collect in one place a strong group of the major articles in selected fields, adding notes and introductions conducive to improved understanding. Editors will select articles containing substantial historical data, so that students – at least those who approach the subject as an objective phenomenon – can advance, not only their comprehension of debated points, but also their grasp of substantive aspects of the subject.

Marxism, under assault elsewhere, has survived well in the study of the slave South largely, as J. William Harris points out, because of the influence of Eugene Genovese and Elizabeth Fox-Genovese. Appropriately, since work on the history of slavery helped to launch the 'new economic history,' advanced work by economists has in this field been in the forefront of revisionism. As in other areas, however, the influences from students of gender and from cultural anthropologists have made themselves felt, and these have also begun to transform our understanding of the history of slavery.

Jack R. Censer

INTRODUCTION

For the past twenty-five years the Old South in the United States has been the focus of some of the most interesting, innovative, and influential historical scholarship. In addition to the continuing vigor of old debates, both established and younger scholars are producing exciting work in the study of culture and the interaction of gender, race, and class in the Old South. The essays presented here include some of this diverse scholarship and introduce some of the central debates about the nature of society and culture in the Old South. They also offer some outstanding examples of current methodological and theoretical models available to historians.

I

A brief consideration of the historiography on slavery and the Old South is helpful for a full understanding of current debates. We may begin with the work of Ulrich B. Phillips, whose work dominated the historiography of US slavery in the first half of the twentieth century. Phillips was a scholar of great range and fine style, and it is understandable that his deeply researched work found great influence.[1] At the same time, Phillips's works were profoundly flawed by his racist assumptions about blacks. While Phillips did not totally repress all evidence of the cruelties of slavery, he argued that the system in the Old South was, by comparison with ancient Roman slavery, "essentially mild," and that slave plantations were "on the whole . . . the best schools yet invented for the mass training of that sort of inert and backward people which the bulk of the American negroes represented."[2] Vigorous

1

dissent from black scholars failed to have much impact on the general acceptance of Phillips's interpretation of the slave South.

It should not be necessary to explain in detail why such interpretation of the Old South eventually lost its influence. As racial attitudes of scholars (and, of course, others) changed, so did their understandings of slavery. Attacks on Phillips's assumptions and evidence mounted, and in 1956 Kenneth Stampp published a new and comprehensive study of slavery, *The Peculiar Institution*. Stampp, like Phillips, was thoroughly at home with the documentary evidence on slavery. He stated at the outset his assumption that "Negroes are, after all, only white men with black skins, nothing more, nothing less." Stampp portrayed slave masters not as kindly paternalists, but as businessmen in an essentially dirty business. They ruled primarily by force and fear. The consequences for black slaves were indeed fearful, including a stripping away of their African culture without having it replaced by anything else substantial. "The Negro," therefore, "existed in a kind of cultural void . . . more or less in a bleak and narrow world." Three years later, Stanley Elkins, in another influential study, went even further in arguing that slaves in the US had been psychologically infantilized by the slave experience, in effect turned into the "Sambos" depicted by apologists of slavery like Phillips.[3]

II

The work of Stampp and Elkins proved to be but the beginning of a sustained outpouring of research and writing on the slave South that has continued to this day. A number of developments in the 1960s helped to spark this research. Perhaps most important was the reassessment of black history that accompanied the rise of the Civil Rights Movement and the subsequent growth of black nationalism. This reexamination of black history took several forms – a determination to see slaves as more than helpless victims of their own history, a greater awareness of evidence in the past of the kinds of pride and courage that were so prominent among black Civil Rights activists, a search for the origins of what some saw as a separate African–American culture in the United States. Thus this scholarship often included explicit rejection of the arguments of Stampp and Elkins about the effects of slavery. The scholarship of the period was marked not only by new attitudes but by the use of sources and evidence that had been previously neglected. Such sources included the large collection of autobiographies of runaway or former slaves, the thousands of interviews of ex-slaves recorded in the 1930s as part of a Works Progress Administration Project, and the rich body of black song and folklore.[4]

Much of this research reached fruition in the 1970s. Among the most influential of the books inspired by the new attitudes and sources were John Blassingame's *Slave Community* (1972), Lawrence Levine's *Black Culture and Black Consciousness* (1977), and Herbert Gutman's *Black Family in Slavery and Freedom, 1750–1925* (1976). Each of these in its own way argued that slaves had created a partly autonomous culture which helped slaves resist white values and white oppression.[5]

III

A quite independent source of new directions in the study of slavery was the rise of the "new economic history" – the application of economic theory and statistical techniques to the study of the past. The "new economic history" was launched in large part by the publication in 1958 of "The economics of slavery in the antebellum south," by Alfred H. Conrad and John R. Meyer.[6] Conrad and Meyer offered evidence that slave plantation agriculture was highly profitable, as profitable, for example, as investments in railroad stocks. The article sparked a number of subsequent studies of slavery. Many were based on massive sets of data collected from sources such as the manuscripts of the US census and analyzed with the aid of new computer technology.[7] This line of research, too, reached a climax of sorts in the decade of the 1970s, with the publication of *Time on the Cross*, by Robert William Fogel and Stanley Engerman.[8] Fogel and Engerman synthesized the work of the new economic historians of slavery and presented the results of their own large research project.

Fogel and Engerman made a number of highly controversial assertions in *Time on the Cross*. Going beyond the now-accepted idea that slavery was profitable, they argued that slave plantations were actually more efficient than northern farms. Fogel and Engerman concluded from this that black slaves had been efficient and effective workers because they had adopted a strong work ethic even as slaves. Planters, they claimed, had learned to use positive incentives, rather than punishment, to motivate slaves. (They also argued that abolitionists as well as historians who had called slavery an inefficient and wasteful system were helping to propagate a racist image of blacks as lazy and careless.) Fogel and Engerman made other surprising claims – that slaves had a more than adequate diet, that planters seldom divided slave families, and that slaves shared white "Victorian" attitudes about sexual behavior and morality.

Criticism descended upon Fogel and Engerman from many directions. Economists faulted them for incorrect inferences from inadequate data and for inappropriate applications of economic theory. To many, their portrayal seemed to show slavery as an even more benign system than the one portrayed by Phillips, and hardly the "time on the cross" implied by their title.[9] Some historians concluded that *Time on the Cross* had demonstrated the limits, rather than the possibilities, of the new economic history.

IV

A development of the 1960s that deserves separate mention was the influential and controversial scholarship of Eugene D. Genovese. Beginning with a series of articles, brought together with new material in a collection called *The Political Economy of Slavery* (1965), Genovese developed a new interpretation of society and culture in the Old South. According to Genovese, slavery in the South was essentially a relationship between classes (rather than races) and he went on to argue that this class relationship was the key to understanding southern society and culture. Here Genovese was following the interpretation of historical development laid out by Karl Marx in the nineteenth century. Marx had argued that every society since the earliest era of human history had been driven by struggles between a dominant ruling class and a subordinate exploited class.[10] History had developed through a sequence of stages, each based on a different core conflict: masters against slaves in ancient society; feudal lords against serfs in medieval society, and capitalists (or "bourgeoisie") against workers (or "proletarians") in modern industrial societies such as nineteenth-century England and the United States. Still, Marx himself thought southern slaveowners had more in common with capitalists than with either ancient slaveowners or feudal lords. Taking issue with Marx's own understanding of the slave South, Genovese argued that slavery had created a unique, non-bourgeois culture – "a special civilization built on the relationship of master and slave." At the heart of this unique culture lay "paternalism," a world-view that valued personal, family-like relationships over the impersonal workings of the capitalist market. Genovese's willingness to accept slave planters' defense of their world as part of a genuine set of beliefs, rather than mere hypocrisy, even led him to defend some aspects of the almost discredited work of Ulrich B. Phillips.[11] In another long essay, Genovese analyzed the work of proslavery writer George Fitzhugh. Fitzhugh had defended slavery by bitterly attacking the injustices of the wage labor system at the heart of modern capitalism. Because Fitzhugh went so far as to imply strongly, without quite explicitly saying so, that white factory workers ought to be reduced to slavery for their own good, most of Fitzhugh's contemporaries had seen him as a somewhat odd extremist. Genovese claimed, however, that Fitzhugh was the best guide to the logic of planter ideology.[12]

Genovese's most important work, *Roll, Jordan, Roll: The World the Slaves Made*, appeared in 1974. In this book Genovese drew on a wide range of sources to describe and explain the slaves' side of the master–slave relationship. The result was a complex argument that elaborated the idea of "paternalism" both in theory and in the day-to-day world of slaves. The slaves, he argued, had to a considerable extent accepted the paternalist vision of the planters, seeing the plantation as indeed a kind of family. This partial acceptance was the key to the planters' "cultural hegemony" – their ability to get their natural antagonists to accept some of the basic ideological premises on which slavery rested.

At the same time, Genovese argued that the slaves had turned the premises of paternalism to their own advantage. They had forced masters to agree, if grudgingly, that slaves had certain rights and privileges even under slavery. The slaves took much from the culture of the masters, especially their Christianity. But the slaves had worked out their own version of a Christian world-view. Included in this slaves' world-view was a rejection of the moral premises on which slavery was based. Thus planter paternalism had not prevented blacks from immediately abandoning the master–slave relationship when the Civil War made this possible.

Roll, Jordan, Roll was controversial, not only because Genovese was a Marxist, but also because he argued that the most important power of the masters was their cultural power, rather than physical coercion. Nevertheless, Genovese's work, and *Roll, Jordan, Roll* in particular, has become the most important and influential scholarship on society and culture in the Old South. His work has consistently shown a number of important strengths. It is based on vast research in a tremendous variety of source material – from the plantation records mined by Phillips to the folklore of slaves. In addition, his attention to comparative material from other slave systems of the Western Hemisphere and from European history gives his work additional authority. Genovese has also been able to incorporate into his own interpretation much of the best scholarship of others, even those who disagree with his interpretations. Finally, Genovese has created a synthesis which is logical and coherent and which offers solutions to a number of historical questions – for example, why the United States had fewer slave revolts than other slave societies, and why southern planters were willing to fight a Civil War to defend their way of life. As a recent review put it, Genovese "has been able to construct an explanation of nearly every aspect of the southern way of life," and thereby "set the agenda for much of the research on antebellum southern history undertaken in the past two decades."[13]

V

Scholars have continued in the past decade to follow the lines of inquiry prominent in the 1960s and 1970s, while also opening up new areas to intense study. The essays in this volume represent some of the most important and provocative examples of the new scholarship.

Eugene Genovese himself, often in collaboration with Elizabeth Fox-Genovese, has continued to develop and modify his basic arguments, responding to criticisms and incorporating others' research at times, but never yielding on the essential argument that the Old South was a non-capitalist, paternalist society, not a bourgeois capitalist one. Essays excerpted here lay out the most recent restatement of this theme, and also include commentary on alternative interpretations.

The research of economists has also continued. A key section of Robert William Fogel's new synthesis of this research is included here. Like Genovese, Fogel has responded to criticisms of his (and Stanley Engerman's) work, but not retreated on the most important claims about the nature of the antebellum South's economy, and, by implication, its culture and society. Sterling Stuckey's contribution here is also in many ways a development from earlier studies of slave folklore and religion, as he argues that the African roots of slave culture laid the basis for the development of black nationalism. Norrece Jones's study of planter control of their slaves shows that in-depth mining of familiar sources can still yield vital insights into the master–slave relationship.

But scholars of the Old South, like historians in many other fields, have also mined new veins of research. Often borrowing from the methods and theories of anthropologists, they have focused more attention on culture – the culture of the masters as well as the culture of slaves. Many, including Stuckey, have been less willing than Genovese to see the culture of either master or slave as determined primarily by a class relationship between them. An example of such an approach is the essay by Bertram Wyatt-Brown. Wyatt-Brown is the author of *Southern Honor: Ethics and Behavior in the Old South* (1982), one of the most influential books in southern history published since *Roll, Jordan, Roll*. In that book, he argued that the South had a culture based on "honor" that could be traced far back into early European history. His description of this system of belief was not incompatible with many of Genovese's descriptions of planter mentality, but Wyatt-Brown was little concerned with the economic base for such a culture. In the essay included here, Wyatt-Brown turns again to the question of honor in the Old South, this time in an analysis of the alternative systems of honor that, he argues, met in the master–slave relationship.

A second area of focus that has resulted in major new work on the Old South is the interrelated study of women and the family. Such study is particularly relevant to the claim that the Old South was "paternalist," since a paternalist world-view is based on the idea that social relationships are and ought to be organized hierarchically along family lines, with the male as benevolent father-figure at the top.[14] Paternalism thus dictates a particular and subordinate place for women. Elizabeth Fox-Genovese's essay here analyzes women's place in the Old South in just this way, and argues in addition that white women in the planter families accepted and accommodated to their subordinate place. Steven Stowe's discussion of planter courtship rituals neither clearly supports nor clearly undermines a paternalist interpretation of planter culture. Joan Cashin's study of migrating planter families does show that men held the power in these families, but there is little evidence in her essay of the voluntary subordination of women. The final essay, Deborah White's study of slave women, also draws on work by anthropologists, and, again unlike Genovese, places little stress on the direct cultural influence of masters on these women.

Some of the essays here, such as those by Fogel and Stuckey, dissent openly from the paternalist interpretation of the slave South's society and culture. Others disagree by implication. It is true that the essays do not add up, in any simple way, to an alternative interpretation. The slave culture described by Stuckey seems difficult to reconcile with the world of work described by Fogel, and the picture of family life that emerges from Jones's research is not obviously the same as the one we see in White's essay. Nevertheless, the cumulative impact of such research is quite significant, because recent scholarship, some of the best of which is represented here, offers powerful challenges to each major aspect of Genovese's paternalist interpretation. It remains to be seen whether this research becomes the basis for a new and widely accepted interpretation of society and culture in the slave South.

A note on editorial practice: cuts in the texts of essays are indicated with ellipses, and when explanatory comments have been added in the text itself, these are enclosed in square brackets. Editor's explanatory notes appear at the bottom of the page. Notes from the original essays appear at the end of each chapter. None of the authors' original notes have been entirely omitted, but some notes have been cut because of space limitations. In notes, as in the text, omissions are indicated by ellipses.

NOTES

1 Most notably in Ulrich B. Phillips (1919) *American Negro Slavery* (New York, reprinted Baton Rouge, La., 1966); see also his *Life and Labor in the Old South* (Boston, 1929).
2 Phillips, *American Negro Slavery*, 342, 343.
3 Kenneth Stampp (1956) *The Peculiar Institution: Slavery in the Antebellum South* (New York); Stanley Elkins (1959) *Slavery* (Chicago). For a stimulating account of this period of slavery historiography, see August Meier and Elliott Rudwick (1986) *Black History and the Historical Profession, 1915–1980* (Urbana, Ill.), 239–76.
4 The WPA narratives were published under the editorship of George Rawick (1972) *The American Slave: A Composite Autobiography* (Westport, Conn.).
5 Other significant books on slave culture published in the decade include Leslie Howard Owens (1976) *This Species of Property: Slave Life and Culture in the Old South* (New York); Thomas L. Webber (1978) *Deep Like the Rivers: Education in the Slave Community* (New York); Albert Raboteau (1978) *Slave Religion: The Invisible Institution in the Antebellum South* (New York).
6 *Journal of Political Economy* 66 (1958): 95–130.
7 An important collection of these studies was William N. Parker (ed.) (1970) *The Structure of the Cotton Economy of the Antebellum South*, a special issue of *Agricultural History* 44 (1970).
8 Robert William Fogel and Stanley Engerman (1974) *Time on the Cross: The Economics of American Negro Slavery*, 2 vols (Boston).
9 Many of the criticisms are collected in Paul David *et al.* (1976) *Reckoning with Slavery: A Critical Study in the Quantitative History of American Negro Slavery* (New York).
10 The literature on Marx and Marxism is too vast to do more than suggest places for interested students to begin. Marx's most influential single volume was *Capital*, vol. I (1867). Students who wish introductions can turn to a sympathetic account by G. A. Cohen (1980) *Karl Marx's Theory of History: A Defense* (Princeton, N.J.); and to a brief critical introduction in Peter Singer (1980) *Marx* (New York). Students should, in any case, be aware that there are several competing interpretations of Marx's thought and not all Marxists agree with one another.
11 Thus, Genovese wrote an introduction, including much praise, for a paperbound reprint of Phillips, *American Negro Slavery*.

12 Eugene D. Genovese (1969) "The logical outcome of the slaveholders' philosophy," in *The World the Slaveholders Made* (New York).

13 Drew Gilpin Faust (1987) "The peculiar South revisited: white society, culture, and politics in the antebellum period, 1800–1860," in John B. Boles and Evelyn Thomas Nolen (eds) *Interpreting Southern History: Historiographical Essays in Honor of Sanford W. Higginbotham* (Baton Rouge, La.), 79, 80.

14 The study of southern women owes much to the pioneering work of Anne Firor Scott, especially in her (1970) *The Southern Lady: From Pedestal to Politics* (Chicago); the publication of Catherine Clinton (1982) *The Plantation Mistress: Woman's World in the Old South* (New York), was the first of a number of major recent studies of women in the Old South.

Part I

THE OLD SOUTH AS A PATERNALIST SOCIETY

1

THE FRUITS OF MERCHANT CAPITAL

The slave South as a paternalist society

Eugene Genovese and Elizabeth Fox-Genovese

In a collection of essays, The Fruits of Merchant Capital: Slavery and Bourgeois Property in the Rise and Expansion of Capitalism, *Eugene Genovese (in collaboration with Elizabeth Fox-Genovese) made the most recent summary and restatement of his basic interpretation of the Old South as a unique society and culture, that should be distinguished sharply from the capitalist, bourgeois society and culture of contemporary Britain or the US North. As explained in the Introduction, the authors' theory and methods are Marxist, though not all Marxists agree with their particular use of Marxian theory.*

This selection includes parts of four of the essays in Fruits of Merchant Capital. *The first, "The Janus face of merchant capital," outlines the basic Marxist argument at the heart of the analysis. Here and elsewhere, the authors argue that modern systems of slavery in the Western Hemisphere need to be understood as one aspect of a long economic and social revolution by which feudalism in Europe was transformed into industrial capitalism. The second essay is a comparative overview of the history of slave economies in the Western Hemisphere; only those sections dealing explicitly with the US South are included here. Both argue that the Old South, as a slave society, could not have been essentially "capitalist," even though slaveowning planters had to make compromises with the capitalist world in which their society was embedded. Excerpts from two other essays follow. Both were written in response to other writings on slavery, and especially in response to the publication of* Time on the Cross, *by Robert Fogel and Stanley Engerman, and the subsequent controversy over Fogel and Engerman's interpretation.*

Readers will want to be aware that the discussion below follows Karl Marx's definition of capitalism as a system based on wage labor, rather

13

than simply one based on private property or profit-seeking in the market. For Marx, much of social and political life was determined by the relationship between a ruling class that owned or controlled the "means of production," such as land, factories, or machines, and the usually much larger group of people who labored for those owners. Societies will differ, depending on the nature of that basic relationship, which, according to Marx, was always one of basic conflict. Under slavery, masters literally own their workers and force them to work. Under feudalism, the ruling class owns all the land, and uses this control as well as their political power to bind serfs to the land and make them work part of the time for the owners. What made capitalism different, according to Marx, was its division between capitalist owners of the means of production (called "bourgeoisie" after the French designation for the merchants and artisans who lived in medieval towns), and wage workers who were no longer physically coerced to labor. Instead, these workers were "free" to buy and sell their labor for wages by the hour, day, or week, seeking the highest wage they could find. (Marx also argued that capitalist owners would always be able to keep wages unfairly low, and that the "freedom" of wage workers was little more than the freedom to starve.) Slavery in the United States is something of an anomaly because it flourished in a country which in most respects was clearly capitalist by any definition. For Genovese, however, a society based on slavery, rather than wage labor, cannot be "capitalist" or "bourgeois."

In this first excerpt, the authors outline their argument that the slave South was an "essentially hybrid" system, embedded in, but not truly of, the world of capitalist industry.

Briefly here . . . we shall try to defend and elaborate the following theses:

1 Changes in the social relations of production, rather than in the sphere of circulation and exchange, determined the emergence of the capitalist mode of production, roughly, by the sixteenth century. Specifically, the separation of the laborers from the means of production and the attendant transformation of labor-power into a commodity proved decisive.

2 The history of capitalism as a world-conquering mode of

production cannot be separated from the creation of a world market, but the emergence of that market must be understood as a new quality, not as a mere quantitative extension of older long-distance markets in luxuries and other goods specific to the seigneurial ruling class and even the early national state. The emerging world market passed through centuries of violent economic purges, political upheavals, and class struggles in the simultaneous process of becoming a large-scale market for the means of production associated with modern industry; of creating a vast source of indispensable raw materials; and of generating a mass effective demand for consumer goods, which itself rested on nothing so much as the protracted separation of the labor force from the means of production. In short, notwithstanding the revolutionary impact of the world market on the productive sector, that market itself developed out of the prior revolution in social relations within the productive sector.

3 Merchant capital did play a revolutionary role in the rise of capitalism, but only within limits that must be clearly delineated. Under certain specific historical conditions, analyzed with particular effectiveness by Karl Marx, Maurice Dobb, and other contributors to the debate over the transition from feudalism to capitalism, merchant capital acted as a powerful solvent of feudal social relations and as an agent of primitive accumulation.[1] But these contributions of merchant capital to capitalist development, while necessary, occurred only under definite conditions of production and represented the great, if spectacular, exceptions to its common role throughout history. On balance, indeed overwhelmingly so, merchant capital proved conservative: it fed off existing modes of production, however backward. Normally, merchants and financiers adjusted their interests to those of the prevailing ruling classes and resisted all attempts to introduce revolutionary transformations into the economy, into politics, into class relations. In a word, they normally lived as parasites on the old order.

4 The conservative – indeed, the increasingly reactionary – role of merchant capital appeared in especially vicious form in the African slave trade and the slave–plantation systems of the Americas. These systems, spawned to no small extent by merchant capital, developed along different routes: as an

adjunct of Portuguese feudalism in Brazil; as an adjunct of British capitalism in the Caribbean; as a pawn and a prize in the bitter struggle between capitalism and a residual feudalism in France; and, most ominously, as the breeding ground of an essentially hybrid system in the Old South, which raised a regionally powerful ruling class of a new type, at once based on slave relations of production and yet deeply embedded in the world market and hostage to its internationally developed bourgeois social relations of production. In this essential respect, the Old South emerged as a bastard child of merchant capital and developed as a noncapitalist society increasingly antagonistic to, but inseparable from, the bourgeois world that sired it.[2]

In the following pages Genovese and Fox-Genovese turn to their interpretation of the nature of the "hybrid" society of the slave South and its dominant class of slaveowning planters. Planters were not "feudal" lords or "seigneurs" – a French equivalent – but, more importantly, neither were they "bourgeois" in the Marxist sense – producers hiring (and profiting from) wage laborers and organizing their private and public worlds around their need to control the physical means of production. An important distinction here as well is that between "merchant capitalism," or the search for profit through the buying and selling of goods, ("exchange"), and industrial capitalism, based on search for profits through the buying of labor power in order to produce goods.

The slaveholders of the Old South constituted a new social class that cannot be identified as feudal, seigneurial, or capitalist. In essential respects they were prebourgeois, akin to the great landed classes of Europe but certainly not to be equated with any of them. In one crucial respect they were akin to the modern bourgeoisie: they produced for a world market and had to think and act like businessmen in much of their endeavors. But then, the rise of a world market, not to mention the much earlier appearance of substantial regional markets, compelled all the great landowning classes to think and act like businessmen in some important respects, even as they fought to arrest the growing power of the bourgeoisie.

The slaveholders arose on the foundations of merchant capital. Whereas merchant capital fastened upon precapitalist labor

16

systems in many areas, it in effect created new ones in many other areas. Slavery had not died out in western Europe, but it had become moribund and marginal. Merchant capital carried it abroad on a grand scale and breathed into it a health and vigor never before experienced. But here too, the parasitic and passive aspects of merchant capital reappeared. Everywhere, the ruling classes and the societies engendered by slavery took their character less from the merchant capital that had spawned them than from discrete conjunctures of metropolitan and colonial structures dominated by ruling classes rooted in production. In the United States the slaveholders, while becoming economic hostages to the world market, succeeded in subjecting merchant capital to their political sway. The Old South, more than any other slaveholding country, became a slave society in the strict sense: its politics, economy, and culture were primarily determined by slave, not feudal or bourgeois, relations of production. In saying that it was in but not of the capitalist world, we say that it offered a special case of the general effect produced by merchant capital – a unique social formation that, notwithstanding much to admire, would prove deadly not only to millions of black victims but to the world at large.

Let us anticipate criticism. Did not the slaveholders, whom we call precapitalist and to whom we attribute "paternalism," behave just as exploitatively as those capitalistic slaveholding entrepreneurs of Conrad and Meyer, Fogel and Engerman, Gray and Stampp?* No doubt. But did any precapitalist ruling class behave less exploitatively? Did, for example, Roman slaveholders or medieval lords or Mongol conquerors or Byzantine imperial bureaucrats exploit and oppress subject peoples with less determination than capitalist classes have done? If so, what a pity that ancient slavery and medieval serfdom ever ended. We find altogether charming this rosy view of the world before the advent of capitalism. As socialists we are delighted, if not altogether convinced, to hear that the bour-

---

* See Alfred H. Conrad and John R. Meyer (1958) "The economics of slavery in the antebellum South," *Journal of Political Economy* 66: 95–130; Robert William Fogel and Stanley Engerman (1974) *Time on the Cross: The Economics of American Negro Slavery* (Boston); Lewis Cecil Gray, *History of Agriculture in the Southern United States* (reprinted Gloucester, Mass., 1958); Kenneth Stampp (1956) *The Peculiar Institution: Slavery in the Antebellum South* (New York).

geoisie invented exploitation and oppression. At issue is neither exploitation (the expropriation of the social surplus) nor oppression (the more general features of domination), but the historical forms of exploitation and oppression. Such changing historical forms have carried those material, ideological, and psychological shifts which have provided the essential content of historical process.

In essential respects the slaveholders of the Old South had much more in common with northern Americans of all classes than they did with, say, Russian boyars or Prussian Junkers. But in historical analysis, ostensibly marginal differences count for everything. That the slaveholders were discernibly American in much more than a formal national sense remains self-evident, but no more so than their uniqueness within the country as a whole. In insisting on the precapitalist nature of the Old South and its ruling class, we are attempting to isolate those special features of material, ideological, and psychological development which made the South just different enough to bring on a long and bloody war. The South had a plantation economy embedded in a world market, but it also had a huge subsistence sector that severely circumscribed the penetration of market relations into the regional economy as a whole. The South, in other words, may be said to have had a market economy only in a very restricted sense. And it did not have a market society. At the root of the restrictions on a regional market economy and of the absence of a market society lay the absence of a market in labor-power. The whole point of the extreme proslavery argument was precisely that the South must not allow itself to be transformed into a market society. Here we return to the central feature of Marx's definition of class as the relation of individuals to the means of production, for the confrontation of master and slave shaped the essential differences between the societies of North and South.

Some critics have fairly asked: "How could the plantations have been more capitalistic than they were?" But if we understand the criteria that underlie the question, we might ask how the export-oriented landed estates that arose in Russia during and after the reign of Ivan IV could have been run more capitalistically in time and place. We reply that in the narrow sense perhaps the slave plantations could not have been run any more capitalistically than they were. But then, the question can again be shifted: "How could Soviet factories be run much more capitalistically than they are?" Or, "How could American society, with its expanding government sector and collective corporate structure, be much more socialistic than it already is?" And indeed, a whole school of economists has arisen to assure us that the two social systems are converging. Yet, the systems differ in their material interests, ideology, and psychological makeup. No socialist country could compete effectively without taking full account of the exigencies of the world market and without absorbing many solidly "capitalistic" practices; and capitalism probably would have collapsed long ago if it had not proven sufficiently flexible to absorb many "socialistic" practices. We remain at what some may see as the margin, but that margin contains irreconcilable antagonisms.

With the rise of a worldwide capitalist mode of production, every attempt to resurrect an archaic social system or to defend a dying one had to bend before the political and economic power of the world market and its competitive demands. In the Old South under slavery, as in a Europe still encumbered by a residual feudalism, the difference between the buying and selling of labor-power and the extra-economic compulsion of direct human labor – the difference in systems of property – constituted the essence not only of a divergence of material interests but of the deepest moral sensibilities.

The following pages from "The slave economies in political perspective" argue for the multiple consequences – in politics, ideology, psychology, and domestic life – for the Old South of an economy based on slave, rather than wage, labor. As the title suggests, the authors argue that slave economies need to be understood as social and political systems, and that a purely economic interpretation ignores crucial aspects of any society based on slave labor. In particular, slaveowners must be seen as a social class with a distinct psychology and distinct political interests, and not merely a collection of profit-seeking individuals.

The economic interpretations of the slave economies of the New World, as well as those social interpretations which adopt the neoclassical economic model but leave the economics out,

19

assume everything they must prove.* By retreating from the political economy from which their own methods derive, they ignore the extent to which the economic process permeates the society. They ignore, that is, the interaction between economics, narrowly defined, and the social relations of production on the one hand and state power on the other. For any economic system remains not merely a method of allocating scarce resources, but a system that, at least on the margin and frequently more pervasively, commands those scarce resources. Even an international market such as that which prevailed in the Atlantic world during the eighteenth and early nineteenth centuries depends heavily upon the state formations that guarantee the ultimate command of economic goods. Neoclassical economists achieve their theoretical sophistication by falling silent on the social relations of production that ultimately determine the prices of commodities in the market. They mystify reality by abstracting prices from the social relations of production and by then assuming that their abstraction provides an effective analytic substitute for those social relations.

Even in a society like our own, in which most facets of human life pass through the market, there remain pockets of non-priced labor – for example, the household work of many women and the early reproduction of human capital. In the eighteenth-century Atlantic world, merchant capital organized the market and fed off it, but it did not penetrate all productive sectors evenly. Typically, merchant capital organized the surplus production of larger or smaller domestic units of labor before the transformation of labor-power into a commodity. In this respect, the slave plantations of the Old South and elsewhere had much in common with the households and farms of the northern North American colonies and states.

The southern slaveholders' recourse to a domestic metaphor [i.e. paternalism, with the slaveowner as father-figure to all on the plantation] to explain their relation to their labor force thus simultaneously evoked the declining seigneurialism of their remote historical origins and certain neoAristotelian features

---

* "Neoclassical economics" refers to the style of economic analysis of markets, often highly technical, typically found in most western capitalist societies; the name indicates its descent from the "classical" economics of Adam Smith and other early modern writers.

of the domestic bases of merchant capital in what would prove to be more progressive sectors. But the political basis of their command of labor no longer required notions of the social household. Repudiating patriarchy and hierarchy in the public sphere, the government of the new United States turned more directly to the language of the market to justify its exercise of political power. The political systems rested upon the equal participation of propertied male individuals and left the transmission of sovereignty within the various domestic units to the discretion of the members of the political community. Political power thus remained impregnated with the duality that characterized merchant capital as well. It left unresolved the discontinuity between the public and the private spheres, just as merchant capital left unresolved the discontinuity between relations of exchange and relations of production. It tolerated – and may even have depended upon – pockets of authoritarian command that contradicted its most cherished principles of equality.

Historically, merchant capital proved a proverbial Janus, looking at once forward and backward. It bound within the market system both archaic and revolutionary social relations. It even generated rationalized and, in time and place, efficient variants of archaic relations of production, above all the slave economies. Within the economic sector, the decisive threshold lay at the transformation of labor-power into a commodity [i.e. in the form of labor hired for wages, rather than coerced, as in feudalism or slavery]. But merchant capital could not itself cause this transformation in the manner suggested by some scholars, most notably Immanuel Wallerstein.* Rather, it contributed to organizing economic space and exchange in a way that permitted the eventual emergence of a fully developed capitalist system. An understanding of this process requires full attention to the role of politics, and especially of state power, in assuring the ruling class an adequate command over its resources, including labor, and an adequate share of the international market. From this perspective, it should come as no surprise that the abolition of slavery in the United States occurred not through a simple economic transfer of resources,

---

* Author of *The Modern World System*, 2 vols (New York, 1974 and Cambridge, 1980).

or through internal social reform, but through a bloody civil war.

The export-oriented colonial economies spawned by western European expansion produced some of the greatest anomalies in the history of capitalism, among the most arresting of which was the coexistence of high profits and high growth rates with manifest retardation of economic development. Critics of Robert William Fogel and Stanley L. Engerman's *Time on the Cross* have called into question their claims for the relative efficiency of southern agriculture, based as they are on the application of a factor-productivity index method few economists think appropriate and fewer historians think tenable at all. But the South undoubtedly did enjoy an impressive growth in total and per capita wealth from colonial times to secession.

No one, not even those classical political economists who attacked slavery as an inefficient system, could reasonably deny that it could generate high profits and attendant growth rates under three conditions: fresh land, a steady supply of cheap labor, and a high level of demand on the world market. The economic indictment of slavery has focused on structural consequences. The origins of the prosperity of the slave economies lay primarily in the force of the world demand for certain staples under narrow conditions of production; and the high levels of profit and growth disguised deep structural weaknesses that condemned slave societies to underdevelopment, eventual stagnation, and political disaster. . . .

Gavin Wright has suggested that those who see the Old South as backward err, and that they ought to see it as dependent.* He makes a good point, so far as it goes, and we hardly wish to quarrel with his insistence on the dependent nature of the southern economy. But economics must be understood politically: dependence spells backwardness. The South, like other slave–plantation societies and colonies, exhibited an impressive rate of economic growth for a prolonged period, but it failed the test of development, which alone could have guaranteed that political viability without which economic viability has little meaning.

In a slave economy, even one so strong and well developed as that of the Old South, the redirection of independent mer-

* Author of *The Political Economy of the Cotton South: Households, Wealth, and Markets in the Nineteenth Century* (New York 1978).

chant capital could take only two general forms on a scale large enough to be historically significant. It could take the ordinary route into bourgeois production, or it could take the alternative route into the production peculiar to slavery itself. Since no slave society ever generated an industrial revolution, the first route led to the transfer of a significant portion of the capital out of the slaveholding region altogether – or, rather, it would have if the second route had not lain open and proven more attractive.

That second route led to increased investment in slaves and the means of production associated with them. Herein lay the secret of the paradox of growth without politically viable development. For the transfer of capital from the merchant to the industrial sector in a slave society encourages quantitative growth while it inhibits the qualitative development normal to the expansion of capitalist production.

The important problems of speculation in slaves for reasons of status and prestige and of the consumption patterns of the slaveholders remain unsettled, but they need not detain us here.[3] The specifically economic argument for the expanded investment in slaves, presented by such formidable economists as Conrad and Meyer, and Fogel and Engerman, end in the same place. In a slave economy, the capital pushed out of the non-slave sectors, including the commercial, flows overwhelmingly into the slave sector.

Thus, no one need be surprised by the generally friendly and mutually supportive relations between planters and factors or, more broadly, between the agrarian slaveholding and urban commercial and financial interests.* Those relations, which had innumerable parallels throughout the world, eloquently announced the deeply conservative nature of merchant capital. To cite them as evidence of "capitalism," as an array of scholars regularly do, is to misunderstand totally the normal function of merchant capital in economic history in general and during the rise and expansion of capitalism in particular. For if the merchants' profit derived, as it surely did, from the prevailing system of production on which merchant capital fed, then only extraordinary circumstances would lead the merchants as a class to disrupt the productive sector. In

---

* Factors were wholesale merchants specializing in selling cotton or other staples and supplying credit and supplies to planters.

Charleston and Natchez, as in Bordeaux and Nantes, the great merchants happily married their daughters off to the sons of the great landowners. And why not? Those conjugal unions provided a splendid symbol of the marriage of merchant capital to the powers that be – a political and economic marriage sanctioned by several thousand years of history.

To this view of merchant capital, of the social content of the slave regime, and of the structure and prospects of the slave economy, Fogel and Engerman have replied with a bold alternative. In particular, in *Time on the Cross* they argue that the slave states not only achieved a growth rate and levels of profitability comparable to the best but also achieved something that economists mysteriously call "viability." If by viability they mean that, at the secular level, more money was being earned than spent, then we must answer that that much may be taken for granted in a competitive market world. If, more seriously, they mean that the rate of return equaled the interest rate, then they have fudged the problem.

At issue is the flexibility of the slave system: its ability to reallocate resources when faced with the secular decline of decisive sectors. In this sense, economists could judge the slave economy viable only if they were able to demonstrate that the planters could and would shift capital to the free labor sector whenever it proved profitable to do so. But they could not provide any empirical justification for such long periods of depression as that of the late 1830s and 1840s, and they would have to ignore the structural characteristics of the slave economy, as well as the social and psychological characteristics of slave society. It is difficult to believe that a regional ruling class of resident planters, whose lives had been formed by a social relation based on the theoretical assertion of absolute power over other human beings and by pretensions to community lordship, could blithely dispense with the very foundations of their social and psychological existence merely in response to a balance sheet of profit and loss.

The standard economic interpretations err in assuming that the slaveholders can be understood as ordinary capitalists who functioned as units in the marketplace. When they are perceived as a social class, having discrete material interests, moral sensibility, ideological commitment, and social psychology, then the question of the economic viability of their system takes on an entirely different meaning. Since their interests, material and ideological, clashed with those of the dominant class of the larger capitalist world, the question of viability reduces to one of military and political power: was their economy strong enough and flexible enough to support their pretensions and guarantee their safety as a ruling class? A long economic slump or a growing fear of isolation and incipient decline could, from this point of view, be expected to generate, not a shift of resources to a free labor economy inside or outside the South, but mounting pressure for war, conquest, or some alternative political solution.

Thus, those economic interpretations which assume that the slaveholders lived, thought, and acted like ordinary bourgeois assume everything they must prove; they cannot begin to illuminate the titanic struggle for power that rent the American Union; and they reduce the impressive complexity of slavery as a social system to the behavior pattern of a single industry, if indeed not a single firm. Yet, all the non-Marxist critics of Fogel and Engerman restrict themselves to technical matters or to superficial complaints about exaggerations and excessive claims. For, in truth, all of them object only to the extreme formulation of assumptions and derivative theses that they themselves share.

Once these misplaced assumptions from neoclassical economics are dropped, the anomalies and paradoxes become less puzzling. Consider, for example, the very different results of soil exhaustion and wasteful agricultural methods in the North and South. The waste and destruction resulted primarily from an enormous abundance of land, rather than from slavery *per se*, for it simply did not pay to conserve resources. But, as soil exhaustion and agricultural depression struck the eastern areas of the free states, capital shifted, not only to the West but into commercial and industrial, as well as agricultural, diversification within the East itself. In the South, the older areas, locked into a slave economy, found it difficult to adjust and fell back toward subsistence. In the end, slave sales sustained the older regions and allowed the slaveholders to keep going. But the region, even while showing modest economic recovery, the bases of which remain debatable, remained at an

25

economic level that undermined the slaveholders' political power. . . .*

The entire economic history of the Old South, from the rise of King Cotton at the beginning of the nineteenth century to the Second World War, reflected the force of international demand. When the world market was good, as during the 1830s and 1850s, profits soared, and growth proceeded apace; when the market slumped, depression and retrogression set in. So long as slavery existed, no foundation for industrialization or economic diversification was laid. Those who insist that the South had developmental possibilities, the realization of which only the periodic return of high cotton prices prevented, have many hard questions to answer. They cannot point to a single slave society in world history that realized such possibilities, or to any presocialist country that carried through an industrial revolution without first severing the laboring classes from the means of production.

Since the South had no effective substitute for cotton as a staple, the comparative disadvantage to the older regions did not generate a significant internal shift of resources. Maryland constituted a nightmare model for the planters of the Lower South, especially those in such depressed cotton states as South Carolina. The pronounced sale of slaves to the Cotton Belt and the inability of the planters to find an adequate substitute for tobacco was steadily transforming Maryland into a free state. Virginia was undergoing a similar transformation, albeit slowly. Delaware was a slave state in name only. The slave sector in Missouri was declining relative to the free, and Kentucky was no longer secure. The fears of the cotton planters of the Lower South were realized during the secession crisis, when Maryland, Missouri, Kentucky, and Delaware, as well as the western counties of Virginia and the eastern of Tennessee, remained loyal to the Union.

In other words, although the derived demand for slaves demonstrated considerable flexibility within southern labor markets, the political consequences were emerging as ominous. This very mechanism was gravely weakening the social regime in the slaveselling states and thereby the political power of the slaveholders in the slave-importing states as well. To

* Omitted here are sections that discuss other slave economies in the Western Hemisphere.

26

make matters worse, the renewed cotton prosperity of the 1850s threatened to speed up the process of dissolution in the Upper South. With cotton prices once again at ten cents per pound, the southeastern planters shifted previously withdrawn land back into cotton production. Thus South Carolina, which had been exporting slaves since about 1820, found itself facing a labor shortage that promised to bid even more slaves away from Virginia and Maryland and that, for good measure, stimulated renewed interest in the reopening of the African slave trade – a measure that could only provoke the most bitter political quarrels within the South as well as between South and North. . . .

Consideration of some special features of the growth of the cotton economy may help clarify the argument. The spread of short-staple cotton dramatically raised the supply during the 1830s – the period known as the "flush times" of Alabama and Mississippi. Speculative slavebuying ran high, fed by a politically induced expansion of bank notes. Regional growth reached eye-catching proportions, and the boldest and ablest of the planters accumulated huge fortunes. Typically, however, the supply outstripped the demand, and by the early 1840s the British textile manufacturers had stocked hundreds of thousands of bales. The panic of 1837 and the ensuing depression therefore hit the South doubly hard, for even when the worst should have been over, years of low prices continued while inventories were slowly worked off. Not until the end of the 1840s did prices recover, if we except 1838 and 1846, when good prices accompanied short crops occasioned by droughts.

During this long depression, the southern press sparkled with calls for diversification, manufacturing, reallocation of resources, and elimination of middlemen's profits by promotion of direct trade with Europe. Conventions of planters and of merchants solemnly resolved upon reform and self-reliance. In the end, nothing much changed. Economists and historians continue to argue about the "causes," but the difficulties inherent in the system as a system cannot be explained away. When shift of capital to industry [i.e. shifting slaves from agriculture into industry], difficult enough under slavery, could be effected, the labor force, to produce adequately in manufacturing, had to be given incentives that drove the planters to protest against the subversion of discipline in the countryside.

When that problem could be kept within safe limits, the weakness of the home market, with its huge population of slaves and white subsistence farmers, took its toll. Since the system depended on export crops, the pressure to switch to manufactures came precisely at the worst time – that is, when purchasing power was low and when northern firms, facing gluts of their own, were ready to undersell newcomers. Direct trade with Europe remained a will-o'-the-wisp since imports could not keep pace with exports, and ships would have to return in ballast. A shortage of capital and entrepreneurship plagued all such attempts. Those who remain fixated on growth rates have yet to explain this dearth. And they have yet to deny that much of the accumulated wealth not sunk back into slaves and quantitative expansion was raked off by northern and European factors, shippers, commission merchants, insurance agents, and bankers, so that much of the multiplier effect of southern investment benefited others.

We confess to finding it absurd that Marxists should have to fight so hard to convince neoclassicists that the liberation of entrepreneurship historically accompanied the free market, especially the market in labor-power, and that entrepreneurship, like science, technology, education, and investment in "human capital" in general, arose as a function of freedom and everywhere suffered in the absence of freedom.

A few statistics on investment in human capital will suggest both the historical problem and the basis for so many diverse historical interpretations. Here, the problem concerns only the Old South, for the slaveholding societies in the rest of the hemisphere remained entirely backward in this respect. In the South, pupils made up less than 6 per cent of the white population, whereas in the North they accounted for more than 18 per cent. And since the blacks lived overwhelmingly in the South and formed the backbone of the labor force, their inclusion would cut the southern ratio by almost a half. Illiteracy statistics showed 7.5 per cent for southern whites, as against only 2 per cent for northern. The South had a white population less than half that of the North (roughly six million as opposed to thirteen million), but it had less than one-third the schools, one-fourth the libraries, and one-half the library books. In each case, and in others that could be cited, the southern investment in "human capital" was concentrated heavily in the Upper South, with the cotton states – the heart of the slave economy – backward.

Still, the South's record did compare favorably with that of many other countries, and it has even been argued, most impressively by Fogel and Engerman, that the South deserved to rank as a major industrial power. Here again, the abstraction of statistics from the social and political context obscures the actual historical problems. The intrinsic strength of investment in human capital – its contribution to "viability" – like the economic performance in general, ultimately emerged as a political question. The southern slaveholders, beyond doubt, felt themselves gravely threatened by the outside world during the last three decades or so of their regime. Thus, only one kind of comparison makes sense: how well were they doing relative to those northern elements whose rising power threatened them so? Or, to what extent could their regime take advantage of the astonishing development of the national economy, with its ability to attract immigrant labor, advanced technology, and foreign capital without foreign control, and its ability to launch a broad-based industrial revolution capable of raising it to world power? The question answers itself. However much growth the slave economy displayed in the abstract, every passing year weakened the political and military power of its ruling class relative to those it had to confront.

The transportation system, too, took its toll, even before its weaknesses compromised the Confederate military effort. Of what use are the statistics that show the South with more miles of railroad than this or that country, if the structure of the system is left out of account? Those who set out to exploit colonies, and who in so many cases impoverished them, often built roads and railroads as the first order of business. The southern leaders themselves built their transportation system colonial-style: it bound the staple-producing plantation districts to the ports and largely bypassed the upcountry. In general, and by design, the system did not facilitate commodity exchange within a national or regional market; it facilitated exports. Here, too, it resembled other export-oriented colonies based on some form of dependent labor.

Those who wish to construct abstract models of growth and

development could doubtless show that a concerted attack on these and related problems remained a theoretical possibility. Historically, the slaveholders had no such option. They had a common stake in slave labor as an investment, as a fountainhead of material interest, and as the basis of their social system, ideology, and social psychology. They could solve none of these problems without falling upon each other in a war of conflicting particular interests, but their class roots in slave labor set them off from the outside world and threw them collectively on the defensive. Disunity had to be avoided and divisive internal political issues kept within limits. When the degree of political unity necessary for a common policy arrived, it was based on secession, territorial expansion, and if necessary, war – on the militant defense of slave property. . . .

Notwithstanding the parallels and similarities between the earlier and later cycles of slave-based production in all parts of the hemisphere, a marked dissimilarity was evident in the slave reproduction rates, and the unique performance in the Old South had important economic implications. The political and economic history of the Atlantic slave trade set the stage for that unique performance. One after another, the southern states closed the trade after the Revolution in response to the moral pressure of the time and, probably much more important, to the panic engendered by the great revolution in Saint-Domingue and the renewed awareness of the explosive potential of heavy ratios of blacks to whites and of African-born to American-born slaves.

This fear was nothing new. The southern colonies had periodically reduced the trade or shut it down completely in response to slave insurrections and conspiracies. In this way, black militancy had a profound effect on the early course of southern economic as well as political and social development. But the attitude of the southern states also reflected directly economic factors. Specifically, the deepening depression in the tobacco colonies simultaneously caused a loss of interest in slave imports and a rising interest in slave exports to the Deep South. The closing of the African trade drove slave prices upward, with attendant capital gains for the planters of the slaveselling states. Conversely, South Carolina, alone among the slave states, reopened the African trade in an effort to replenish losses from the American Revolution and to stock slaves before the expected closure of 1808, for a promising new staple, upland cotton, was offering fresh opportunities.

The most dramatic part of this story came during the nineteenth century, during which the black population increased threefold after the closing of the African slave trade. This period, 1800–60, with its extraordinary demographic expansion, was precisely the period of the rise of the Cotton Kingdom and the territorial expansion of the slave system. Thus, the slave regime matured in the United States under special conditions.

The positive demographic performance predated the abolition of the African slave trade, although it was undoubtedly strengthened by it. Intermittent tobacco depression and periodic taxation of imports in response to fear of slave revolt provided a functional equivalent for the economic effects of abolition, but only because they proceeded within a specific social structure. In Virginia and Maryland and to a lesser extent in the Lower South, the planters, from an early date, were residents not absentees. Their exceptionally close life with their slaves provided some protection against the tendency of the absentee-overseer system to concentrate on quick returns at the expense of long-term investment. The South Carolina coast, however, resembled nothing so much as Barbados and was dominated by a ruling class whose "callous disregard for human life and suffering," in the words of Forrest McDonald, "was probably unmatched anywhere west of the Dnieper."[4] As might be expected, the natural increase of slaves lagged badly and matched Virginia's levels only at a much later date, when conditions had changed.

The living conditions of the slaves, which proved so conducive to reproduction, undoubtedly reflected considerable initiative by the slaves themselves. For example, the calculations by Fogel and Engerman of the nutritional value of the slaves' basic diet have come under heavy attack, but most participants on both sides of the debate have slighted the most interesting question. The slaves did not rely on the basic diet of fat pork and cornmeal provided by their masters. Rather, as Sutch has seen, they supplemented it by fishing, hunting, raising fowl, and keeping gardens.

The total economic performance reflected the specially favored circumstances of the North American economy. While indebtedness remained a pressing problem, as in all the slave-holding countries and colonies, the southern planters during the nineteenth century did not have to mortgage themselves to the African slave traders. If many southern planters, in speculative bursts, bought slaves unwisely in the domestic slave trade, their misfortune was balanced by the capital gains that accrued to those in less productive areas who were selling. The large tracts of cheap land made possible a shift to food production and a retreat toward autarky during periods of low tobacco or cotton prices. In the smaller islands of the West Indies, planters had to import food for their slaves, and a collapse of sugar prices or the wartime interruption of trade, or such natural disasters as hurricanes, threatened starvation. Famine did not trouble the United States during the nineteenth century, and severe underfeeding occurred only exceptionally.

These circumstances hardly justify sweeping generalizations about the entrepreneurial rationality of the master class. They suggest a very different kind of economic flexibility, appropriate to a regime that had managed to cushion itself against the vicissitudes of the market by retaining, if not creating, a significant non-market sector within the heart of its export-oriented economy. And this flexibility – this particular form of adjustment to the world market – suggests nothing so much as the historical experience of merchant capital in its mobilization of precapitalist labor systems within an expanding international capitalist mode of production.

At the root of the interpretation sketched here lies a particular evaluation of the historical role of merchant capital, which Marx first advanced and Maurice Dobb developed. Specifically, it insists that merchant capital has exerted a conservative influence in all except the most extraordinary circumstances and that under seigneurial and other precapitalist modes of production it has generally retarded industrial development while stimulating economic growth. Modern colonial and plantation economies, based on monoculture and subjected to the sway of merchant capital, embodied features of two different economic systems. They arose within a developing world capitalist mode of production and, from the beginning and virtually by definition, functioned within a world market. But they simultaneously rested on slave or other dependent labor systems that deprived them of the best social and ideological as well as economic advantages of a market in labor-power, in contradistinction to that market in labor which slavery's capitalization of labor made possible.

Thus, among other ramifications, the macroeconomic structure of the plantation sector of the world economy had only an indirect relation to the microeconomic structure of individual plantations, considered as firms. Both exhibited economies of scale in the production of crops that can command a viable if sometimes speculative price on a market external to the system of commodity exchange and labor control within the individual firms.

Whatever the contribution of economies of scale, the slaveholders' most powerful advantage over the yeomen was, as Gavin Wright has pointed out, financial. So long as the economy depended upon monoculture and the export market, with little chance to shift resources internally, those with the capital to command land and slaves had disproportionately large opportunities. In other words, the very dependence of the slave system on merchant capital created massive if temporary opportunities for the ruling class to amass great wealth.

The colonial expansion of capitalism not only absorbed pre-capitalist economic systems; it created them. The enserfment of the Russian peasants during and after the sixteenth century, the second serfdom in eastern Europe, the economic exploitation of the highland Indian communities of Mexico and Peru, and the rise of plantation-based slave regimes in the American lowlands constituted varying expressions of colonial capitalist expansion. They represented nothing so much as the power of merchant capital to adjust unfree labor systems to the rising demand of western European mass markets, which themselves, however paradoxically, arose on free labor – on the emergence of labor-power as a commodity. Within this process, slavery represented a major advance over quasi-seigneurial alternatives, for it permitted greater economic rationalization and a more flexible labor market.

What slavery could not do, despite its economies of scale and its financial advantages, was to lay the foundations for sustained growth and qualitative development. Nowhere did it advance science and technology, generate self-expanding home markets adequate to encourage industrial diversification, accumulate capital within its own sphere for industrial development, or encourage the kind of entrepreneurship without which modern industry would have been unthinkable. It produced spectacular growth in response to the demand of an outside society but simultaneously guaranteed stagnation and decline once that support was withdrawn.

Fogel and Engerman have reasonably stressed the long periods of prosperity for the slaveholders and economic growth for the slave economies as prima facie evidence of viability. Their argument, while reasonable by the standards of the bourgeois economics they share with most of their critics, reopens the question of what bourgeois economists and historians, whether for or against Fogel and Engerman, mean by viability. From our point of view, viability can refer only to the political security of the human beings who commanded the regimes – the slaveholders. And at that, there remains the theoretical possibility, noted by Fogel and Engerman themselves, that a socially retrogressive regime might achieve such viability by inflicting unspeakable horrors on its people.

That trifle aside, nothing in the interesting and discretely valuable new work in economic history undermines the thesis that slavery condemned the slaveholders to a political fate which makes all appeals to the prosperity of *longue durée** beside the point. For the specific kind of economic stagnation suffered by their economies closed the road to an industrial revolution – to that economic development without which the slaveholders remained at the mercy of their enemies. That the confrontation with those enemies took half a century or longer to unfold poses interesting secondary questions but does not weaken the primary argument.

All slave societies in the New World met the same economic fate and left wrecks in their wake. That of the Old South, however, had a special quality. In striking contrast to the West Indies and in partial contrast to Brazil, the Old South produced a slaveholding class capable of seizing regional political power and of deeply influencing national politics for more than a half a century. Thus, the structural economic deficiencies of the regime did much more than create painful problems of readjustment once the world demand schedule for staples

* Long term – literally "long duration."

34

slackened. Rather, they confronted a powerful retrograde social class with the prospect of defeat and disaster.

Only in this political context do discussions of the economic viability of slavery take on meaning. And in the end, the historical verdict sustains the older view against all revisionist caveats: northern freedom, not southern slavery, generated the political, economic, and military wherewithal for the nation's survival, development, and rise to world power.

The following pages, from the critical review essay "Poor Richard at work in the cotton fields: the psychological and ideological presuppositions of Time on the Cross *and other studies of slavery," elaborate some of the consequences of the Old South's class structure and its culture of paternalism. Much of the argument takes the form of disputing the contention of* Time on the Cross *that slaves and masters shared "Victorian" family values. According to Genovese and Fox-Genovese, the South's culture was not Victorian but "paternalist." It was based on differing, if overlapping, conceptions of masters and slaves, and derived from the fact that they shared (in different ways) "membership in a plantation family," with the planter as father-figure. This culture and psychology, according to the authors, derived logically from an economy based on slave plantations. This analysis is in many ways a summary of the one developed in much greater detail in* Roll, Jordan, Roll.

Mintz reminds us that both masters and slaves in the New World confronted a new social and economic environment, to which they could apply only a limited portion of their original cultural legacy.[5] The masters, who enjoyed the commanding advantage of power, had the upper hand in shaping the institutions that would govern the public life of the community. Physical environment and economics, as well as unconscious psychological factors, may have powerfully influenced their elaboration of social, legal, and political norms, but they retained the option of institutionalizing at least some of their most cherished and consciously held values. We can, as Mintz argues, "probably assume that the behavioral norms of slaves, be it in the United States or in the West Indies, were at some expectable variance from the norms of the society in which they were compelled to live."[6] In other words, just as the masters retained some portion of their heritage, which they adapted to New World conditions, so did the slaves retain aspects of their African heritage, which they adapted to the constraints imposed by enslavement.

The cultures of the New World slave societies, in short, resulted from the struggles between those who were becoming the slave and master classes. From the first purchase of a black by a white, there were slaves and masters in the New World. But the classes that composed the slave societies resulted from historical processes that included non-slaveholding whites and, eventually, some free blacks. Blacks, as well as whites, contributed mightily to these emerging cultures. Blacks, like whites, brought to the New World their own beliefs and practices. And even when they could not preserve the specific forms or the social meaning of those beliefs and practices, their participation in the evolving slave societies remained profoundly influenced by the structures of psychological identity and response they brought with them.

A bountiful supply of land suited to the production of scarce raw materials and the possibility of employing slave labor, among other New World conditions, permitted the southern slaveholders to practice economic rationality within the world market and in response to European cultural possibilities. These conditions did not free them from the economic and social, or cultural and psychological constraints imposed by their historical development. Their economic success long remained dependent upon European demand for southern commodities, and, psychologically, the slaveholders remained products of centuries of European ontogeny. Their social, political, and cultural institutions developed between two poles. Only a herculean suspension of disbelief could cast them as rational capitalist entrepreneurs in a historical context in which the most advanced European businessmen still showed a marked preference for investment in land, office, or royal finance, rather than for reinvestment in business. European culture, including the English, still devotedly espoused the aristocratic and gentlemanly virtues. Even the novels of Richardson and Defoe, so permeated with the values of bourgeois individualism, presented the leisured, paternalistic, and morally sensitive landed gentry as the ultimate cultural model.[7]

The Protestant Reformation and the English Revolution, not to mention the gradual rise of capitalism, had firmly buttressed individualistic self-assertion in all realms of life, but they had not eradicated older notions of social responsibility. A modified seigneurial ideal still prevailed as the ultimate goal of individual endeavor. The intense anxiety and flight from the aggressive energies inherent in any thorough individualism had characterized the Reformation and continued to plague Protestants and capitalists alike until it attained its most dramatic embodiment in the Victorian morality celebrated – somewhat anachronistically, let it be noted – by Fogel and Engerman. The reaction to the ideological revolution of bourgeois individualism took many forms in different countries and cultures. In its most general manifestation, it invariably included a reassertion of "the sanctity and purity of the family circle" in general and paternal authority and responsibility in particular.[8] The general reaction makes excellent historical and psychological sense. The family had constituted the prototype for both the seigneurial and the feudal systems and constituted an essential component of their ideological hegemony. What could be more natural than to follow the path drawn by Luther when he revolted against the authority of the church in the name of the higher authority of God and to repudiate the constraints of traditional institutions in the name of the deeper principle upon which they rested – that of the family.

Fogel and Engerman clearly understand the social, cultural, and ideological importance of the southern family, black and white. They acknowledge that in the South more significantly than in the North, "The relationship between its ruling and its servile class was marked by patriarchal features which were strongly reminiscent of medieval life" (I: 29). Rather than pursuing the dynamics and implications of their insight in the historical context, however, they immediately turn to planter regulation of slave family life. They concede that the planters did not view "the slave family purely as a business investment" since the planters took their Victorian attitudes seriously, and then argue that the coincidence of "morality and good business practice . . . created neither surprise nor consternation among most planters" (I: 129–30). One might wonder, here as elsewhere, about their celebration of black culture and achievement, since they reduce both to a mere reflex of the masters' wills and to the internalization of white norms. Yet, whatever Victorian morality the planters did espouse – and where, in *Time on the Cross*, are Steven Marcus's "Other Victorians"? – must have been either a very recent and fragile import from England or the discrete product of a specifically southern historical process that stretched back almost two centuries and involved both blacks and whites.*

Fogel and Engerman not only fail to deal with the historical development of southern paternalism, let alone with the possibility that its force might have derived precisely from a psychological reaction to the business success and ownership of men that contradicted traditional and liberal values; they also neglect the contributions of blacks to the forging of that paternalism. Rather, they present an improbable picture of a strong black family inculcated by that enlightened combination of white business practice and morality and pallidly reflecting white Victorian practice. Not that they are wrong about the strength of black family life under slavery. But by their own criteria, they are wrong to treat the black family, or the black work ethic, as an achievement of black people under adversity and as a source of black cultural vigor; for, in their account, it represents a success only according to modern white criteria. Unwittingly, they have rested their case for black achievement upon a total black identification with white norms – which, after all, is what Elkins said in the first place.** Despite their deep and admirable hostility to racism, they have, by a series of implicit culture-bound assumptions, moved perilously if unconsciously close to the very position they seek to combat.

If black slaves had arrived in the South with no previous nuclear family tradition, or with a family tradition widely at variance with prevailing white norms, and if they had then completely identified with – or assimilated or observed – those white norms, they could hardly have drawn an abiding source of strength from that family life. For if, in the absence of comparable indigenous family patterns, they had, like the proverbial blank slate, accepted the imprint of another culture, the patterns they received would have had no roots in their preslavery experience as a group and would have remained

* See Steven Marcus (1966) *The Other Victorians: A Study of Sexuality and Pornography in Mid-Nineteenth Century England* (New York).
** The reference is to Stanley Elkins (1959) *Slavery* (Chicago), who argued that the slave's African culture was utterly destroyed by slavery, especially the slave trade, and that slaves subsequently identified psychologically with their totally powerful masters.

psychologically grounded in the experience of slavery itself. Consequently, with the disappearance of slavery, the family institution would have lost much of its psychological force and, if they had opposed slavery, much of its cultural appeal. Alternatively, if an identification that led blacks to accept the white family pattern had been rooted in a negative affect [a technical psychological term meaning a strongly felt emotion], the end of slavery would have provoked a conscious rejection of family life along with the repudiation of the master and all he stood for.

In fact, African culture included stable marriage relations and a deep love for and appreciation of children. Traditional African religions, which circumscribed the sense of guilt, encouraged the appreciation of children independent of notions of original sin and without compulsive concern for measures to enforce presumed moral self-betterment.[9] Rather, they strengthened the sense of shame and community responsibility and interpreted morality in a collective spirit. Thus, slaves could effect a partial identification with the marriage patterns of their masters while maintaining their own cultural reasons for doing so. Psychologically, such an identification might still include a number of negative affects, including resentment of the master as ultimate father, as usurper of the power that should accompany the role of black husband and father, as evil father who could break up marriages at will – he had to do so only once for the affect to retain its force. But it would also include a strong positive affect grounded in black culture and psychology and would, accordingly, remain partially independent of the specific experience of slavery. Fogel and Engerman, by evaluating the black family without reference to the African past and, even more important, without reference to independent Afro-American norms, fall into Elkins's reductionist pit, notwithstanding their diametrically opposed conclusions.

Both blacks and whites had good reasons for a large psychological investment in family life as a source of psychological strength and positive self-image independent of their reciprocal relations. In addition, those reciprocal relations, and their respective rejections of the full implications of slavery itself, reinforced the importance of the family as the proper and most viable image of the larger social order. Membership in the plantation family at least partially mitigated the slave's sense of degradation and offered him or her a positive identification with the master and mistress. Extensive psychiatric work has demonstrated that children invariably seek a positive image of the parent with whom they identify, no matter how cruel or vindictive that parent may actually be.[10]

Such positive identifications come at a price. The negative aspects of the parent figure are recognized on some level even when consciously denied in the interests of creating a positive self-image. Normally, the repressed negative aspects, particularly anger at a figure too powerful or too necessary to be directly challenged, surface in some other form. Fogel and Engerman err in their unquestioning acceptance of the ex-slave narratives' reports of the "good master." Reflection upon the frequency with which ex-slaves testified to the good qualities of their own master but readily described masters of neighboring plantations as mean or bad might have made Fogel and Engerman more thoughtful. If an interest in reasonable comfort and a positive sense of themselves encouraged many slaves to see their master as essentially good – to accept his self-proclaimed role as benevolent paternalist – that interest and positive sense would not have prevented the slaves from registering the master's negative qualities or merely his human weaknesses, and would not have prevented their projecting them onto another member of his class.

The discretely good qualities, the general striving for humanity and decency, even the economic rationality of the masters, are not at issue. Most masters could be placed on a scale somewhere between the purely rational entrepreneur and the psychological pervert. No amount of decency, however, could obliterate the central fact of southern life. The slaves did not face the objective laws of the market directly; they faced the individual, human will of another man against whom they had no direct, sanctioned recourse. None of Fogel and Engerman's revisions of the traditional picture of material conditions and economic efficiency alters that fundamental power relation and its psychological and cultural implications. . . .

The final selection from Fruits of Merchant Capital, *from "The debate over* Time on the Cross: *a critique of bourgeois criticism," discusses the political implications of some of the debates about slavery in the Old South. For example, the authors suggest some interpretations of slavery can be used to support black nationalist–separatist political goals, while others are more likely to be cited in support of "liberal–integrationist" policies. Included is a critique of the analysis of slave family values by Herbert Gutman, author of* The Black Family in Slavery and Freedom *and one of the strongest critics of* Time on the Cross. *This selection may serve as a summary and restatement of the basic idea of the paternalist interpretation: that values of both masters and slaves were each shaped by those of the opposite class, locked as they were into confrontation by the nature of the slave plantation economy.*

Those who claim that the Old South had a bourgeois economy and social system must delineate its bourgeois culture and attendant social psychology. Fogel and Engerman conjure up slaves with a bourgeois work ethic and a Victorian sexual code who responded primarily to an economically rational incentive system. Their bourgeois critics provide no alternative except a slave force that responded productively to the whip and yet managed to secure a degree of privacy adequate to the development of a wholly autonomous culture miraculously sealed off from the actions of the masters, whip and all.

The particular Marxist alternative presented here suggests (a) a ruling class spawned by the expansion of European capitalism but increasingly shaped by the precapitalist nature of its relation to the labor force; (b) a pervasive if slowly developing social psychology and attendant ideology mediated by the determined struggle of the contending classes respectively to maintain and to challenge the system of superordination and subordination – mediated, that is, by a struggle for the surplus, which for some meant their very freedom; and (c) the absorption of both problematics within a framework that situates the sociopolitical struggle for power on social rather than personal terrain. A full defense of this line of interpretation will have to be deferred, although it has been prefigured in our own published work and with appropriate qualifications and independent judgments, in the work of other Marxists. This body of work, whatever its shortcomings, has addressed the central issues, much as Fogel and Engerman have. . . .

Marxist critics have tried, without success, to compel a discussion of the more immediate political implications of the debate. With no pejorative intent, we must characterize *Time on the Cross* as a liberal–integrationist attack on both racist and black nationalist interpretations of slavery. Fogel and Engerman apparently accept the characterization, but the silence from their bourgeois critics remains disturbing. Indeed, that silence remains the more disturbing since the bourgeois critics have directed some of their heaviest fire, and certainly much of their impassioned hostility, against what they see as an attempt to interpret black culture as a carbon copy of white. Once more, however, their own views lie buried, and their attempt to bolster their case by invoking sociological theory succeeds only in adding to their embarrassment and confusion. The problem of the black family may stand for the larger problem of the evolution of black culture in slavery. Although Gutman has taken the lead among the bourgeois critics – properly so, in view of his impressive command of the sources and the breadth of his learning in American social history – the others, to a man, have either followed him or, worse, ignored the issue.* Here too, the ideological component of the debate, which they have largely obscured, rises to plague them.

Gutman, in [his] essays and in his subsequent book on the black family, has had to face the thorny problems that confront all demographers and empirical researchers.** Moving backward and forward in time, and sorting out census schedules, birth records, and marriage registers, he has pieced together evidence of family solidarity and widespread kinship networks to produce a valuable addition to our knowledge of the history of the black family. Having demonstrated the existence of family units at different productive units of different sizes, Gutman attempts to assess the import of his empirical work. For him, slave family connections became the primary source of Afro–American culture. He argues, with considerable emphasis, that those family bonds dated from the passage to the New World and therefore owed nothing to the culture of

---

* Gutman's criticisms of *Time on the Cross* can be found in his (1981) *Slavery and the Numbers Game: A Critique of Time on the Cross* (Urbana, Ill.), and in his essay co-authored with Richard Sutch, "Sambo makes good, or were slaves imbued with the Protestant work ethic," in Paul David *et al.* (1976) *Reckoning With Slavery: A Critical Study in the Quantitative History of American Negro Slavery* (New York).

** See Herbert Gutman (1976) *The Black Family in Slavery and Freedom, 1750–1925* (New York).

the masters. "Young slaves everywhere learned from other slaves about marital and familiar obligations and about managing difficult daily social realities."[12] The family thus functioned, in the Parsonian fashion, as the principal agent of "socialization."

Regrettably, neither Gutman nor his associates in the debate define "socialization," and his implicit Parsonianism hardly does justice to Talcott Parsons.* Parsons's severest critics must praise his determined effort to locate his sociological theory in specific relation to economics and social psychology – an effort that formed the core of his life's work. Yet Gutman and, more astonishingly, the economists associated with him discuss socialization divorced from any political economy and from any psychology of cultural transmission. Accordingly, the theoretical underpinnings of his and their work crumble. No wonder, then, that they arrive at the incredible if implicit conclusion that the slaveholders imparted nothing of importance to the culture of the slaves and indeed made no attempt to do so. Virtually any contemporary document suffices to refute this assertion.

It is especially saddening to see Gutman, who writes with such deep feeling about the struggle of black people to shape their own lives, implicitly, and no doubt inadvertently, trivialize their extraordinary effort to embrace and transform a Christianity they initially had to learn from the whites – a Christianity that, among other things, manifested itself in the marriage ceremonies he so lovingly describes. Indeed, where did those marriage ceremonies themselves come from? Surely not from Africa. They came, as Gutman would be the first to acknowledge, from the blacks' own struggle to live with dignity even as slaves. But that struggle necessarily included an acceptance of the inescapability of having to draw upon a variety of sources, and it especially included the wisdom to extract from the whites, slaveholders or no, whatever commended itself as wholesome.

Neither Gutman nor any of his associates notice that their thesis resurrects, in inverted form, the discredited sociology of Gabriel Tarde and of Ulrich B. Phillips, who followed him,

---

* Talcott Parsons (1902–79), an influential sociologist who sought to create a systematic and comprehensive theory of society in such works as *The Social System* (Glencoe, Ill., 1951).

and that it falls victim to the same objections.* Nor do any of them consider the corollary to their own argument – that blacks could not have contributed much to white culture in the South. Gutman has filed the technically correct complaint that he nowhere speaks of the development of the black family as "autonomous," and his associates could also say as much. But it is enough to point out that nowhere do he or any of those associates point to a single positive slaveholders' influence on black culture generally or on the black family in particular.

Conversely, at the Rochester conference [which met to discuss the findings reported in *Time on the Cross*], Fogel and Engerman faced repeated assault for insisting that blacks had merely absorbed white culture and had modeled their family life, sexual mores, and work ethic according to white norms. They even faced charges of "racism." They have heatedly denied the charge and expressed astonishment that anyone would read them as saying any such thing. Yet almost everyone in fact hears them saying just that. Fogel and Engerman are by no means dissembling here. Rather, for them, the blacks did not copy the whites; blacks advanced, as the whites had been advancing, toward acceptance of bourgeois values, which should be understood as non-racial and altogether wonderful. Hence, Fogel and Engerman commit the ghastly error of accusing the abolitionists and many historians of being racists for insisting that blacks could make little progress while they remained slaves. Fogel and Engerman, in short, define progress as progress toward capitalism and define good values as bourgeois values. They praise the blacks for having achieved so much – for having absorbed so much of the bourgeois ethos – even while suffering as slaves. Our readers do not have to be told what Marxists think of this flagrantly ideological mess. But what needs to be kept in mind is that, once again, Fogel and Engerman are plunging into a labyrinth in an effort to rescue the very bourgeois premises they share with their fuming critics, who show not the slightest interest in baring their own assumptions.

The related questions of black culture in slavery and the meaning of black nationalism become all the more urgent in

---

* Gabriel de Tarde (1843–1904) was a French sociologist whose theories distinguished between inventive and imitative persons; for Phillips see the introduction to this volume.

view of Gutman's book on the black family, which in its interpretation of black cultural development implicitly takes extreme black nationalist ground. His associates among the bourgeois critics of Fogel and Engerman do not seem to have noticed this small implication of Gutman's work, which they have so warmly embraced while reaffirming their own commitment to liberal–integrationist ideology and politics. Neither Gutman nor any of his associates show the slightest sympathy for black nationalism, although none of them can be so naive as not to notice that their social history lends heavy support to the black nationalist interpretation of the black experience. It is especially unfortunate that Gutman ignores the pioneering work of Sterling Stuckey, Vincent Harding, Amiri Baraka, and other black scholars whose work on black cultural history compels all who write on black history to confront the national question.* The bourgeois critics not merely fail to meet the challenge – they ignore it. And they thereby deny the most serious claims of the people whose lives they study and in whose defense they claim to write. On the decisive questions, they join Fogel and Engerman on liberal–integrationist ground, albeit with much inconsistency and confusion. We have been privy to a family quarrel among liberals.

Marxists claim no magic formula for resolving the thorny theoretical problems presented by black America as a nation within a nation. But since W. E. B. Du Bois, we have, in different ways and with different judgments, struggled with the problem, not as an abstraction but in class terms. Marxists have distinguished between bourgeois and proletarian influences on nationalism in general and on nationalist politics in particular. For example, the argument of *Roll, Jordan, Roll* identified the roots of black nationalism in the measure of success scored by Afro–American slaves in their struggle for spiritual as well as physical survival. Black nationalism emerges as a historically authentic development, not as a pathological response to oppression. The slave class made the decisive cultural contribution, the implications of which are the more telling since those slaves metamorphosed, with

* Vincent Harding is author of *There is a River: The Black Struggle for Freedom in America* (New York, 1981); Amiri Imamu Baraka is a poet, playwright, and political activist (who earlier wrote under the name of LeRoi Jones); for Sterling Stuckey, see Chapter 4 below.

emancipation, into a rural proletariat. But, for reasons suggested in *Roll, Jordan, Roll*, the slaves alone could not have forged or sustained a degree of cultural autonomy appropriate to their needs. The very idea of a "slave culture" is absurd. The class struggle had to pass on to broader terrain. The survival of black slaves required the building of bridges across class lines to free blacks, North and South.

This viewpoint remains debatable. Fogel and Engerman, by rejecting it root and branch, provide a coherent integrationist alternative, wrong though it may be. Here as elsewhere they meet their responsibilities as engaged scholars. Would that their excellent example were more generally followed.

NOTES

The Editor gratefully acknowledges permission to reprint material from *The Fruits of Merchant Capital: Slavery and Bourgeois Property in the Rise and Expansion of Capitalism*, by Eugene Genovese and Elizabeth Fox-Genovese. Copyright © 1983 by Elizabeth Fox-Genovese and Eugene D. Genovese. Reprinted by permission of Oxford University Press, Inc., and the authors.

1 See Karl Marx, *Capital: A Critical Analysis of Capitalist Production*, 3 vols (Moscow, 1961), esp. I: 146–76, 564–774; III: 262–599; Maurice Dobb (1947) *Studies in the Development of Capitalism* (New York); Rodney Hilton *et al.* (1978) *The Transition from Feudalism to Capitalism* (London); V. I. Lenin (1956) *The Development of Capitalism in Russia: The Process of the Formation of a Home Market for Large-Scale Industry* (Moscow). See also the seminal contribution of Eric Hobsbawm in Trevor Aston (ed.) (1967) *Crisis in Europe, 1560–1660* (New York), chaps 2 and 3.

2 For a sketch of our views on the several slave systems of the New World and their relation to European metropolises, see Eugene D. Genovese (1969) *The World the Slaveholders Made: Two Essays in Interpretation* (New York).

3 For an original defense of some of the propositions we have been arguing and for a cogent criticism of Fogel's work on the "specification problem" and other matters, see Jon Elster (1978) *Logic and Society: Contradictions and Possible Worlds* (Chichester), 208–18.

4 Forrest McDonald, (1965) *E Pluribus Unum: The Formation of the American Republic, 1776–1790* (Boston), 65.

5 Sidney W. Mintz, "History and anthropology: a brief reprise," in Stanley Engerman and Eugene D. Genovese (eds) (1974) *Race and Slavery in the Western Hemisphere: Quantitative Studies* (Princeton, N.J.), 485.

6 Ibid., esp. 490.

7 Esp. Samuel Richardson (1972) *The History of Sir Charles Grandison*,

ed. Jocelyn Harris, 3 vols (London). Cf. Ian Watt (1957) *The Rise of the Novel* (London).

8 "Victorian" usually applies to the period after 1830 and particularly mid-century and after. Fogel and Engerman apply the term to a society with roots in the seventeenth century, and they treat that society as a homogeneous unit. The term is, furthermore, inappropriate, since it remains a matter of debate whether American society and culture were ever truly Victorian. See George Fitzhugh (1960) *Cannibals All!*, ed. C. Vann Woodward; Walter Houghton (1957) *The Victorian Frame of Mind* (New Haven, Conn.); W. L. Burn (1968) *The Age of Equipoise* (London); Bernard Bailyn (1955) *The New England Merchants of the Seventeenth Century* (Cambridge, Mass.); Perry Miller (1953) *The New England Mind* (Cambridge, Mass.); Lyle Koehler (1981) *A Search for Power: The "Weaker Sex" in Seventeenth-Century New England* (Urbana, Ill.). A fuller treatment of the earlier period can be found in Allen Kulikoff (1986) *Tobacco and Slaves: The Development of Southern Cultures in the Chesapeake, 1680–1800* (Chapel Hill, N.C.).

9 Cf. Eugene Genovese (1974) *Roll, Jordan, Roll* (New York).

10 E.g. John Bowlby (1973) *Attachment and Loss*, vol. II, *Separation: Anxiety and Anger* (New York), 177.

11 Gutman (1976) *Black Family in Slavery and Freedom* (New York), 17.

2

WITHIN THE PLANTATION HOUSEHOLD

Women in a paternalist system

Elizabeth Fox-Genovese

In this excerpt from her book, Within the Plantation Household: Black and White Women of the Old South, *Elizabeth Fox-Genovese discusses women's place in the paternalist, hierarchical world of plantation slavery. The prescribed and actual roles of women are necessarily an important aspect for any group – for Fox-Genovese, the planter class – that interprets its world through a metaphor of family relationships.*

Here, Fox-Genovese insists that plantation mistresses were quite different from the women of the new urban bourgeoisie – the wives of the businessmen and professionals often referred to as the "middle class" – of the antebellum North. As historians have shown in recent years, many of these middle-class women had adopted the idea that men and women properly belonged to "separate spheres" of life. That of women was the "domestic sphere," the private world of home, where women should raise children, care for their husbands, and provide proper moral and religious guidance for their families. Men, by contrast, belonged to a public sphere of work and public affairs (including politics). Usually people thought of these "spheres" as literally separate, as men would leave home each day to work in offices, shops, or factories. Women did not see the idea of separate spheres as implying that women were inferior to men. On the contrary, within their own domestic sphere women were superior to men. Thus some historians see the idea of separate spheres as a step in the direction of the modern feminist idea of complete equality for women and men in all spheres.

Women in the South, according to Fox-Genovese, were different. The difference was rooted, she argues, in the special nature of the plantation as a producing "household," quite unlike the domestic "homes" of the North's middle-class women. Plantation mistresses, unlike their northern counterparts, continued to be intimately involved in the world of production. At the same time, it was a world still dominated by men – the masters of the plantations. In the world of paternalism, women were, as they ought to be, subordinate to men.

The selection reprinted here includes a brief excerpt from Fox-Genovese's theoretical discussion of the southern household, followed by her extended treatment of Louisa McCord. McCord was the daughter and wife of South Carolina planters, and, highly unusual for southern women, published essays on political economy and current issues, including nineteenth-century feminism. In these essays she firmly endorsed the subordination of women in the public sphere and also endorsed what she saw as the conservative values of her own slave-based society. Fox-Genovese admits that McCord is an exceptional person in many respects, but, nevertheless, "mapped . . . the logic of women's place in a slaveholding society" better than other women. The procedure is analogous to Eugene Genovese's earlier argument that proslavery theorist George Fitzhugh, in many ways the most extreme proslavery writer, was the one who laid out best the logic of the world of the slaveholders.

Antebellum southern women, like all others, lived in a discrete social system and political economy within which gender, class, and race relations shaped their lives and identities. Thus, even a preliminary sketch of the history of southern women must attend scrupulously both to their immediate conditions and to the larger social system in which the immediate conditions were embedded and by which they were informed. We have, in a sense, two views: the view from within and the view from without – the view of the participants and the view of the historians. Women do not normally experience their lives as manifestations of the laws of political economy, although they may register sharply the vicissitudes of economic fortunes. The papers of southern women are accounts of troubles with servants and children, of struggles for faith, of friendships, and of turning hems. These intimate personal details and perceptions constitute a valuable record in themselves and suggest patterns of a larger social experience. We inevitably abstract from historical evidence in order to construct a narrative or an analysis. The most significant differences among historians occur at this stage of abstraction, which itself influences the ways in which we interpret and organize the specific evidence. Southern history abounds in these debates, which afford some of the most lively and theoretically informed writing in American history. But the debates have not yet taken adequate account of the history of southern women. Nor has the experience of southern women significantly penetrated the "larger" debates, which badly need closer attention to gender.

Southern women belonged to a slave society that differed decisively from the northern bourgeois society to which it was politically bound. Slavery as a social system shaped the experience of all its women, for slavery influenced the nature of the whole society, not least its persisting rural character. Southern slave society consisted largely of a network of households that contained within themselves the decisive relations of production and reproduction. In the South, in contrast to the North, the household retained a vigor that permitted southerners to ascribe many matters – notably labor relations, but also important aspects of gender relations – to the private sphere, whereas northerners would increasingly ascribe them to the public spheres of market and state. The household structure and social relations of southern society had multiple and far-reaching consequences for all spheres of southern life, including law, political economy, politics, and slaveholders' relations with yeomen and other non-slaveholding whites. And it had special consequences for gender relations in general and women's experience in particular.[1]

The persistence in the South of the household as the dominant unit of production and reproduction guaranteed the power of men in society, even as measured by nineteenth-century bourgeois standards. During the period in which northern society was undergoing a reconversion of household into home and ideologically ascribing it to the female sphere, southern society was reinforcing the centrality of plantation and farm households that provided continuities and discontinuities in the experience of women of different classes and races. Variations in the wealth of households significantly differentiated women's experience, but the common structure as a unit of production and reproduction under men's dominance provided some basic similarity. Effectively, the practical and ideological importance of the household in southern society reinforced gender constraints by ascribing all women to the

domination of the male heads of households and to the company of the women of their own households. In 1853 Mary
Kendall, a transplanted New Englander, wrote to her sister of
her special pleasure in receiving a letter from her, for

> I seldom see any person aside from our own family,
> and those employed upon the plantation. For about three
> weeks I did not have the pleasure of seeing *one white
> female face*, there being no white family except our own
> upon the plantation.

The experience of black slave women differed radically from
that of all white women, for they belonged to households
that were not governed by their own husbands, brothers, and
fathers. But even black slave women shared with white women
of different social classes some of the constraints of prevalent
gender conventions.[2] . . .

Louisa Susanna McCord – daughter of Langdon Cheves of
South Carolina, planter, statesman, and president of the Bank
of the United States – combined the typical life of a woman
of her class with an atypical career as the author of articles
on political economy and social theory, including the woman
question. At the relatively advanced age of thirty, she married
a respected jurist, David J. McCord, with whom she had three
children. She spent much of her life before the Civil War
quietly in Columbia or on one of their nearby plantations. In
Columbia she benefited from the lively intellectual circle that
centered on South Carolina College. An outspoken and polemi-
cally effective defender of slavery and the subordination of
women, she testified in her poetry and drama to a deep sensitivity to women's experience. Hardly typical, either in the
range of her interests or in her manner of representing them,
she none the less offers an essential perspective on many other
women's private feelings, for she mapped, more clearly than
any of her peers, the logic of women's place in slaveholding
society.

Little given to personal, much less confessional, narratives,
Louisa McCord wrote more of political economy than of
women's condition. She left no diaries or journals and few
letters. She preferred to consider women's lot from the objective perspective of society rather than from the subjective perspective of their personal experience. On the rare occasions on

which she wrote of that experience, she did so obliquely. Her reflections on women's feelings rarely assumed the first person, singular or plural. She did not invite the identification of other women in some purported sisterhood. More the Roman matron than the winsome young lady, she offered a forbidding picture of women's obligations. She scoffed mercilessly at any notion of women's rights that did not insist upon their duties. Yet in her political economy and antifeminist polemics, as well as in her poetry and drama, she captured the social conditions that grounded the personal identities of the women of her class. Her intrinsic and compelling merits entitle her to more attention than she has yet received. A fiercely biting and intellectually gifted polemicist, she wrote out of the marrow of her class, her race, and her gender. Her writings differed in voice and focus from the personal reflections of less talented and less politically and theoretically sophisticated "ordinary" slaveholding women, yet they made explicit attitudes and values that other women took for granted.

More traits united Louisa McCord with other slaveholding women than separated her from them. The apparent differences derived primarily from the variations in their voices, styles, and intended audiences. Most slaveholding women wrote subjectively, in a personal voice and for members of their own families. Even those who wrote for publication, notably the novelists, remained close to that personal perspective and invited their readers' identification with the stories of other women. Louisa McCord wrote primarily from an objective perspective, in an intentionally political voice, and for an enlightened audience. She wrote as a woman, but primarily in the voice of a latter day Roman matron who measured personal feelings against their social consequences. She worked, normally with success, for an impersonal voice and an objective perspective, although even she had occasional lapses. She was wont to mobilize her considerable wit, satire, and charm in the service of her causes rather than in the service of herself – or, as she would have said, in the service of narrow personal ambition, which she deplored in all, especially politicians and belles. The case for Louisa McCord as guide to the imaginative worlds of slaveholding women lies not in her personal voice, but in her evocation of the dynamics of the external world in which those imaginative worlds were inscribed. Through political economy, political and social theory, drama, and poetry she articulated the worldly constraints within which other slaveholding women sought identity.

Louisa McCord wrote for the intellectual elite of the South and, beyond it, for the Republic of Letters of the Western world. She surely did not intend her political economy for a primarily female audience, for it would have taken considerable effort to find a southern woman who could even approximate her mastery of a subject taught only in men's schools. Even her literary work did not readily fall into a distinct domestic or female discourse. She vigorously attacked Harriet Beecher Stowe and Harriet Martineau as apostles of misguided, dangerous, and muddle-headed notions, much as she attacked the men – George Frederick Holmes and George Fitzhugh, among other worthies – with whom she disagreed. She granted Martineau and Stowe the grudging respect of bothering to attack them at all, although she gave them no quarter in dismissing their ideas as muddle-headed.*

Louisa McCord did not keep a journal, at least not one that has survived or to which she ever referred. For whatever reasons – and they probably included temperament and education – she directed her authorial ambitions toward intellectual and political debates, toward the context of women's lives more than toward personal experience. Born 3 December 1810 in Charleston, to Langdon Cheves and Mary Elizabeth Dulles, she spent the years from 1819 to 1829 in Philadelphia, where her father was serving as director of the Bank of the United States. There she received an education appropriate to a young woman of her class, and then some. With her sister, Sophia, she attended an academy and then was tutored at home in French – which she learned to read, speak, and translate fluently – and Italian as well as in history, music, astronomy, and the related cultural graces that constituted the light academic course her father considered appropriate for his daughters. She also shared in her brothers' instruction in mathematics, for which she displayed a precocious "passion." According to family legend, as a 10-year-old she was so taken with the

* For Harriet Martineau and Harriet Beecher Stowe, see below; George Frederick Holmes and George Fitzhugh were southern proslavery writers.

subject that, being barred from instruction in it, she concealed herself behind the door of the room in which her brothers were being tutored. There her father found her and, being touched by her interest, permitted her to join the lessons.[3]

From her early years, exposure to her father's friends and associates gave her a formidable apprenticeship in and abiding passion for politics.[4] In 1830, after the Cheves's return to Charleston, she inherited her own cotton plantation, Lang Syne, from an aunt and began to manage it, presumably under the direction and advice of her beloved father. During the same year, her sister Sophia married Charles T. Haskell and settled on a plantation nearby. A letter from their mother, Mary Cheves, reported that both of them adapted well to their new responsibilities, especially the making of clothes for their people. Even Louisa Cheves, who had never had much experience with sewing, cut out and made up pantaloons, "Jackson" coats, shirts, and clothes for the women and children.[5]

Little evidence remains of Louisa Cheves's life during the following decade, although it apparently left her with a jaundiced perspective on the status of belle, which so many young women of her class relished. In 1839, she reported to her brother Langdon that she and Anna, her younger sister, had finally returned home. "I have surmounted a summer at the Springs, which thank Heaven *est finie* and I am again released from playing belle, which, nolens volens, seems some how or other to be my destiny when I go into company." Never again would she "go to matronize Miss Anna in the gay world" without donning "a cap, or some such distinguishing mark of age." She would give none the excuse to think that her "venerable self stepping close on nine & twenty had any ambition to pass as young Lady, any more." She vowed to "pin a piece of paper with *'aged twenty-nine'* on my shoulder, and if that don't scare off the young seventeen year-olders who come to flirt with me, the dear knows what will." She confessed to being "tired to death with rivalling Nan in their good graces." But she was talking "of bygone ills which really seem now like the confused bustle of a dream," for they have been going through "such very different scenes of late that the contrast seems unreal." She had been attending General Hayne's widow, who was in dreadful spirits and health. Had it not been for the sudden death of her friend and the misery of his widow, she might have judged the bustle and "fooleries" of the Springs "more indulgently, tho' at best, *vraiment*, they don't suit my fancy."[6]

Apart from time she spent at Lang Syne, Louisa Cheves lived an active social life in the company of her family and friends. She made and received calls and engaged in the social rounds of her set. Continuing to see her father's political friends, she deepened her understanding of the issues of the day and strengthened her fierce loyalty to the South. Many years later, she jotted innumerable notes for a memorial that would do justice to the father she deeply revered. "I have never known or read of any man equal for completeness of character (This is the verdict I think not a natural prejudice in his favor but of my well-sifted reason)." Her father never stooped to imperfect means, however worthy the cause. He never swerved from his pursuit of truth, never changed "the right to suit circumstance," never sacrificed probity to interest or ambition. His only limit lay in his conviction that one should "never act wrongly because right is unattainable," but must "wait if the glimmer of truth may prevail, when the cloud of wrong is too heavy." He delighted "in the happiness of young people." She recalled seeing him "standing & beating time to the joyous dancing of our young friends too happy for the languor of fashion & showing how he enjoyed &c."[7] The only other hint of Louisa Cheves's feelings during her protracted spinsterhood appear in the collection of poems, *My Dreams*, which she published – or her husband had published for her – in 1848, eight years after her marriage. And even those poems testify more to the love that she had found than to the loneliness of the years before she found it.[8] . . .

Louisa McCord's passing experience of spinsterhood apparently undercut any inclinations she might once have had to identify with adolescent fantasies of love, belles, and even young wives. She did not aspire to collect tokens of admiration for her person. It was as if she willed herself to become a matron even before marrying and bearing her own children. By 1851, when she published *Caius Gracchus*, she was able to portray Gracchus's young wife Lucinia with sympathy, but with scant trace of identification.[9] In "Woman and her needs" (1852), she scathingly castigated any trace of women's personal ambition for fame, especially that of the belle. Women, she

wrote, degrade themselves when they refuse to submit themselves to "a faithful adherence to the laws of God and nature."
Those women who "forget the woman's duty-fulfilling
ambition to covet man's fame-grasping ambition" give way to
"mistaken hungering for the forbidden fruit." This "grasping
at notoriety belonging (if indeed it belongs properly to any)
by nature to man, is at the root of all her debasement. Look
at the ballroom belle for instance." She errs not "because there
is harm in the ball-room enjoyment of youth; in the joy-waking
music, or the spirit-rousing dance; but because she would be
talked of, and forgets duty, conscience, and heart, in the love
of notoriety."[10] . . .

By the time Louisa Cheves married Col. David J. McCord
in 1840, she had forged a strong, independent character. Yet
her fifteen years of marriage to a respected lawyer consolidated
the apprenticeships of her youth and laid the foundation for
the strengths she displayed during her own widowhood and
the travail of the Confederacy. The testimony to her love for
her husband remains strong, if indirect. Her poetry, much of
which she probably wrote before meeting him, and her drama
Caius Gracchus, which she wrote before he died, both evoke
the place of love in a woman's life, but only one poem, "'Tis
But Thee, Love, Only Thee," explicitly portrayed her own
experience. Her marriage remained her great silence, but every
word she published testified to its centrality. For Louisa
McCord published only during the years of her marriage. And,
according to family legend, she would never have published
her most personal writing, the poems of *My Dreams*, had David
McCord not sent them to a publisher without her permission.[11]

Louisa McCord's silence evokes, as poignantly as do the
words of others, the importance of marriage to her and to her
countrywomen. Slaveholders' marriages were as likely as the
marriages of members of other classes to contain misery, infi-
delity, and even violence. But slaveholding women, in their
own way, echoed the sentiments of the articulate freedman
who harangued his brothers: "The Marriage Covenant is at
the foundation of all our rights."[12] Louisa McCord believed,
although she never said in so many words, that marriage
constituted the bedrock of adult women's natural and,
especially, their social identities. Where others sought the truth
of women's experience in personal feeling, she sought it in

their social roles or in the logic of nature. Her poem "Pretty Fanny" represents a young woman who challenges her "Grandame" about the desirability of marriage. The grandmother does not dispute:

> That man's a heartless, false deceiver;
> Believes from him, a maiden's ways,
> 'Tis Heaven's best mercy to deliver;
> Owns that wives have much to suffer;
> That such fate 'tis wise to dread.

And Fanny ponders,

> How that false deceiver, – man
> With his tongue could do such wonders,
> More than Grannie's wisdom can.

During Fanny's pondering, her prudence falls asleep, and "love's radiance beaming" intrudes, "Oped such worlds to her wild dreaming/That quite forgot was poor old Grannie." Fanny, like her grandmother before her, "soon was what she dreaded,/And a wedded life her lot." Only in one poem, "'Tis But Thee, Love, Only Thee," does Louisa McCord evoke love from a personal perspective. In it she wrote that, as in the glancing of sunbeams, "There my love, I think on thee," so in "fear, or dark misgiving," only one angel hovers near, "Who but thee, love? only thee!"

> Thus in hope, and thus in sorrow,
>   Fancy paints thy shadow near,
> Thou the brightener of each morrow,
>   Thou, the soother of each care.
> And the sun which gives me light,
> And the star which gilds my night,
> And the lingering hope to cheer me,
> 'Tis but thee, love! only thee![13]

Louisa McCord's sociological and precociously naturalistic perspective encoded the wisdom of those slaveholding women who bemoaned their own marriages and even those who rejected the married state, as well as the wisdom of those who delighted in their marriages. Marriage provided the standard against which they assessed their own lives. And how else could it have been among a preeminently rural social class that presided over a slave society, in which women had no viable adult alternative to marriage except widowhood? If women were fortunate, marriage anchored their personal and social lives.[14] . . .

Louisa McCord's attack on women's quest for personal fame was derived, I suspect, from intimate personal knowledge of the temptations she deplored. She, not unlike Emily Dickinson, had wrestled with those tendencies in herself and had vanquished them young . . . Louisa McCord may have been troubled by her spinsterhood and the prospect of its permanence, but by the time her writings were published she had integrated her personal experience into a theoretical perspective on society and her place as a woman in it. In her view, the personal experience of women must serve the larger good of nature's purpose and society's needs. Louisa McCord may be counted among the lucky – or the deserving – in having found such deep personal satisfaction in meeting her self-defined responsibilities. During the years of her marriage she divided her time between Columbia and Lang Syne, in the management of which she continued to take an interest. She especially attended to the "comfort & well-being of a large number of slaves (to whom she was ever a kind and attentive mistress)." The demands of her life ensured that she could give only episodic attention to her own writing, although her husband encouraged her. Their identical worktables stood in different corners of the library at Lang Syne, and, according to their daughter, they delighted in the time spent there.[15]

Louisa McCord's daughter, Louisa, remembered her father as a warm man "who dearly loved a joke," told wonderful stories, and "loved to give dinner parties, not stylish dinner parties . . . but with good cooking, good friends, and best of all, good talk." She especially remembered his "quiet, witty voice and keen bright eyes" and his close attention to his children, whom he watched with the utmost enjoyment, especially when anything in them "seemed to come up to his ideas." Louisa McCord appears to have loved those qualities in him, although she did not count on him always to attend to domestic responsibilities. He entranced the children by occasionally calling them into his room to read to them; for "the reading was sure to be something so original, so different from anything we ever heard from anybody else – so delight-

fully funny." But their mother read to them every day, beginning, as soon as they could understand, with Scott's novels,
which continued as a standby but were gradually supplemented by "French books." She undertook much of their
schooling and occasionally chafed at her husband's lack of
assistance. "I school them all morning," she wrote to her
cousin Mary Middleton, "& of course in the afternoon am too
stupid & tired to do any thing for myself." Until another
solution could be found, she remained a schoolmistress. "Mr
McCord offers to read a little history & geography with them,
but I do not count much upon his help. He does not like
trouble much."[16]

Louisa McCord none the less benefited from considerable
assistance in her domestic responsibilities. Her daughter fondly
recalled Maum Di, who had primary charge of the McCord
children. "Maum Di was our stay and comfort in trouble, our
companion and sympathizer in happiness." According to
family legend, on one occasion the younger Louisa ran to
Maum Di with the complaint that "Mamma with her busy-
body gone and slap me!" But Maum Di could also enforce
standards and was known to inform the young ladies that they
were nothing more than "little ha'ad head spitfires." As the
children grew older and no longer needed her attention, Maum
Di gradually assumed charge of the pantry, where she made
the preserves and cut the sandwiches for tea. Maum Di had
two sisters, both of whom also helped with the children, but
Maum Rache in particular took turns with Maum Di in putting
them to bed and occasionally sleeping in the nursery. Normally, one of two younger slave women, Fanny or Nora, slept
there and also assisted in dressing the young ones. The slave
women rivaled Louisa McCord in shaping her children's early
cultural life, for their stories and music provided sources of
endless bliss.[17] . . .

Sally Baxter, who subsequently married Frank Hampton,
visited the McCords at Lang Syne in 1855 and wrote a description to her father in New York. Nothing she could say could
give him an idea of the beauty of the place. The plantation
was "considered rather a model place even in South Carolina"
where there were so many fine ones. Not very large, it
included only about three thousand acres and two hundred
slaves but of the slaves only about fifteen had not been born

on the place. Nobody could pity the condition of those slaves: "well tended, well cared for, they idolize their mistress, who, in her turn, devotes her whole time and energy to their improvement and comfort." Sally Baxter wished that her father could see Mrs McCord's review of Mrs Stowe's *Uncle Tom's Cabin*. Mrs McCord, like the other members of the Cheves and McCord family, "is hotly engaged in the strife and almost all her feeling and intellect seem to be expended on that one topic." But above all, he should see "this kind of life on a plantation and among the slaves themselves," for it embodied "what southern life is."[18]

McCord never wrote directly on motherhood as woman's vocation, but she regularly evoked it. She left none of those tracts on mother's nurture which readily flowed from the pens of northern women. Nor did she leave private testimony to her feeling for her children, as did many of her southern counterparts. Her dedication of *Caius Gracchus* contains the most direct expression of her feelings as a mother: "To My Son." The moving testimony of the dedication describes the mother's heart as "that quenchless fount of love," which can never "idly rest/From the long love which ever fetters it/In bondage to her child." Reading these lines, one day, her son may catch "the shadow of my love,/Thy soul may guess its fullness." A mother's heart might throb and even break, "but never never/Could deem her child a thing of vice or shame." Even more than this passage, her many references to women's roles as mothers provide an objective perspective on her countrywomen's subjective experience.[19]

For Louisa McCord, women's natural, personal, and social identities converged in the role of mother, which she delineated in a manner that departed significantly from the model that was being offered to white, middle-class women in the North. Nature might endow all women with an instinct for motherhood, but the realization of that instinct depended upon the broad social relations in which it was embedded as well as upon the character of the individual woman. Other women endorsed her view, in the same breath writing of their difficulties in governing their children and their servants and reminding themselves of their duties to both. Louisa McCord's doughty defense of women's true vocation as mothers rested not upon a sentimental view of women's "empire" in the home, but upon a view of southern society as a slave society.[20] Her theory of gender relations proved inseparable from her theories of class and race relations. Her political economy thus furnishes the context for her discussions of women.

Louisa McCord established her intellectual reputation as a political economist, notably as the translator of and enthusiastic commentator on the work of the French political economist Frederic Bastiat. Although she probably read Bastiat after her formation as a woman of strong views on political and social questions, she embraced his work as the commanding formulation of her own convictions.[21] Bastiat's unmitigated defense of liberal political economy, understood primarily as free trade, derived from his understanding of the logic of French capitalist development, but it rested on a social conservatism that proved eminently adaptable to Louisa McCord's own understanding of the needs of southern slave society. She had to ignore Bastiat's resolute condemnation of slavery, but she somehow rose coolly to that task.[22]

In effect, Louisa McCord passionately espoused liberal, free trade principles as they affected the relations between free, preferably propertied, white men in the marketplace. Free trade governed the relations among men, understood as the delegates and lords of households, but should, under no conditions, penetrate the walls of the household to influence its internal relations. This implicit notion of the household, which became explicit in the writings of her fellow proslavery theorist, Henry Hughes of Mississippi, permitted her to bind the liberal free trade principles of bourgeois political economy to apparently contradictory particularistic and hierarchical proslavery convictions. Unfortunately – at least for her antislavery, antiracist admirers – her deep and systematic commitment to racial slavery strengthened her position and helped her to avoid the deepest contradictions that plagued the thought of her impressive predecessor, Thomas Roderick Dew.[23] Yet the central implications of her political economy for her views on "the woman question" lay in her arbitrary divorce of the principles of the market, which must govern political economy in the aggregate, from the principles of social and gender relations. She understood gender as a social condition that must conform to the overriding claims of social order.

Louisa McCord never fully faced the inescapable contradiction between the market, the wondrous workings of which she so admired, and the social views that articulated her commitment to slavery as the foundation of the southern social order. She appears to have reasoned from the specific case of the needs of social order in a slave society to the general case of woman's proper identity and role, but she presented her views on women as if they reflected a general or natural law. Precocious in this respect as in others, she foreshadowed the systematic sexism of late nineteenth-century thought even as she hearkened back to older, traditional views.[24] But she cast both tendencies in her own thought in the common language of early nineteenth-century bourgeois culture. Her observations on women can, superficially, be read as corresponding to those of European and American bourgeois culture. To settle for that reading is to miss entirely the true referents for her words – is to misunderstand her thought and that of other women of her class.

Louisa McCord defended the innate differences between men and women as staunchly as any bourgeois sentimentalist of true womanhood. She even used the term "true woman."[25] She peppered her writings on women with evocations of motherhood, women's duty, women's charity, the unique power of women's love, and almost every imaginable prevailing piety. She forcefully insisted upon woman's special excellence and mission. But she offered a quintessentially southern interpretation of that common vocabulary. She equated gender spheres with moral and physical attributes. She had a high opinion, as well as extensive personal experience, of women's talents and capabilities, but she viewed them as confined within clearly defined channels. Above all, she dismissed with unveiled contempt the concept of systematic individualism and its permutations and corollaries, especially the concept of universal rights.

Louisa McCord, like other southerners who expressed themselves less rigorously, viewed rights as particular, not general. Rights, like the duties that must accompany them, adhere to particular functions. "It is the high duty of every reasoning mortal to aim at the perfecting of his kind by the perfecting of his individual humanity. Woman's task is, to make herself the perfected woman, not the counterfeit man." Elsewhere, she underscored the concept:

God, who has made every creature to its place, has, perhaps, not given to woman the most enviable position in his creation, but a most clearly defined position he has given her. Let her object, then, be to raise herself in that position. Out of it, there is only failure and degradation.[26]

Her view of the perfected woman owed nothing to the bourgeois ideal of female passivity. Freed from any universalist notion of woman's possible equality with man, she felt no need to protect men from women's legitimate self-assertion or strivings. She assuredly held women to possess the same intellectual capabilities as men. Conversely, she castigated any irresponsible celebration of the higher powers of intuition: "The rule of intuitions is the rule of brute force." In attacking intuition as women's distinctive mode of understanding social relations, she was attacking the women's rights advocates who advanced it as justification for their own claims. Man, too, she impatiently reminded them, has his "spontaneities and intuitions," with "the indisputable advantage of being backed by physical force, which will secure, as it always has secured, male supremacy, in case of a clash between contending spontaneities."[27]

She gave no quarter to Harriet Martineau, Fanny Wright, Elizabeth Smith, and their fellow champions of women's rights, ridiculing them mercilessly and always returning to the absurdity of their claim for universal equality. "*Fraternité* extended even to womanhood! And why not? Up for your rights, ladies! What is the worth of a civilization which condemns one half of mankind to Helot submissiveness?" Reform of this kind would destroy civilization. For reform, as she time and again insisted, betokens an entire ideology, not piecemeal tinkering with social arrangements. Touch one part of the system and you destroy the whole. She likened women's rights reformers to Sganarelle, the doctor in Molière's play *Le médecin malgré lui*, who decided that the heart lies on the right hand side of the human body. When his opinion was challenged, he replied that it used to lie on the left side, "but we have changed all that." Martineau's views, according to Louisa McCord, followed that enlightened model:

If Miss Martineau and her sisterhood should prove powerful enough to depose *Le Bon Dieu*, and perfect their

63

democratic system, by reducing *His* influence to a *single vote*, we do not doubt that, according to the approved majority system, it will be clearly and indisputably proved that Cuffee is Sir Isaac Newton, and Mrs Cuffee, Napoleon Buonaparte, and Miss Martineau herself may stand for Cuffee, unless, indeed, she should prefer (as some of her recent works seem to indicate) to have it decided that she is *Le Bon Dieu* himself.[28]

She never settled for some fatuous notion that all is for the best, much less that women's lot is uniformly a happy one. "Woman's condition certainly admits of improvement (but when have the strong forgotten to oppress the weak?)." But she saw no amelioration that could result from the projects of the prophets of women's equality. Woman does suffer from *"compression."* But so may man. "Human cravings soar high. Perhaps there is no human being, not born in a state of imbecility . . . who does not suffer, or fancy that he suffers, from compression." The solution surely did not lie in encouraging everyone to pout for the moon. Instead, it lay in striving for perfection, rather than in agitating for reform. "Here, as in all other improvements, the good must be brought about by working with, not against – by seconding, not opposing – Nature's laws." Above all, women should be mindful that, should they attain the equality they claimed to want, they would rapidly find themselves more oppressed than ever before. In sum, "are the ladies ready for a boxing match?" If so, they would be bested. For whatever men's and women's respective virtues, men would carry the day with respect to physical strength. Man, being "corporeally stronger than woman," has used his strength unjustly and has "frequently, habitually (we will allow her [Martineau] the full use of her argument,) even invariably, oppressed and misused woman." But surely the abuse is not to be corrected by

> pitting woman against man, in a direct state of antagonism, by throwing them into the arena together, stripped for the strife; by saying to the man, this woman is a man like yourself, your equal and similar, possessing all rights which you possess, and (of course she must allow) possessing none others. In such a strife, what becomes of corporeal weakness?[29]

Louisa McCord had no doubt of the outcome. The woman would lose, the world would become a "wrangling dog kennel," and life would be as nasty, brutish, and short as anything Hobbes imagined. Worse, it would become a topsy-turvy, dyspeptic nightmare – "a species of toothache, which, by some socialistic, communistic, feministic, Mormonistic, or any other such application of chloroform to the suffering patient, may be made to pass away in a sweet dream of perfection." So, with impatience, Louisa McCord dismissed all the "isms" that pretend to fell Evil, "which the poor, ignorant world has so long imagined inexplicable and incurable." So she warned against any pretense of transforming the order of God and Nature. "Wo to the world which seeks its rulers where it should but find its drudges! Wo to the drudge who would exalt himself into the ruler!" Thus her argument returns to the problem of Cuffee and of slavery as a social system. "Nature is vigilant of her laws and has no pardon for the breakers of them." The struggle for women's rights, as she saw it, challenged natural and divine intentions. Regrettably, it could only be attributed to native American genius. Happily, "our modest Southern sisters" had not succumbed to its deceptive appeal. It remained "entirely a Yankee notion."[30]

"Woman," Louisa McCord wrote, "is designed by nature, the conservative power of the world."[31] Catharine Beecher would doubtless have concurred. McCord intended a compliment to her gender, the capacities of which she, like Beecher, held in high esteem. All the more reason that she could not bear to see social disorder promulgated upon the world in the name of women's rights. The defense of women's rights constituted the cutting edge of all the baleful "isms" she deplored. Her countrywomen's accounts show that they agreed, even if few cast the question, as she did, in an objective perspective. In truth McCord, like many other slaveholding women, celebrated many of the same qualities in women as did Beecher, yet in using the same words she frequently meant different things. For Beecher represented the conservative wing of northern individualism, whereas McCord openly espoused hierarchical distinctions among human beings. Beecher, drawing the core of her identity from her New England heritage, declared war on many aspects of its Calvinist foundations, notably the institution of the church and original sin. McCord, who did not openly enter the lists of religious controversy, unmistakably drew upon the values of institutions and original sin to justify modern slavery and the subordination of women that it necessarily entailed. It gives one pause to imagine just what she would have thought of Beecher's emphasis on women's scientific management of their kitchens.[32]

The current view of Mary Chesnut and other slaveholding women as critics of slavery and "patriarchy" appears to dismiss Louisa McCord as exceptional. That view rests on a misunderstanding. Louisa McCord never denied women grounds for discontent: she opposed generalizing from individual unhappiness. Ever mindful of the prevalence of evil and of the frailty of human nature, Louisa McCord admitted that southern society left room for improvement, but she denied that the need for improvement justified "reform."

To Louisa McCord "reform," Yankee style, meant nothing less than revolution. She shrewdly linked the goals of the agitators for antislavery and women's rights to those of the French revolutionaries of 1848 and, before them, to those of the Jacobins. Behind the sanctimonious talk of individual right and universal equality, she believed, lurked the specter of landless men and women who thronged the streets, erecting barricades and toppling civilization. Louisa McCord had her private moments of despair, but she endured them as the inevitable dark side of everything she valued.

She drew her strength from the particularist, hierarchical slave society she so steadfastly defended. Elitist to her core, she anticipated all the tendencies that threatened it. At her least attractive, she embraced the pseudoscientific theory that consigned blacks to subhumanity and that her neighbor in Columbia, the Reverend Dr James Henley Thornwell, the great Presbyterian theologian and jewel of the southern church, denounced as unscriptural and infamous. She admired modern science, bourgeois political economy, and modern culture, but she sought to bend them to the service of her class and society – to the perpetuation of a slaveholding elite within a slave society. Women's clearly defined roles as women – in a word, gender relations – constituted an integral aspect of this project. Women who challenged those prescribed roles threatened the foundations of slave society, of Christian society, of all civilized society; women who accepted them inevitably accepted limitations. In return, they gained protection against their weakness, respect for their particular excellence, and an unchallenged status as ruling ladies.[33]

Caius Gracchus offers a marvelous panorama of Louisa McCord's view of the world and her own place in it. *Gracchus* features the widowed Cornelia; her son, Caius; her daughter-in-law, Lucinia; her infant grandson; a variety of senators and citizens; and, as a setting, Rome in turmoil.* The plot carries Caius to his death at the hands of the corrupt Senatorial party and confirms the collapse of the Republic. Significantly, Caius himself bears heavy responsibility for the defeat of his cause. For, heedlessly, he has mobilized the lower ranks of the citizenry and unleashed on Rome the irresponsibility of the landless mob. The senators are a bad lot, from whom Rome deserved deliverance, but not at the price of the rabble's triumph. Although bad representatives of their kind, the senators none the less represent the shreds of proper order. The mob represents wanton anarchy.

Some years before the loss of her husband, and a good decade before the loss of her son, Louisa McCord depicted herself in *Caius Gracchus* as a widow who understands the implications of political choices better than the son she cherishes. She never explicitly wrote of her identification with Cornelia, although the bust of her as a Roman matron suggests that she and others took it for granted. Certainly the neoclassical overtones of republican motherhood persisted longer in southern than in northern culture. To take but one example, at the famous dinner, during the height of the Nullification controversy, at which Andrew Jackson toasted "our Federal Union – It must be preserved," the eighteenth toast was to Virginia – likened to the mother of the Gracchi. But the sensibility was general and McCord, although not usually given to displays of personal vanity, had reason to hope that she embodied it. As her tragedy ineluctably unfolds, she further

---

* Caius (usually Gaius) Gracchus and his brother Tiberius were "tribunes of the people" in ancient Rome, who championed the poor against the interests of the aristocrats. Both were killed – Tiberius in 133 BC and Gaius in 121 BC – in disorders provoked by their policies. Their mother, Cornelia, was famed for her devotion to her sons.

depicts herself as possessed of a genuinely public vision. When Lucinia seeks to bind Caius to herself and their son, to retreat to private comforts rather than face the destiny his actions have set in motion, Cornelia gently chides her:

> Alas! I cannot in your cause, my child.
> Our life is for the world. Man doth forget
> His every highest purpose, scorning it;
> And from the level of his high intent
> Doth thus degrade himself.[34]

After Caius's departure, Cornelia experiences her own moment of crippling grief. Yet after a thoughtful pause, she reproves herself for weakness:

> My task is not yet done. Up! up! and work!
> Life yet has duties, and my comfort is
> Yet to fulfil them. Daughter! Daughter! wake!
> We must go seek our boy, who waits us still,
> To show us how his wooden horse can trot!
> Oh! what a motley is this struggling world![35]

It is tempting to leave Louisa McCord there, with her own words that testify to her double grasp of the duties that pertain to life and station and their incarnation in children's toys. Such were the boundaries and the furniture of the imaginative worlds of slaveholding women: duties to their society and their class, made manifest in daily responsibilities to succeeding generations of their families, white and black. But there is more. Although few slaveholding women matched Louisa McCord's breadth and depth of cultural literacy, many of them participated in the same discourse. Louisa McCord presented her self-portrait as Cornelia in the form of a Shakespearean tragedy. Phrases in her poetry unmistakably echo Keats. She liberally sprinkled her writings with French and Latin phrases. And, in choosing Cornelia as her model, she had to know that she was invoking the image of a woman widely celebrated among the leading men of southern politics and letters, who were well read in ancient history. To Robert Y. Hayne, Henry W. Washington, Nathaniel Beverley Tucker, and Benjamin F. Perry, among others, Cornelia, mother of the Gracchi, whose jewels were her sons, stood as a Roman beacon to the true men of the South – just as, to so many of their women, she stood as the embodiment of the virtues of republican mother-hood that they aspired to emulate.[36]

Louisa McCord, and innumerable women of her class, wrote in the idiom of the canon, which they adapted to their own specific perceptions. Identifying with the canon, they accepted a discourse predominantly fashioned by men. They regularly employed the generics "he" and "man" to represent the aspirations of humanity, including their own. Writing privately, they wrote directly as women. But when they moved to inscribe their personal experience in the general culture, they accepted man as its embodiment. Their experience as women influenced their appropriations from the canon, but they never wrote as if that experience should result in a separate women's culture. In this respect, they lagged behind or ran ahead of their northern sisters. But then, they assumed culture to be more a matter of class than of gender. Even if they took second place to their men in education and intellectual ambition – and Louisa McCord did not – they viewed themselves, together with the men of their class, as heirs and custodians of a great Christian civilization.

NOTES

The Editor gratefully acknowledges permission to reprint material from *Within the Plantation Household: Black and White Women of the Old South*, by Elizabeth Fox-Genovese. Copyright © 1988 by the University of North Carolina Press. Used by permission of the author and the publisher.

1 See Elizabeth Fox-Genovese (1983) "Antebellum Southern house-holds: a new perspective on a familiar question," *Review* 7: 215–53. In addition, among many works on the economic transformation of northern households, see Christopher Clark (1979) "The household economy, market exchange, and the rise of capitalism in the Connecticut Valley, 1800–1860," *Journal of Social History* 13: 169–90, and esp. "Households, market and capital: the process of economic change in the Connecticut Valley of Massachusetts, 1800–1860" (Ph.D. diss., Harvard University, 1982); Michael Merrill (1977) "Cash is good to eat: self-sufficiency and exchange in the rural economy of the United States," *Radical History Review* 4: 42–71; Rolla Milton Tryon (1917) *Household Manufactures in the United States, 1640–1860* (reprinted New York, 1966), 164–87, 242–376; Douglas C. North (1961) *The Economic Growth of the United States, 1790–1860* (Englewood Cliffs, N.J.); Percy W. Bidwell (1921) "The agricultural revolution in New England," *American Historical*

Review 26: 683–702; George Rogers Taylor (1951) *The Transportation Revolution, 1815–1860* (New York); Paul E. Johnson (1978) *A Shopkeeper's Millenium: Society and Revivals in Rochester, New York, 1815–1837* (New York); Anthony F. C. Wallace (1978) *Rockdale: The Growth of an American Village in the Early Industrial Revolution* (New York); Jonathon Prude (1983) *The Coming of Industrial Order: Town and Factory Life in Rural Massachusetts, 1810–1860* (New York). For a helpful overview, see Steven Hahn and Jonathon Prude (eds) (1985) *The Countryside in the Age of Capitalist Transformation: Essays in the Social History of Rural America* (Chapel Hill, N.C.). For an examination of the impact that the separation of home and work had on northern women, see esp. Nancy Cott (1977) *The Bonds of Womanhood: "Woman's Sphere" in New England, 1780–1835* (New Haven, Conn.); Linda Kerber (1980) *Women of the Republic: Intellect and Ideology in Revolutionary America* (Chapel Hill, N.C.); Ann Douglas (1977) *The Feminization of American Culture* (New York); Carroll Smith-Rosenberg (1985) *Disorderly Conduct: Visions of Gender in Victorian America* (New York); Joan Jensen (1986) *Loosening the Bonds: Mid-Atlantic Farm Women, 1750–1850* (New Haven, Conn.); Ruth H. Bloch (1978) "American feminine ideals in transition: the role of the moral mother," *Feminist Studies* 4: 100–26; Mary P. Ryan (1981) *Cradle of the Middle Class: The Family in Oneida County, New York, 1790–1865* (New York); Nancy A. Hewitt (1984) *Women's Activism and Social Change: Rochester, New York, 1822–1872* (Ithaca, N.Y.); Kathryn Kish Sklar (1973) *Catherine Beecher: A Study in American Domesticity* (New Haven, Conn.); Catherine Beecher (1841) *A Treatise on Domestic Economy* (reprinted New York 1977).

2 Mary Kendall to "Sister Lydia," 20 June 1853, Hamilton-Kendall Family Papers, Georgia Department of Archives and History.

3 On Louisa McCord's life, see Jesse Melville Fraser, "Louisa C. McCord" (M.A. thesis, University of South Carolina, 1919); Margaret Farrand Thorp (1949) *Female Persuasion: Six Strong-Minded Women* (New Haven, Conn.), 179–214; Louisa McCord Smythe, "Recollections of Louisa McCord," and correspondence between Louisa McCord Smythe and Jessie Melville Fraser, Dulles–Cheves–Lovell–McCord Family Papers (DCLM), South Carolina Historical Society (SCHS). [Omitted here are further references to women's education in the South.]

4 Fraser, "Louisa C. McCord."

5 Margaret Thorp refers to the letter from the mother, but does not indicate its location (*Female Persuasion*, 190). On Louisa Cheves's inheritance of Lang Syne, see Louisa Smythe to Miss Fraser, 5 May 1920, DCLM, SCHS.

6 Louisa Cheves to Langdon Cheves, 7 October 1839, Cheves Family Papers, South Caroliniana Library (SCL).

7 Fragmentary notes in Louisa S. McCord's hand, in the DCLM, SCHS. The notes, which have a slightly obsessive quality, would appear to be those which Louisa McCord drafted to prepare her heated response to Benjamin F. Perry's sketch of her father in

Reminiscences of Public Men (published as vol. 2 of *The Writings of Benjamin F. Perry* (1889; reprinted Spartanburg, S.C., 1980), 83–7. Perry's portrait was gracious enough but did not begin to satisfy McCord's very high opinion of her father. See McCord (1870) "Langdon Cheves: a review of 'Reminiscences of Public Men'," *XIX Century* 2: 885–8.

8 Louisa McCord (1848) *My Dreams* (Philadelphia).

9 Louisa McCord (1851) *Caius Gracchus: A Tragedy* (New York).

10 McCord (1852) 'Woman and her needs,' *DeBow's Review* 13.

11 Fraser, "Louisa S. McCord".

12 Not many of the women whose papers I have read complained directly about violence to themselves, but many included reports of the cruelty of other women's husbands. For one woman who complained about her own husband, see Susan Davis (Nye) Hutchinson Diary, Southern Historical Collection. For other views of slaveholders' marriages, see esp. Carol K. Bleser (ed.) (1981) *The Hammonds of Redcliffe* (New York); "Perrys of Greenville: a nineteenth century marriage," in Walter J. Fraser, Jr., R. Frank Saunders, Jr., and Jon L. Wakelyn (eds) (1985) *The Web of Southern Social Relations: Women, Family, and Education* (Athens Ga.) 72–89; and her "Southern wives and slavery" (paper presented to the Organization of American Historians, 1986); Steven M. Stowe (1987) *Intimacy and Power in the Old South: Ritual in the Lives of the Planters* (Baltimore). . . .

13 McCord, *My Dreams*, 185–9, 160–1.

14 Most commonly, those who claimed to reject the married state were adolescents. See, for example, Kate S. Carney Diary, SHC . . .

15 Caroline Lee (Whiting) Hentz Diary, 7 June 1836, SHC; unsigned memo on Louisa McCord, in DCLM, SCHS (prob. Louisa Smythe); Smythe, "Recollections of Louisa McCord," SCHS.

16 Smythe, "Recollections of Louisa McCord," SCHS; Louisa S. McCord to Mary Middleton, 17 July 1852, Middleton Family Papers, SCHS.

17 Smythe, "Recollections of Louisa McCord," SCHS.

18 Sally Baxter to George Baxter, 15 April 1855, in Ann Fripp Hampton (ed.) (1980) *A Divided Heart: Letters of Sally Baxter Hampton, 1853–1862* (Spartanburg, S.C.), 20–3. See also McCord (1853) "Uncle Tom's Cabin," *Southern Quarterly Review* 23: 81–120; D. D. Hall (1960) "A Yankee tutor in the South," *New England Quarterly* 33: 82–91; (1853) "Stowe's key to Uncle Tom's Cabin," *Southern Quarterly Review* 24: 214–54; and, of course, Harriet Beecher Stowe (1852) *Uncle Tom's Cabin* (Boston).

19 McCord, *Caius Gracchus*, dedication. See Anne L. Kuhn (1947) *The Mother's Role in Childhood Education: New England Concepts, 1830–1860* (New Haven, Conn.); Sklar, *Catherine Beecher*; Mary P. Ryan (1982) *The Empire of the Mother: American Writing About Domesticity, 1830–1860* (New York); Charles Strickland (1985) *Victorian Domesticity: Families in the Life and Art of Louisa May Alcott*

(University, Ala.). For southern women's private writings about their feelings as mothers see, for example, Sarah A. (Haynesworth) Gayle Journal, SHC. . . .

20 Ryan, *Empire of the Mother*.

21 Frederic Bastiat (1848), *Sophisms of the Protective Policy*, transl. by Mrs D. J. McCord (New York); Louisa McCord (1849) "Justice and fraternity," *Southern Quarterly Review* 15: 356–74; McCord (1849) "The right to labor," *Southern Quarterly Review* 16: 138–60.

22 Eugene Genovese and I have discussed Louisa McCord's political economy elsewhere; here I shall only evoke its essential features as they bear upon her general views on the twin social questions of gender and slavery. Genovese and Fox-Genovese (1984) "Slavery, economic development, and the law: the dilemma of the southern political economists," *Washington and Lee Law Review* 41: 1–29.

23 See Hughes (1854) *Treatise on Sociology, Theoretical and Practical* (reprinted New York, 1968); Stanford M. Lyman (1985) *Selected Writings of Henry Hughes* (Jackson, Miss.); Allen Kaufman (1982) *Capitalism, Slavery, and Republican Values: Antebellum Political Economists, 1819–1848* (Austin, Tex.); Genovese and Fox-Genovese, "Slavery, economic development, and the law."

24 Elizabeth Fee (1976) "Science and the woman problem: historical perspectives," in Michael S. Teitelbaum, (ed.) *Sex Differences: Social and Biological Perspectives* (Garden City, N.Y.), 175–223.

25 E.g. McCord, "Enfranchisement of woman," 325.

26 McCord, "Woman and her needs," 282, and "Enfranchisement of women," *Southern Quarterly Review* 21 (1852): 322–41. See also Eugene Genovese and Elizabeth Fox-Genovese (1986) "The religious ideals of southern slave society," *Georgia Historical Review* 70: 1–16.

27 McCord, "Woman and her needs," 278. In fact, she hedged on the question, sometimes claiming that at least some women (she had to take account of herself) were as intelligent as men, sometimes suggesting that there might be innate differences for which discrepancies in education could not account. See also A. G. M., "The condition of women," *Southern Quarterly Review* 10 (1846): 148–73; "Women physiologically considered," *Southern Quarterly Review* 2 (1842): 279–311; and "Men and women of the eighteenth century," *Southern Quarterly Review* 22 (1852): 63–77.

28 McCord, "Enfranchisement of women," 325.

29 Ibid., 324–5, 332, 334; McCord, "Woman and her needs," 275.

30 McCord, "Woman and her needs," 268, and "Enfranchisement of women," 322, 330.

31 McCord, "Woman and her needs," 289.

32 On Beecher, see Sklar, *Catherine Beecher*, 244–57, esp. 246–7.

33 For a sample of views on Louisa McCord's views on slavery and the races, see "Negro and white slavery – wherein do they differ?", *Southern Quarterly Review* 20 (1851): 119–32, and "Diversity of the races: its bearing upon negro slavery," *Southern Quarterly*

Review 19 (1851): 392–419. [Other references to Southern racial thought are omitted here.]

34 McCord, *Caius Gracchus*, act 5, sc. 1. On the mother of the Gracchi, see Charles M. Wiltse (1949) *John C. Calhoun: Nullifier: 1829–1839* (Indianapolis, Ind.), 70. The *Ladies Magazine*, the first Georgia publication for women, proclaimed in its announcement that mothers were the key educators and cited Cornelia and her jewels – her sons (Savannah, Ga., 1819). See Bertram Holland Fleming (1944) *Early Georgia Magazines: Literary Periodicals to 1865* (Athens, Ga.), 14.

35 McCord, *Caius Gracchus*, act 5, sc. 1.

36 See Hayne's "Speech on Mr Foote's resolution," 21 January 1830, as quoted, with approbation, in Henry Augustine Washington (1982) "The social system of Virginia," in Michael O'Brien (ed.) *All Clever Men Who Make Their Way: Critical Discourse in the Old South* (Columbia, Mo.), 228–62; N. Beverly Tucker (1845) *Series of Lectures on the Science of Government . . .* (Philadelphia), 371; Perry, *Writings*, 2: 59.

Part II

MASTERS AND SLAVES

3

AMERICAN SLAVERY
A flexible, highly developed form of capitalism
Robert William Fogel

It will be recalled that the publication of Time on the Cross, *by Robert Fogel and Stanley Engerman, raised a storm of controversy for both its interpretations and methods. The controversy has subsided, but the research of economists on the history of slavery has continued. In his* Without Consent or Contract: The Rise and Fall of American Slavery, *Robert Fogel again summarizes and synthesizes this research. Fogel has retreated from some of the more controversial interpretations put forward in the earlier book, but, as the title of this chapter indicates, not from what he considers the most important of all the findings reported in* Time on the Cross. *This is the contention that slavery was not merely profitable for the owners, but a very efficient economic system. If, for Eugene Genovese and Elizabeth Fox-Genovese, slavery made compromises with capitalism without becoming capitalist, Fogel makes the case here that slavery flourished because it was a "highly developed form of capitalism." As the excerpt below, from Chapter 3 of Fogel's book, makes clear, Fogel's standards for making such judgments are those of "neoclassical" economists – for example, the ability and willingness of slaveowners to respond flexibly to market signals and organize production with maximum efficiency. Compare his analysis of the economics of slavery with that in the essay by Genovese and Fox-Genovese, in Chapter 1, above.*

Evidence of the responsiveness of slaveowners to prices and other economic signals is quite evident throughout the period from the Revolution to the Civil War. Production in all of the major southern staples waxed and waned in response to prices. Indigo disappeared as a commercial product in less than a decade (between 1792 and 1800), once the price turned against it. Planters in upper Georgia and South Carolina who moved into tobacco during the post-Revolutionary boom in demand moved out of it after the War of 1812, shifting from tobacco to cotton as the demand for cotton surged upward and the price of tobacco declined toward depression levels. Planters in Maryland, Virginia, and North Carolina shifted between tobacco and grains in response to changes in their relative prices. Tobacco production in these states languished from the early 1790s to the mid-1840s, when tobacco prices leaped sharply upward and remained above the long-term trend until the outbreak of the Civil War. Eastern planters, responding rapidly to each new surge in demand, more than doubled tobacco output between 1849 and 1859, pushing its price back toward a normal level.[1]

By far the most dramatic evidence of the responsiveness of slaveholders to market signals was the way in which they adjusted to the booming demand for cotton. As late as 1809 cotton was a secondary crop for southern agriculture, with production concentrated mainly in South Carolina and eastern Georgia. Just 7 per cent of the crop was raised to the west of this area and probably just 10 per cent of the slave labor force across the entire South was engaged in its production. During the next three decades the cotton crop increased nearly tenfold and the share of the western states leaped from 7 to 64 per cent.

The depression decade of the 1840s interrupted this dual process of mammoth increases in the size of the cotton crop and a westward shift in the locus of its production. But the process resumed during the next decade when booming world markets led to a doubling of the crop. By the eve of the Civil War the westward shift was completed, with three-quarters of the richest crop in southern history coming from states which, at the start of Washington's administration, had been virtually uninhabited.[2]

The correlation in the geographic movements of cotton and slaves was dictated by biology and economics.[3] Cotton could be grown successfully in a long belt stretching mainly from South Carolina through Texas. The bounds of this belt were determined largely, but not exclusively, by climatic conditions since the cotton culture requires a minimum of two hundred frostless days and ample rainfall. Temperature set the northern boundary, and rainfall the western one.

Not all land within these boundaries was equally suitable for cotton. The black-belt lands of Alabama and Texas were more congenial to it than the sandy soils of the Carolina Piedmont or the marshes of the coastal plains, except for long-staple cotton. The best cotton lands of all were the alluvial soils of the Mississippi flood plain. As long as tobacco and grains were the principal market crops of the South, as they were down to the end of the eighteenth century, it was efficient to concentrate labor and other resources in regions that bordered on the Chesapeake Bay. But as the demand for cotton grew relative to other commodities, efficiency dictated a reallocation of labor and other resources to the best western lands.

Between 1790 and 1860 some 835,000 slaves were moved into the western cotton states. The tempo of interregional slave movements accelerated with time. The traffic during the last half of the seventy-year period was three times as large as during the first half. The main exporting states were Maryland, Virginia, and the Carolinas. Together they supplied over 85 per cent of the migrants. The four largest importers were Alabama, Mississippi, Louisiana, and Texas, which together received about 75 per cent of the displaced blacks. The impact of the movement of slaves on the rates of growth of the slave populations of the exporting and importing states was quite substantial. By 1860 the exporting states had just 60 per cent of the slave population they would have had if they had grown at the national average. On the other hand, the slave population of the importing states swelled to several times the level that would have been obtained if these states had grown at the national average.[4]

The westward shift of cotton and slaves was also stimulated by breakthroughs in transportation. The response of slave-owners to steamboats and railroads reveals the eagerness with which they sought to bend the industrial technology of the nineteenth century to their advantage. Although the steamboat was originally developed on the Hudson River, it was on the Mississippi that this innovation achieved its swiftest and most impressive successes. Steamboat traffic grew at phenomenal rates after 1811 and there were such major improvements in boat design and in engines that efficiency rose fourfold in a quarter of a century, which sent the cost of river transportation plummeting downward.[5]

It is sometimes argued that the preference of slaveowners for steamboats over railroads revealed their antipathy toward new technology. But the first US railroad, the Baltimore and Ohio, was constructed in Maryland beginning in 1828. Other southern cities including "Norfolk, Charleston, and Savannah each feverishly projected lines westward to gain control of such commerce as might be developed in the interior." It was not lack of enthusiasm for the railroad but practical economics that made steamboats the preferred means of transporting the region's freight. Down to the end of the antebellum era, the steamboat was not only cheaper but more reliable than the railroad and often speedier in the delivery of cotton and other bulky commodities. Even so, southern enthusiasm for railroads led to the construction of more than 9,500 miles of railroad track by 1860, about one-third of the nation's total, and more than the mileage of France, Germany, or Great Britain, the European leaders.[6]

The South was also in the forefront of the effort to gather and disseminate economic intelligence. Southern planters had at their fingertips reports on the transactions in cotton, tobacco, rice, sugar, and other commodities, not only for all of the leading southern markets but also for the leading cities of the North and of Europe. Produce exchanges, cotton exchanges, brokerage houses, and financial institutions published (first weekly, then daily) listings of commodity prices and other economic indicators in bulletins and newspapers commonly called "Prices Current." It was determination to exploit every avenue for gathering economic information that caused the South to string telegraph lines across the entire region as soon as that means of communication was developed. The first two cities to be connected were Baltimore and Washington in 1844. By 1852 every major southern city was linked to the new network. It was a point of pride that New Orleans had telegraphic communication with New York sooner than Chicago did.[7]

Cliometricians have not as yet been able to resolve the

debate over the form of the interregional slave movement.*
Were most slaves sold by owners in the East to traders who
transported them to western markets where they were resold,
or did the majority go West with owners who relocated plantations? Estimates of the proportion shipped to the West by
traders range between 16 and 60 per cent.[8]

Cliometric analyses of the slave trade have, however, demonstrated the business acumen with which masters valued
their chattel and the limited role of sentimentality in effecting
their economic decisions. How many masters were constrained
by emotional attachments to individual slaves, by antipathy to
the business of slave trading, or by a loathing to tear husbands
from wives is still a matter of conjecture. Such sentiments
were, however, balanced against the interests and con-
veniences of the masters. There were planters who, like George
Washington, said that they were determined to resist all but
the most urgent pressures to enter the market for slaves,
although in Washington's case the flight of his cook led him
to consider the purchase of a replacement. Others were more
like Jefferson, who made no apologies for selling recalcitrant
slaves and purchased new ones when he was shorthanded.[9]

When they did enter the slave market, masters assessed
each purchase with as much shrewdness and concern for value
as any western horse trader or northern manufacturer. Probate
records and invoices of slave sales reveal that the prices were
systematically affected by such characteristics of slaves as their
age, gender, health, skills, and reliability. There were also
distinct seasonal patterns in slave sales. As one might expect
in an agricultural economy, the largest proportion were sold
during the first quarter of the year, the quarter between the
end of the harvest and the beginning of planting. Moreover,
the prices that slaves brought were 10 per cent higher during
this slack season than during September, which was close to
the peak of the harvest.[10]

Age had by far the greatest influence on prices, as shown
by Figure 1.[11] Although prices varied at each age, as one would
expect of slaves who differed in health, attitudes, and capabilities, the distribution displays a quite definite pattern. On aver-

* "Cliometrics" is a term coined from "Clio," the Greek muse of history, and
"econometrics," the term encompassing the statistical techniques used by
economists.

age, prices rose until the late twenties and then declined. The decline was slow at first but then became more rapid, until advanced ages were reached. Masters put a price on each skill and defect of a slave (see Figure 2). As compared with a male field hand of the same age, blacksmiths brought a premium of about 55 per cent and carpenters about 45 per cent.[12] Slaves who were in poor health or who were crippled sold at substantial discounts. Masters even put a price on "virtues" and "vices." Slaves labeled as runaways, lazy, thieves, drunks, suicidals, or having "heredity vices" sold for average discounts of up to 65 per cent as compared with slaves of the same age who were "fully guaranteed."[13]

The slave trade was one of the ugliest aspects of American slavery and probably was one of the most effective issues in rallying support for the antislavery cause. Foes of slavery condemned the practice on moral and political grounds, arguing that the interstate traffic in people provided the planters of the older states with the bulk of their profit and was indispensable for maintaining the profits of slaveholders as a class. Yet, interstate slave trading could not have accounted for a significant fraction of the profits of the slaveowning class and may actually have reduced their collective profit.[14] Professional traders, those who purchased slaves in one state and resold them in another, did earn a regular profit for that "service," and may even have reaped some windfall gains. Since such windfalls came at the expense of other slaveholders, they were merely transfers within the slaveholding class and so did not add to its total profit.

Whether or not the masters as a class actually profited from the westward movement turns on a complicated set of trade-offs.[15] Slaveowners understood that from the purely economic standpoint, the westward march of slavery was not an unmixed blessing. Virginia planters complained loudly and frequently about the depressing effect of western tobacco on the world price of that commodity. Recent cliometric work has confirmed the suspicions of Virginians that the competition from western tobacco did more to depress the prices of their slaves than the interstate slave trade did to raise it. The doubling of slave prices in Virginia during the late 1840s and the 1850s owed relatively little to the western demand for slaves

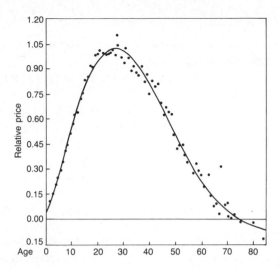

Figure 1 Averages of prices relative to age for male slaves in the Old South. Each point represents the average price of slaves at a given age. The curve fitted to these points is called an age–price profile. Notice that the average price of slaves remained positive until the mid-seventies. This means that although some slaves in their early seventies were too sick to earn their upkeep, other slaves at that age earned enough to support themselves as well as the disabled members of their cohort and still leave a profit for their masters.

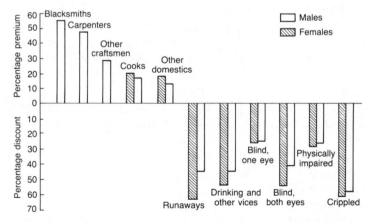

Figure 2 Premiums and discounts in slave prices for various skills and "defects." This diagram shows that there was little difference between the way in which planters priced their slaves and the way they priced their other capital assets. They were as precise in valuing human attributes as those of their livestock or equipment. The premiums and discounts are measured relative to the price of a healthy field hand of the same age and gender (the zero premium).

and much to the resurgence in the European demand for tobacco during those years.[16]

While the tobacco interests (eastern and western combined) may have suffered from the westward movement, the cotton interests probably did not. Some eastern cotton planters were made worse off, but the gain to planters in the West more than offset these losses. Cotton planters as a class gained for two reasons. One is that the world demand for cotton increased so rapidly that bringing the highly fertile western lands into production did not reduce the total revenues of cotton planters. The other is that by responding so quickly to the burgeoning world demand for cotton, on lands far more suited for cotton than existed anywhere else in the world, US planters slowed the expansion of cotton production in the West Indies, Brazil, India, and elsewhere. As a consequence, the US share of the world's market for cotton rose quite dramatically as the westward march progressed. Cotton growers in the West Indies and India could compete quite well with cotton grown in Virginia and the Carolinas, but not with cotton coming from the Alabama black belt or the Mississippi alluvium.[17]

The congressional battles of the 1840s and 1850s over the extension of slavery into the territories were not due to the degradation of eastern soils, or any sort of land shortage whatsoever. Analysis of census data reveals no evidence of the decline in labor productivity on the farms of the Old South that would have been caused by a decline in the quantity or quality of land per worker. In fact, the cotton boom put very little pressure on southern supplies of land because cotton was not a land-intensive crop.[18] The 1850 crop was grown on just 6 per cent of the improved land in the farms of the cotton states. If slaveowners had been confined to the counties that they already occupied in 1850, and if they had been barred from adding to the total acreage already improved in 1850, they could still have doubled cotton production over the next decade merely by shifting about one-fifteenth of the land normally planted with other crops into cotton.[19] This is quite close to what actually happened. Much of the increase in cotton production during the decade of the 1850s, especially the leap in production after 1856, came not from the spread of the culture to new counties or new farms, but from the expansion of output in counties that were already major producers at the beginning of the decade.

The surging demand for cotton during the 1850s put far more pressure on the South's labor supply than on its supply of land. Between 1850 and 1860 southern farmers shifted about 3 million acres of land from corn to cotton, but this shift did not release enough labor because cotton required about 70 per cent more labor per acre than did corn. To meet this extra labor requirement planters drew slaves out of the cities and from the small slave farms by bidding up the price of slave labor. And so the decade of the 1850s witnessed both a decline in the urban share of the slave population and a rise in the share of the slave population working on gang-system farms that specialized in cotton. The surging demand for slave labor by cotton planters after 1846 pushed the real price of slaves to higher levels than they had ever previously achieved, not because the demand for cotton increased more rapidly during the 1850s than during all previous decades, but because the share of the slave labor force demanded by cotton planters at these prices was larger than ever before.[20]

The struggle over the expansion of slavery into the territories, despite the rhetorical references to economics, was almost a purely political issue. Radical abolitionists denounced the "political" antislavery leaders for paying too much attention to the territorial issue. As the radicals saw it, this issue only served to divert the abolitionist movement into harmless channels, and so they called on antislavery leaders to fight slavery where it was, rather than where it was not. On strictly economic grounds, the radical position was sound. Slavery could not have been damaged economically by denying it access to lands in Kansas, or anywhere else outside of the states in which it was already well established by the 1840s. Yet, Republican leaders rejected the advice of the radicals because they and their chief southern opponents saw the territorial issue as the crux of the political struggle against slavery.[21]

THE RELATIVE EFFICIENCY OF SLAVE LABOR

It was Benjamin Franklin who initiated efforts to measure the relative efficiency of slave and free labor. In an essay written in 1751, at a time when men such as Montesquieu and Hutcheson believed that slavery, at least in the context of the New World, was more efficient than free labor, Franklin set forth an accounting of the cost of slave labor that showed the opposite. Although his statement on this issue was extremely brief, and although the quantitative evidence he set forth was not sufficient to warrant his conclusion, Franklin's statement was highly influential in both France and England. In 1771 Pierre Samuel DuPont de Nemours, a prominent French abolitionist and a member of the Physiocratic school of French economists, set forth a lengthy elaboration of Franklin's theme. Adam Smith did not explicitly cite Franklin's essay, which had achieved considerable fame by the publication date of the *Wealth of Nations*, but he obviously had it in mind when he asserted that slave labor was more costly than free labor "even at Boston, New York, and Philadelphia where the wages of common labor are so high."[22]

Despite its limitations, Franklin's measure of efficiency was similar to those employed by economists today. Indexes of efficiency are ratios of output to input. One common measure is output per worker, which is usually referred to as an index of "labor productivity." A more comprehensive measure called "the index of total factor productivity" is the ratio of output per average unit of all the inputs (which in the case of agriculture are mainly land, labor, and capital).[23] Franklin used only labor in his denominator and he did not measure the output, but implicitly assumed that the output of a given number of slaves was less than, or equal to, that of a like number of free men. Consequently, if slave labor was more costly than free labor, as Franklin contended, it was also less efficient.

Although modern research on the problem of efficiency has been carried out along the lines suggested by Franklin, there have been significant advances of both a theoretical and empirical nature. The main theoretical advance involves the careful formulation of a distinction between profitability and "technical" efficiency, a distinction that has often been blurred. Technical efficiency refers to the effectiveness with which inputs are used in a productive process. One productive process is said to be technically more efficient than another if it yields more output from the same quantity of inputs.

Profitability does not necessarily imply technical efficiency, especially in the slave context, since even processes that were technically inefficient could have been profitable if masters expropriated some of the income that would have accrued to free labor. Profitability calculations can tell whether or not masters were efficient in the allocation of their resources among alternative investments, but not whether the productive techniques employed in each of these enterprises were technically efficient. The intense investigation of the profitability issue, which extended from the mid-1950s to the mid-1970s, revealed that the slave economy had a considerable degree of "allocative" efficiency, which means that masters were fairly efficient in shifting their resources from place to place, at least within agriculture, in order to exploit opportunities to increase their profits. But it still left open the possibility that slave agriculture was technically inefficient.

Frederick Law Olmsted, the great landscape architect and a critic of the economy and culture of the South, posed the problem of measuring the technical efficiency of slavery in a fairly clear way when he said that a comparison of the relative efficiency of slave and free labor should be made "man with man, with reference simply to the equality of muscular power and endurance."[24] To perform such a comparison it is necessary to take account of differences in the age and gender composition of the slave and free labor forces. About two-thirds of all slaves were in the labor force, which was about twice the proportion among free persons. Such a high proportion could be achieved only by pressing virtually everyone capable of any useful work at all into the labor force. As a consequence, nearly one-third of the slave laborers were untrained children and about an eighth were elderly, crippled, or disadvantaged in some way. Women represented a much larger proportion of field laborers among slaves than among free farmers.

In order to have a valid comparison of labor productivity on slave and free farms it is necessary to convert the labor of children, women, the aged, and the infirm into "equivalent prime hands." One way of doing this is to make use of the "hand" ratings that planters assigned to slaves in order to achieve a rational allocation of their laborers among the various tasks.[25] An even more refined and reliable set of ratings can be obtained from the abundant data on slave prices and on

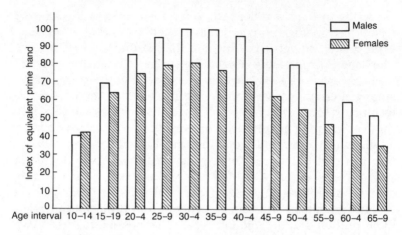

Figure 3 Work-capacity (hand) ratings of slaves, by age and gender (males aged 30–4 equal 100).

annual hire rates. Figure 3 shows that, on average, two women in their fifties did about as much work as one prime-aged male, and three boys in their late teens did about as much work as two prime-aged males. When indexes of labor productivity (average output per equivalent prime hand) are used to compare technical efficiency, they give a marked advantage to slave plantations. By this measure the intermediate and large slave plantations of the cotton belt were nearly twice as efficient as the free farms of the same region in 1860. But indexes of labor productivity exaggerate the relative advantage of slave farms because they do not take account of the fact that the slaves usually worked on more fertile soils and had more work animals and other capital than did the free farmers of the region. The index of total factor productivity overcomes this problem because it takes account not only of the average amount of labor required to produce a given amount of output, but also of the quantity and quality of the land and capital that were employed.

Taking account of the superior land and capital with which slaves worked considerably reduces their edge over free farmers. The advantage of small plantations (one to fifteen slaves) over free farms that was indicated by the index of labor productivity is now almost completely wiped out, and the advantage of the two classes of gang-system farms (those with six-teen or more slaves) is cut in half. Nevertheless, plantations with sixteen or more slaves exhibit a considerable advantage over smaller farms, whether slave or free. The gang-system plantations produced, on average, about 39 per cent more output from a given amount of input than either free farms or slave farms that were too small to employ the gang system.[26] A plantation with sixteen slaves usually had about ten slaves old enough to work in a gang, and ten hands appears to have been the threshold number for the successful operation of a gang.

It is worth noting that most of the advantage made possible by the gang system was achieved by intermediate plantations (those with sixteen to fifty slaves). They had an edge over free farms that was two-thirds of that enjoyed by the large plan-tations (those with fifty-one or more slaves). Part of the extra advantage of the large plantations was due to a degree of labor specialization that was higher than could be achieved elsewhere. On the large plantations, for example, plow hands were almost always men in the prime ages. But on intermedi-ate plantations men in their teens or in their fifties, and some-times the stronger women, were used for plowing. Part of the extra advantage also came from the much higher degree of regimentation than was typical of the large plantations, a regi-mentation that reflected itself not only in field work but in every other aspect of life, including the use of leisure time and the scope for personal choice that slaves were allowed in the selection of marital partners.

While the gang system gave cotton producers who skillfully employed it a clear edge over non-gang producers, it was no automatic guarantee of success. Not all masters were equally adept in the management of their slaves or in the techniques of growing cotton. Planters varied in their mastery of the special characteristics of their particular soils, in the art of combining the production of cotton with that of other crops in such a manner as to keep all hands as fully occupied as possible, and in those planting and cultivating skills that had such important effects on yields at harvest time. As a consequence, the efficiency of gang-system producers varied nearly as much as that of free farmers. This point is brought out by Figure 4, which shows that in both the free and large farm slave cases, the top 10 per cent of the farms were several times more efficient than the bottom 10 per cent.[27]

Figure 4 also demonstrates the advantage that the gang system gave to large plantations. At every rank of the two distributions, except the tenth, large plantations were about 50 per cent more efficient than free farms.[28] So considerable was the advantage of the gang system that only the top 20 per cent of the free farms exceeded the efficiency of the plantation that was just of average efficiency among the large slaveholdings.

The average level of efficiency varied considerably from state to state, among both free and slave farms. The highest levels of efficiency among most classes of farms were generally in those states that attracted the bulk of the interstate slave traffic. Despite the scope of the traffic, the level of efficiency was still not equalized between the slave-importing (New South) and slave-exporting (Old South) regions as late as 1860. One possible explanation is that the planters and free farmers who responded to the opportunities in the New South were more efficient producers than those who remained behind.[29] Another possibility is that movement of slaves from the Old South to the New South simply was not large enough to bring the measured productivity of the two regions into line. The interregional gap in the annual hire or rental rate of slaves provides some support for the second hypothesis. During the last half of the 1850s the average hire rate in the New South exceeded that of the Old South by 38 per cent, which would account for about two-thirds of the difference in total factor productivity between the two regions.[30]

When the technical efficiencies of agriculture in the North and in all farms in the South are compared, the South has an advantage of about 35 per cent.[31] The superior performance of southern agriculture was not due primarily to the high performance of its free farms. Free farms in the Old South were slightly less efficient than northern farms, while the free farms of the New South were somewhat more efficient than those in the North. These differences tended to net out so that, overall, only a small fraction of the edge enjoyed by southern agriculture was due to the superior performance of the free sector. The technical efficiency of the slave farms,

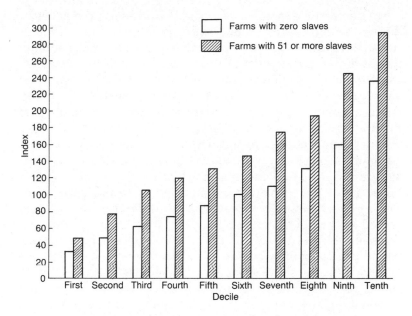

Figure 4 The distribution of efficiency scores of large slave farms
compared with that of free farms, the cotton belt, 1860 (average
total factor productivity on free farms = 100). Shown is the average
efficiency score of farms in each decile (each 10 per cent) of the
distributions of free and large slave farms, when these farms are
arranged according to their efficiency scores. Notice that the top
10 per cent of the free farms were more efficient than most of the
gang-system farms. Many of these very efficient free farmers soon
purchased slaves and some eventually accumulated enough capital
to rise into the ranks of gang-system planters. On the other hand,
the lowest deciles of the large slave plantations were so inefficient
that they could not compete with most of the free farms, let alone
with the majority of the other gang-system plantations. Some
owners of these inefficient plantations were bankrupt. Others sold
out. This process makes it likely that the gang-system plantations
were run by individuals with above-average ability in the
production of southern staples. Consequently, the superior
efficiency of the big plantations was due not merely to inherent
advantages of the gang system but also to the concentration of
cotton farmers of above-average ability in the ownership of such
farms.

particularly of the intermediate and large plantations, accounted for about 90 per cent of the southern advantage.[32]

The cliometric debate on the validity of these findings began during the middle of 1974 and was carried on with such intensity that the convergence of views has proceeded more rapidly than it did on the issue of profitability. Critics of the efficiency computations questioned the way in which the measures of output and of each of the inputs were constructed. They also raised a series of issues regarding the proper interpretation of the findings. Although these issues at first appeared to be of a purely theoretical or statistical nature, they ultimately involved questions about the way that agricultural production was actually carried out in antebellum times.[33]

The effort to resolve these issues led to reconsideration of the working hours of both slaves and free farmers. Researchers turned to the business records of gang-system plantations, some of which kept schedules of what each slave on the plantation was doing on each day of the year. Independent studies of two different samples of these schedules produced quite similar results. Slaves on cotton plantations worked an average of about 2,800 hours per year. The number of days worked per year averaged 281, well below the potential maximum. This shortfall is explained primarily by the almost total absence of Sunday work. Occasionally, a few hands were used on Sundays for special tasks, but such incidents were rare. This nearly total absence of Sunday work is a unique feature of the intermediate and large slave plantations, and it bears on the special nature of the gang system. The balance of the shortfall is explained by other holidays and occasional half days on Saturdays (six days), by illness (twelve days), and by rain and inclement weather (fifteen days).[34]

Plantation records also revealed a surprisingly high degree of regularity in the length of the workweek over the seasons. The workweek averaged 5.4 days over the entire year, with only slight deviations from season to season. The regularity of the workweek is explained partly by the practice of requiring slaves to work a full day on Saturdays if rain forced a postponement of work on a weekday. When considered on an hourly basis, there was somewhat more variation in seasonal work patterns, due partly to variations in the number of daylight hours and partly to the natural demands of agricultural production. The spring, summer, and fall show roughly equal workweeks, ranging between fifty-seven and sixty hours. Although the short period of daylight during the winter led to a significant reduction in the hourly length of the workweek, slaves still averaged about forty hours per week during these months.

Comparable evidence on working conditions in the North revealed that although the length of the workyear varied with the nature of the farm, free northern farmers averaged about 3,200 hours per year. The lowest subregional average, 3,006 hours, was found in the corn and general farming belt; the highest was 3,365 hours in the western dairy region. Thus, the average length of the southern slave workweek was not 10 per cent longer than the average workweek in northern agriculture, as some cliometricians had conjectured, but 10 per cent shorter.[35]

This finding seems paradoxical because of the widespread but incorrect assumption that the length of the growing season (the number of frost-free days) was the principal factor determining the length of the agricultural workyear in antebellum times. Although the number of frost-free days determines which plants can be raised in a particular region, there is little relationship between the length of the growing season and the duration of the period from seedtime to harvest for particular crops. The growing season in South Dakota, for example, is about 150 days but the period from seedtime to harvest is 310 days for winter wheat and only 115 days for spring wheat.[36]

It was the overall mix of farm products, particularly the mix between field crops and animal products, that was the principal determinant of the hourly length of both the workweek and the workyear. The length of the northern workweek was correlated with the degree of specialization in rearing livestock and dairying. Northern farmers specializing in these products generally worked an hour longer on weekdays and Saturdays than those who did not, and they also usually worked a half day on Sundays. So the paradox of the longer northern workyear is resolved by the fact that dairying and livestock accounted for 38 per cent of the output of northern farms, while the corresponding figure for the large slave plantations was hardly 5 per cent.[37]

The discovery that the slave workyear was shorter than the

free workyear does not contradict the proposition that slave labor was more intensely exploited than free labor, but only the proposition that such exploitation took the form of more hours per year. The available evidence indicates that greater intensity of labor per hour, rather than more hours of labor per day or more days of labor per year, is the reason the index of total factor productivity is 39 per cent higher for gang-system plantations than for free farms. The principal function of the gang system was to speed up the pace of labor, to increase its intensity per hour.

Slaves employed on the intermediate and large plantations worked about 76 per cent more intensely per hour than did free southern farmers or slaves on small plantations. In other words, a slave working under the gang system produced, on average, as much output in roughly thirty-five minutes as a farmer using traditional methods, whether slave or free, did in a full hour.

Once it is recognized that the fundamental form of the exploitation of slave labor was through speeding up rather than through an increase in the number of clock-time hours per year, certain paradoxes resolve themselves. The longer rest breaks during the workday and the greater time off on Sundays for slaves than for free men appear not as boons that slaveholders granted to their chattels but as conditions for achieving the desired level of intensity. The finding that slaves earned 15 per cent more income per clock-time hour is less surprising when it is realized that their income per equal-efficiency hour was 33 per cent less than that of free farmers.[38]

Of the many issues raised by the investigation of working hours, perhaps the most intriguing and difficult is the meaning of "harder work" or "more intense labor." These terms are often loosely used, as though their meanings were perfectly obvious. Among the several possible definitions, two are most relevant. The first defines intensity of labor by caloric requirement. Thus, one person (of a standard weight and height) would be said to work more intensely than another if his (or her) caloric requirement per hour of labor was greater. But one person could work more intensely than another even if both required the same number of calories. Such a situation would exist if the amount of motion of the two workers was identical, but one wasted less motion than the other. The slave case probably involved both kinds of intense labor – that is, labor requiring more calories per man hour and labor with less wasted motion. Labor that eliminates wasted motion may result in psychic fatigue and alienation, and so be more obnoxious than labor that permits wasted motion. The unremitting, machine-like quality of gang laborers repelled mid-nineteenth century observers who valued traditional agrarian ways. And trade unions today frequently resist the introduction of practices aimed at eliminating wasted motion, even when workers are compensated by somewhat higher wages.[39]

Of course, the fact that blacks who toiled on large plantations were more efficient than free workers does not imply that blacks were inherently superior to whites as workers. It was the system that forced men to work at the pace of an assembly line (called the gang) that made slave laborers more efficient than free laborers. Moreover, the gang system, as already noted, appears to have raised productivity only on farms that specialized in certain crops.

After the demise of indigo production, only five US crops appear to have lent themselves to the gang system. One of these, hemp, was quite minor and has yet to be analyzed. Of the other four, the advantage of the gang system appears to have been greatest in sugar, and nearly 100 per cent of all cane sugar in the United States was produced on gang-system farms. In tobacco the advantages of the gang system appear to have been small because of the limited opportunities for division of labor, so it is not surprising that as much tobacco was produced by free or small farms as by gang-system farms. Although cotton and rice were intermediate cases, the advantage of gang-system plantations was so substantial that they accounted for the great bulk of the output of both crops.

NOTES

The Editor gratefully acknowledges permission to reprint selections from *Without Consent or Contract: The Rise and Fall of American Slavery*, by Robert William Fogel, with the permission of W. W. Norton & Company, Inc. Copyright © 1989 by Robert W. Fogel.

[In the notes that follow, references to three companion volumes of *Without Consent or Contract* are abbreviated *EM* for *Evidence and Methods* and *TP* for two volumes of *Technical Papers*. These volumes include material on the "technical foundations" of *Without Consent or Contract*, authored by Fogel and others. They are identified by the last name of the author and/or a sequence number for papers printed there.]

1 Lewis Cecil Gray (1933) *History of Agriculture in the Southern United States to 1860*, 2 vols (reprinted Gloucester, Mass., 1958), 610–11, 757.

2 James L. Watkins (1908) *King Cotton: A Historical and Statistical Review, 1790–1908* (reprinted New York 1969), 29–31. [Discussion of missed population is omitted here.]

3 The soils and climates of the various states were not equally advantageous to all southern crops. The Atlantic Coastal Plain just below the Mason–Dixon line and the Central Piedmont Plateau were favorable for raising tobacco and general farming, but could not support a cotton culture. Rice had its greatest advantage in the swamplands along the southeastern coastal flatwoods of Georgia and South Carolina and in the lower Gulf Coastal Plain. Sugar production was confined largely to a handful of parishes in the Mississippi Delta. On regional specialization, see *EM* 21. Cf. Gray, *Agriculture in the Southern United States*, 684, 891, 652, 655.

4 Robert Fogel and Stanley Engerman (1974) *Time on the Cross: The Economics of American Negro Slavery*, 2 vols (Boston), 1: 46. This discussion of the interregional slave trade is based on the estimates of Claudia Goldin, which are presented in vol. 2 of *Time on the Cross*, 183–4.

5 Louis C. Hunter (1949) *Steamboats on the Western Rivers* (Cambridge, Mass.), chaps 1 and 2; Erik F. Haites, James Mak, and Gary M. Walton (1975) *Western River Transportation: The Era of Early Internal Development* (Baltimore), 60–9, 183–4.

6 Sidney Ratner, James H. Soltow, and Richard Sylla (1979) *The Evolution of the American Economy: Growth, Welfare, and Decision Making* (New York), 118–19; Kent T. Healy (1951) "American transportation before the Civil War," in Harold F. Williamson (ed.) *The Growth of the American Economy* (Englewood Cliffs, N.J.), 127; US Bureau of the Census (1862) *Preliminary Report of the Eighth Census, 1860* (Washington, D.C.), 231. The mileage of track in Continental Europe is from Michael G. Mulhall (1892) *The Dictionary of Statistics* (London), 495; in Britain, from B. R. Mitchell and Phyllis Dean (1962) *Abstract of British Historical Statistics* (Cambridge), 225.

7 US Bureau of the Census (1853) *Abstract of the Seventh Census* (Washington, D.C.), 106–18.

8 See, for example, Fogel and Engerman, *Time on the Cross*, 2: 33–54; Richard Sutch (1975) "The treatment received by American slaves: a critical review of the evidence presented in *Time on the Cross*," *Exploration in Economic History* 12: 335–438; Vernon Carstensen and S. E. Goodman (1977) "Trouble on the auction block: interregional slave sales and the reliability of a linear equation," *Journal of Interdisciplinary History* 8: 315–18. For discussion of these estimates and the debate on these questions, see *EM* 22, 23.

9 David Brion Davis (1975) *The Problem of Slavery in the Age of Revolution, 1770–1823* (Ithaca, N.Y.), 171; John Chester Miller (1977)

The Wolf by the Ears: Thomas Jefferson and Slavery (New York), 107, cf. Leonard L. Richards (1979) "The Jacksonians and slavery," in Lewis Perry and Michael Fellman (eds) *Antislavery Reconsidered: New Perspectives on the Abolitionists* (Baton Rouge, La.), 102–5.

10 Kotlikoff, *TP* 3.

11 Figure 1 is taken from Fogel and Engerman, *Time on the Cross*, 1: 72. The curve was developed from data in probate records. For a discussion of Sutch's conjecture on the intercept of the price–wage profile, see Fogel and Engerman, *TP* 21 (9); *EM* 23.

12 The premia and discounts shown in Figure 2 were estimated from data in the probate sample of slave prices by fitting sixth-order polynomials on age and using dummy variables for specific skills and defects. Separate regressions were run on each gender. That blacksmiths and carpenters brought such a large premium does not necessarily imply that more profit could be made by slave-owners if they sold such craftsmen than if they sold ordinary field hands. . . . There was a cost to training craftsmen, which was the foregone product in other occupations during training. If markets were in equilibrium, then the profit rate on craftsmen would have been no greater than that on ordinary field hands.

13 Kotlikoff, *TP* 3.

14 For an elaboration of this point, see Kotlikoff and Pinera *TP* 6.

15 The price planters received for tobacco depended on total output. Production of western tobacco lowered the price of tobacco on the world market. Slaves were valued by the output they could produce but the increase in tobacco production, and decrease in price, could lower the price of slaves overall. If increases in quantity greatly reduced the price of tobacco, then the expansion of tobacco production into the West reduced the price of slaves. See Kotlikoff and Pinera, *TP* 6. Cf. Peter Passell and Gavin Wright (1972) "The effects of pre-Civil War territorial expansion on the price of slaves," *Journal of Political Economy* 80: 1188–1202; Susan Previant Lee (1978) "Antebellum land expansion: another view," *Agricultural History* 52: 488–502; Mark Schmitz and Donald Schaefer (1981) "Paradox lost: westward expansion and slave prices before the Civil War: discussion," *Journal of Economic History* 41: 402–7.

16 Ulrich B. Phillips (1919) *American Negro Slavery* (reprinted Baton Rouge, La., 1966), chart following 370. See *EM* 22, 23, 35.

17 See *EM* 21, 22, 35, 37.

18 Between 1840 and 1860 the productivity of agricultural labor increased nearly as rapidly in these states as in the Northeast, although productivity growth in both of the eastern regions lagged somewhat behind the pace of the North and the South Central states. Far from declining, the average value of farm lands in the three chief slave-exporting states (Virginia, North Carolina, and South Carolina) increased by 60 per cent over the decade of the 1850s, nearly as much as the increase (79 per cent) experienced by the three chief slave-importing states (Alabama, Mississippi, and Louisiana). See *EM* 23, 40, 68; US Bureau of the Census (1895)

Report on the Statistics of Agriculture in the United States (Washington, D.C.), 84–100.

19 Fogel and Engerman, *TP* 13; Ralph V. Anderson, "Labor utilization and productivity, diversification and self-sufficiency, Southern Plantations, 1800–1840," (Ph.D. diss., University of North Carolina, 1974), 53–70. Cf. *EM* 23.

20 See Goldin, *TP* 7, for a fuller discussion of the paradoxical effect of the combined rural and urban increases in the demand for slaves on the share of the slave labor force demanded by cotton planters. See also Fogel and Engerman *TP* 12.

21 Kotlikoff and Pinera, *TP* 6. [The political role of territorial issues is discussed at length elsewhere in portions of *Without Consent or Contract* not included here.]

22 Adam Smith (1776) *The Wealth of Nations* (reprinted New York, 1937), 81. See Leonard W. Larabee and Whitfield Bell (eds) (1961) *The Papers of Benjamin Franklin* (New Haven, Conn.), 225–6; David Brion Davis (1966) *The Problem of Slavery in Western Culture* (Ithaca, N.Y.), 427, 431.

23 For further discussion see Fogel and Engerman (1974) 2: 126–30; *TP* 12, 14, 15.

24 Frederick Law Olmsted (1856) *A Journey in the Seaboard Slave States* (reprinted New York, 1968), 91.

25 On "hand" rating, see chap. 1 [of *Without Consent of Contract*], 27–8. On the procedure for computing Figure 3 from the Parker–Gallman sample see *EM* 24. Cf. *EM* 27.

26 For the procedures underlying this discussion see *EM* 24–31.

27 See *EM* 24–31.

28 It should be remembered that it was the greater intensity of slave labor per hour rather than longer hours that was the source of the greater productivity of the slaves.

29 Those who migrated to the West were also generally younger and a larger proportion of them were men. However, these demographic differences are controlled in the construction of the indexes and so do not affect the comparison.

30 Robert Evans, Jr. (1962) "The economics of American negro slavery," in National Bureau of Economic Research, *Aspects of Labor Economics* (Princeton, N.J.), 197, 216. Since the hire rate reflects labor productivity, about two-thirds of total factor productivity was due to factors which made labor productivity higher in the New South than in the Old South.

31 For discussion of the elements contributing to the efficiency of slave farms see Fogel and Engerman, *Time on the Cross* 1: 191–209, *TP* 12, 13. See also Fogel and Engerman, *Time on the Cross*, 2: 132–9.

32 For a discussion of the issues involved in the North–South comparison see Paul David *et al.* (1976) *Reckoning With Slavery: A Critical Study in the Quantitative History of American Negro Slavery* (New York); Paul David and Peter Temin (1979) "Explaining the relative efficiency of slave agriculture in the antebellum South: comment,"

American Economic Review 69: 213–18; Gavin Wright (1979) "The efficiency of slavery: another interpretation," ibid., 219–26; Schaefer and Schmitz, "Relative efficiency of slave agriculture"; Fogel and Engerman, *TP* 12, 13; Yang, *TP* 14.

33 For a discussion of some of these issues see *TP* 12, 13.

34 Olson, *TP* 11. It is important to note that these estimates of labor time refer mainly to the work of slaves on the master's account and probably exclude most work on their own account, whether on or off the plantation. Cf. p. 28 and n. 34 of chap. 1 [of *Without Consent or Contract*].

35 Olson, *TP* 11.

36 US Department of Agriculture (1912) *Seedtime and Harvest*, Bull. 85 (Washington, D.C.), 35, 36, 43, 44. The relationships between the growing period, the growing season and the period between seedtime and harvest are discussed on p. 14 of this source.

37 See Olson, *TP* 11 for further discussion of the estimates of gross farm income originating in livestock and dairying in the North and the South.

38 Slaves' "pay" is the value of their maintenance plus some cash given to slaves as rewards. For the method of estimating the implicit income of slaves see *EM* 52; cf. Fogel and Engerman, *Time on the Cross*, 2: 116–17, 159–60. The term 'equal-efficiency hour" refers to the adjustment for the higher intensity of labor by slaves than by free agricultural workers. See Olson, *TP* 11 for a fuller treatment of this issue.

39 For a discussion of how caloric intake can be used to measure the intensity of labor see Robert William Fogel (1987) "Biomedical approaches to the estimation and interpretation of secular trends in equity, morbidity, mortality, and labor productivity in Europe, 1750–1980," typescript. The high body mass of slaves which indicates that they consumed enough calories to sustain very intense labor is discussed in *EM* 47. Compare with Robert A. Margo and Richard H. Steckel (1982) "The heights of American slaves: new evidence on slave nutrition and health," *Social Science History* 6: 516–38 and *TP* 24.

4

SLAVERY AND THE CIRCLE OF CULTURE

Sterling Stuckey

In his book Slave Culture: Nationalist Theory and the Foundations of Black America, *Sterling Stuckey makes one of the most sophisticated defenses of the argument that US slaves were "basically African in culture" (an argument the book also extends to subsequent African–American culture). To make his case, Stuckey relies heavily on an extended analysis of slave folklore and religion. He finds that the most important key to understanding slave culture is the symbolism of the circle, especially as it appeared in the "ring shout" of slave religious ceremonies.*

Stuckey acknowledges the achievement of Eugene Genovese's own analysis of slave religion and folklore in Roll, Jordan, Roll, *but obviously cannot agree with Genovese's argument above that "the very idea of a 'slave culture' is absurd." And, while most historians of slavery agree that African influences on the culture of slaves was profound, many would undoubtedly argue that Stuckey pushes his evidence very far. In any case, Stuckey's imaginative use of songs, stories, and ritual observance as sources – a type of analysis he has pioneered in his essay, "Through the prism of folklore: the black ethos in slavery" (*Massachusetts Review *(1968)) – is a model of its kind.*

The excerpt that follows comes from the long first chapter of Stuckey's book. Beginning students may not be aware that, before one can speak of a single "African" cultural influence on US slaves, one must deal with the fact that Africans themselves were divided into numerous ethnic groups which did not all share an identical culture. Thus Stuckey opens with a discussion of ethnicity in Africa and among African–American slaves. His point is to argue that different African ethnic groups shared certain basic values and rituals, and that these values helped to shape a new, common community of feeling among blacks in North America. One of the most important of these shared aspects of

African culture was the symbol of the circle, especially in dance rituals. In the United States, such a ritual dance appeared in many settings and was known as the "ring shout."

The final gift of African "tribalism" in the nineteenth century was its life as a lingering memory in the minds of American slaves. That memory enabled them to go back to the sense of community in the traditional African setting and to include all Africans in their common experience of oppression in North America.[1] It is greatly ironic, therefore, that African ethnicity, an obstacle to African nationalism in the twentieth century, was in this way the principal avenue to black unity in ante-bellum America. Whether free black or slave, whether in the North or in the South, the ultimate impact of that development was profound. . . .

The majority of Africans brought to North America to be enslaved were from the central and western areas of Africa – from Congo–Angola, Nigeria, Dahomey, Togo, the Gold Coast, and Sierra Leone.[2] In these areas, an integral part of religion and culture was movement in a ring during ceremonies honoring the ancestors. There is, in fact, substantial evidence for the importance of the ancestral function of the circle in West Africa, but the circle ritual imported by Africans from the Congo region was so powerful in its elaboration of a religious vision that it contributed disproportionately to the centrality of the circle in slavery. The use of the circle for religious purposes in slavery was so consistent and profound that one could argue that it was what gave form and meaning to black religion and art. It is understandable that the circle became the chief symbol of heathenism for missionaries, black and white, leading them to seek either to alter it or to eradicate it altogether. That they failed to do so owes a great deal to Bakongo influence in particular, but values similar to those in Congo–Angola are found among Africans a thousand or more miles away, in lands in which the circle also is of great importance. Thus scholarship is likely to reveal more than we now know about the circle in Africa, drawing West and Central Africa closer together culturally than they were previously thought to be.

The circle is linked to the most important of all African

ceremonies, the burial ceremony. As Talbot shows, in discussing dance in southern Nigeria,

> The Ekoi also in some of their dances imitate the actions of birds, but the most solemn of them all is perhaps the Ejame, given at the funeral of great chiefs, when seven men dance in the centre of an immense circle made by the other performers.

In that ceremony, the men keep their eyes to the ground and the songs they sing are said to be "so old that their meaning has long since been forgotten," which suggests the ancient quality of dance within the circle, the immemorial regard for the ancestral spirits in a country in which dance exists mainly as a form of worship and appears to have developed as a means of achieving union with God, of "exerting an influence *with his help* on the fertility of men and of crops."[3] Talbot notes the prime importance of rhythm to dance, and his description of "one variety" of dance parallels descriptions of dance in the ancestral circle in the Congo and in America since "the main object appears to be never to lift the feet off the ground and to leave a clear, even, continuous track." The ordinary method of dancing among the people of southern Nigeria – among them Ibos, Yorubas, Ibibios, and Efiks – appears monotonous and unattractive

> since it consists of slowly moving round in a circle – always in the opposite direction to the hands of a clock, widdershins – with apparently little variation in the few steps employed. It takes time to appreciate the variety and detail in the different movements and the unceasing, wave-like ripple which runs down the muscles of the back and along the arms to the fingertips. Every part of the body dances, not only the limbs.[4]

In Bakongo burial ceremonies, according to art historian Robert F. Thompson, bodies were sometimes laid out in state in an open yard "on a textile-decorated bier," as bare-chested mourners danced to the rhythms of drums "in a broken counterclockwise circle," their feet imprinting a circle on the earth, cloth attached to and trailing on the ground from their waists deepening the circle. Following the direction of the sun in the Southern Hemisphere, the mourners moved around the body of the deceased in a counterclockwise direction. If the deceased lived a good life, death, a mere crossing over the threshold into another world, was a precondition for being "carried back into the mainstream of the living, in the name and body of grandchildren of succeeding generations." From the movement of the sun, Kongo people derive the circle and its counterclockwise direction in a variety of ways.

> Coded as a cross, a quartered circle or diamond, a sea-shell's spiral, or a special cross with solar emblems at each ending – the sign of the four moments of the sun is the Kongo emblem of spiritual continuity and renaissance. . . . In certain rites it is written on the earth, and a person stands upon it to take an oath, or to signify that he or she understands the meaning of life as a process shared with the dead below the river or the sea – the real sources of earthly power and prestige."[5]

Wherever in Africa the counterclockwise dance ceremony was performed – it is called the ring shout in North America – the dancing and singing were directed to the ancestors and gods, the tempo and revolution of the circle quickening during the course of movement. The ring in which Africans danced and sang is the key to understanding the means by which they achieved oneness in America. Knowledge of the ancestral dance in Dahomey contributes to that understanding and helps explain aspects of the shout in North America that are otherwise difficult to account for. For instance, the solo ring shouts noted by Lydia Parrish in Virginia and North Carolina are in the ring dances of Dahomey done in group *and* solo forms, the two being combined at times. Thus, as the drums sounded, a woman held a sacrifice under her left arm, slowly dancing in a "cleared space three times in a counterclockwise direction, ending with a series of shuffling steps in front of the drums, while the young women who followed her cried out a shrill greeting to the spirits." Solo dance combined with other patterns of dance:

> With the drums sounding they formed a line of twos, and one couple behind the other they danced in the customary counterclockwise direction about the edges of the cleared space, finally forming a single line in front of

the drums, which they faced as they danced vigorously. Retreating in line to their place on the South side, before the ancestral temple they remained standing there, while one after another of their number danced singly, moving toward the drums and then retreating before circling the dance space.[6]

An impressive degree of interethnic contact, representing large areas of black Africa, at times took place at such ceremonies in Dahomey. F. E. Forbes, who spent two years in Dahomey and kept a journal of his observations, reports that one such instance of ethnic cross play involved "groups of females from various parts of Africa, each performing the peculiar dance of her country." When not dancing a dance with elements unique to a given country, they performed dances common to many different countries of Africa: "the ladies would now seize their shields and dance a shield-dance; then a musket, a sword, a bow and arrow dance, in turns." Finally, "they called upon the king to come out and dance with them, and they did not call in vain." The king's response had its own unifying influence and was understood by the women from the various countries of Africa, just as the response of Daha, the chief observed by Herskovits almost a century later, would have been understood by them as he "twice circled the space enclosed by the 'bamboos' in a counter-clockwise direction before he retired to the portico, where several of his wives solicitously wiped the perspiration from his face and otherwise attended him."[7]

A Kongo ancestral ritual that is profoundly related to counterclockwise dance among the Kongo people occurs, according to Thompson, when they place a cross in a circle to derive the four moments of the sun. While counterclockwise dance in itself achieved as much, the graphic representation does so in more explicit terms, marking off in precise ways the important stages or moments along the way:

> In each rendering the right hand sphere or corner stands for dawn which, in turn, is the sign of life beginning. Noon, the uppermost disk or corner, indicates the flourishing of life, the point of most ascendant power. Next, by the inevitable organic process as we know it,

104

come change and flux, the setting of the sun, and left hand mediam point or disk."[8]

The horizontal line of the cross, referred to as the Kalunga line, deserves attention for we shall later encounter it in American slavery – associated, as in the Congo, with those who were generous, wise and strong "on a heroic scale." Such people, in the imagination of the Kongo people, "die twice . . . once 'here,' and once 'there,' beneath the watery barrier, the line Bakongo call *Kalunga*." According to Thompson, "This is a line marked by the river, the sea, or even dense forest -ation, a line which divides this world from the next."[9] When that line, which extends from dawn to sunset, is evoked by the Kongo staff-cross, it symbolizes the surface of a body of water beneath which the world of the ancestors is found, and this casts additional light on why water immersion has had such a hold on blacks in America and why counterclockwise dance is often associated with such water rites.

The art historian Suzzane Blier has written that the circle is the most frequently employed linear mode of movement in Togo: "In the funeral, circular lines are formed as clockwise movements when linked to women, but are counter-clockwise motion sequences when employed for men." In the funeral, circular movement is used to represent themes of togetherness and containment. For example, when the deceased is carried around the house before being taken to the cemetery, the act "is said to call together the house ancestors so that they will come to the cemetery for the ceremonies to be performed there." The clockwise movement of women in Togo is a significant departure from the counterclockwise movement indigenous to much of Central and West Africa and does not appear to have an analogue in North America. The most likely explanation for its failure to survive in North America is that Africans from Togo who might have continued the clockwise movement in slavery yielded to the overwhelming preference of other Africans for counterclockwise movement.[10]

An indication of the complex rites to which people other than the Bakongo put the circle is found in ethnic groups from Sierra Leone. The connection of the circle to the ancestors and to the young is so various in that country, from which Africans were imported to American markets, that one better understands the strength and varying patterns of the circle in North America by understanding its antecedents in Sierra Leone. The Sierra Leonean Earl Conteh-Morgan's scholarship illuminates the relationship of the circle to the storyteller as dancing in a counterclockwise direction occurs: "Instances of dancing in a circle occur during storytelling time in the villages as the storyteller sits in the middle while the listeners sit around him and listen attentively." Since storytellers, or griots, focus mainly on the history of their people, ancestors are usually the principal subject of a particular chronicle of the past – the ceremony framed, as it were, by the listeners gathered around the storyteller. Depending on the demands of the narration, they either listen or, on signal from the storyteller, become active participants.

> Clapping and dancing usually occur in stories with a song that takes the form of a refrain. The refrain is repeated by the listeners at a signal from the story teller. Although it may not involve physical touching of the storyteller, it none the less gives the whole exercise an air of celebration. It also adds an air of vivid drama in the whole process of storytelling.[11]

Such singing of refrains and clapping of hands as dance occurs in a counterclockwise direction are similar to those of the dance described by Thompson in the Kongo funeral scene. Conteh-Morgan observed counterclockwise dance among the Bundu in Sierra Leone during a burial ceremony, and such dancing around the deceased, given the prominence of sacred dance in traditional societies, would seem to be widespread in Sierra Leone.[12]

The Sierra Leoneans reveal much about the circle in relation to the life process; indeed, the circle may well be the principal African metaphor for it. Among Mende and Temne secret societies, dancing in a circle with people in the center is a common practice on sacred occasions, for example, during rites of passage for young girls. When they are eligible to be selected for marriage by young men, they go through rites in

> the secret house, usually in the bush, or in huts specifically built for that. A couple of days are set aside, or one

big day, when they are brought out into the open for all to see as they participate in final ceremonies.

At this time, the women stand around the girls, who are generally teenagers, clapping and singing as the girls sit in the middle of the circle.

> From time to time, dancing in a circle takes place either by the girls themselves or by the women surrounding them. Touching of the heads or shoulders of those in the center and many types and styles of dancing take place as the music varies in rhythm and tempo.[13]

The circle, among Mende and Temne, is the chief symbol of a ceremony that leads to marriage and the renewal of the life process with the birth of children. Although counterclockwise dance of the Mende and Temne continued in North America as a function primarily of religious activity, it is highly unlikely, considering the mockery that was made of slave marriage in America, that the associated institution of preparation for marriage in the secret house survived even in secrecy in slavery.

Nevertheless, other African institutions and African priests were brought to America in large numbers and, unrecognized by whites, found their places in the circle and elsewhere. Some were among the first and last slave preachers. Herskovits tells us that a variety of them came to the New World, which greatly encouraged the preservation of African values in slavery:

> the river spirits are among the most powerful of those inhabiting the supernatural world, and . . . priests of this cult are among the most powerful members of tribal priestly groups. It will be . . . recalled how, in the process of conquest which accompanied the spread of the Dahomean kingdom, at least (there being no data on this particular point from any other folk of West Africa), the intransigence of the priests of the river cult was so marked that, more than any other group of holy men, they were sold into slavery to rid the conquerors of troublesome leaders. In all those parts of the New World where African religious beliefs have persisted, moreover, the river cult or, in broader terms, the cult of water spirits, holds an important place. All this testifies to the

vitality of this element in African religion, and supports the conclusion, to be drawn from the hint in the Dahomean data, as to the possible influence such priests wielded even as slaves.[14]

Priests were present on the plantations of the South, but whether they were, in specific instances, African-born or products of African influence in America is usually difficult to determine. This distinction is mainly theoretical, since at times one finds their practices, irrespective of the period of slavery, to be of nearly pristine purity and highly esoteric, as when they surface in the folktale. [In folk tales], as in life [Africans] gathered on the principal occasions of worship, above all at ancestral ceremonies, the most important of which in North America was the ring shout, which often was but one aspect, however important, of multifaceted African religious observance. The ring shout was the main context in which Africans recognized values common to them. Those values were remarkable because, while of ancient African provenance, they were fertile seed for the bloom of new forms. Moreover, understanding the function of ancestral ring ceremonies elsewhere in the Americas makes it possible to determine the function of the ring ceremony in its most arcane form in North America. . . .

Marshall Stearns offers a description of ring shouts in South Carolina in the 1950s, some years after John and Alan Lomax saw shouts in various parts of the South. Stearns's description is, in most respects, a characteristic one but also helps us understand an abstruse problem, to be considered later, relating to a particular manifestation of the shout:

> The dancers form a circle in the center of the floor, one in back of another. Then they begin to shuffle in a counterclockwise direction around and around, arms out and shoulders hunched. A fantastic rhythm is built up by the rest of the group standing back to the walls, who clap their hands and stomp on the floor. . . . Suddenly sisters and brothers scream and spin, possessed by religious hysteria, like corn starting to pop over a hot fire. . . . This is actually a West African circle dance . . . a complicated and sacred ritual.[15]

In this next section Stuckey turns to an examination of African

108

*culture as it is manifested in folktales. A central figure in the folktale
he examines most closely is the "trickster." The trickster is a character
who succeeds in the world by using his cleverness and cunning to
overcome physical weakness. Most students will be familiar with
stories about "Brer Rabbit," the best known of these trickster characters. In these tales Brer Rabbit is constantly fooling much stronger,
but less clever animals, such as Brer Bear. Such trickster tales have
their origins in Africa, and were brought to North America by slaves.
Folklorists have pointed out how, in slave tales, Brer Rabbit can be
seen as the clever slave who outwits the master. Stuckey analyzes a
trickster tale below to show how African culture – dance rituals,
ancestor ceremonies, and music – is revealed in black folklore.*

The most stunning illustration of the trickster's involvement
in ancestral ceremonies is contained in the tale "Bur Rabbit in
Red Hill Churchyard," collected in South Carolina by [E. C.
L.] Adams.[16] In this tale, Rabbit is trickster in ways never
before associated with him (except in the work of the great
collector and storyteller William John Faulkner): he is keeper
of the faith of the ancestors, mediator of their claims on the
living, and supreme master of the forms of creativity. As presented in "Red Hill Churchyard," Brer Rabbit is shown as a
man of God, and new possibilities are opened for understanding him as a figure in Afro–American folklore heretofore unappreciated for religious functions. In the Adams tale, ancient
qualities of African culture, some of the most obscure kind,
appear to yield new and original artistic forms within the circle
of culture and are directly related to Anansi and Akan priests
in the Suriname bush. More precisely, the tale reveals African
tradition and the future flowing from it, the ground of spiritual
being and the product of its flowering.

But the Red Hill ceremony seems, on its face, just one of
the many in which Brer Rabbit uses his fiddle as a kind of
magic wand – for example, to realize his will against predators
or in competition for the hand of a maiden. What seems equally obvious, though inexplicable, is the strong convergence of
the world of the living and that of the dead as a function, it
seems, of nothing more than Brer Rabbit's genius with his
instrument. That a deeper meaning lies beneath the surface of
the tale is suggested, even to one without a command of the
African background, by slave folklore, which holds that all

sorts of things, under the right conditions, are possible in the graveyard. Headless horsemen race about, a rabbit is seen walking "on he hind legs wid a fiddle in he hands," and the sacred and the secular are one in moments of masterly iconography as the "buck and wing" is danced "on a tombstone," "It look lik in de Christmas ef de moon is shinin' an' dere's snow on de ground, dat is de time when you sees all kinds er sights." At such times, day appears to light up the night, but the glow is from the moon and "every star in de element . . . geeing light." The "diff'ence been it ain' look as natu'al."[17] The real seems unreal, the unreal real as the story unfolds in the depths of winter in the South.

> De ground was kiver all over wid snow, an' de palin's on de graveyard fence was cracklin; it been so cold. . . . An' I look an' listen . . . an' I seen a rabbit settin' on top of a grave playin' a fiddle, for God's sake.[18]

The dance of the community of animals occurred:

> All kind 'er little beasts been runnin' round, dancin'. . . . An' dere was wood rats an' squirels cuttin' capers wid dey fancy self, and diff'ent kind er birds an' owl. Even dem ole Owl was sachayin' 'round look like dey was enjoying' dey self.[19]

Brer Rabbit got up from his seat on the tombstone, stopped playing and "put he fiddle under he arm an' step off de grave." Then he gave "some sort er sign to de little birds and beasts, an' dey form dey self into a circle 'round de grave." Within that setting, several forms of music were heard:

> Well, I watch an' I see Br'er Rabbit take he fiddle from under he arm an' start to fiddlin' some more, and he were doin' some fiddlin' out dere in dat snow. An' Br'er Mockin' Bird jine him an' whistle a chune dat would er made de angels weep.[20]

Probably a spiritual, the song whistled by Brer Mockingbird is made sadder as Brer Rabbit accompanies him on the violin, the ultimate instrument for the conveying of pathos. But sadness gives way to a certain joy as Brer Rabbit, with all the subtlety of his imagination, leads Brer Mockingbird as they prefigure a new form of music:

Dat mockin' bird an' dat rabbit – Lord, dey had chunes
floatin' all 'round on de night air. Dey could stand a
chune on end, grab it up an' throw it away an' ketch it
an' bring it back an' hold it; an' make dem chunes sound
like dey was strugglin' to get away one minute, an' de
next dey sound like sump'n gittin' up close an whis-
perin'.[21]

The music of Brer Rabbit and Brer Mockingbird resembles the
improvisational and ironic flights of sound that characterize
jazz, especially on Fifty-second Street in New York in the mid-
twentieth century. The close relationship between the music
in Red Hill Churchyard and jazz finds further support in the
behavior of Brer Rabbit, whose style calls to mind Louis Armstrong's:

An' as I watch, I see Bur Rabbit lower he fiddle, wipe
he face an' stick he han'k'ch'ef in he pocket, an' tak off
he hat an' bow mighty nigh to de ground.[22]

That scene and the others recall the broader context of Louis
Armstrong's musical environment in New Orleans, where jazz
was sacred in funeral ceremonies and where African secret
societies were important to its sustenance and definition. A
further consideration of the tale reveals its irreducible foundation in Africa.

The Herskovitses' discussion in *Suriname Folklore* of the drum
harks back to the Akans of the Gold Coast and enables us, by
transferring the power of the drum to the fiddle, to understand
the central mystery of the ritual, which at first glance seems
inexplicable. The drums have a threefold power in the myth-
ology of the bush Negro. Of the first power, the Herskovitses
write, "Tradition assigns to them the . . . power of summoning
the gods and the spirits of the ancestors to appear." After Brer
Rabbit stopped fiddling, wiped his face, and with the other
animals bowed in a circle before the grave, the storyteller tells
us, "de snow on de grave crack an' rise up, an' de grave open
an' I see Simon rise up out er dat grave. I see him an' he look
jest as natu'al as he don 'fore dey bury him."[23] The second
power of the drums of the Akans is that of "articulating the
message of these supernatural beings when they arrive." A
flesh-and-blood character capable of speech, rather than a dis-

embodied spirit, appears as the ancestor in the tale. Consequently, the other characters are able to communicate directly
with him, and he is greatly interested in them:

> An' he [Simon] look satisfy, an' he look like he taken a
> great interest in Bur Rabbit an' de little beasts an' birds.
> An' he set down on de top of he own grave and carry
> on a long compersation wid all dem animals.[24]

The third power of the drum is to send the spirits of the
gods or ancestors "back to their habitats at the end of each
ceremony."

> But dat ain't all. Atter dey wored dey self out wid com-
> persation, I see Bur Rabbit take he fiddle an' put it under
> he chin an' start to playin'. An' while I watch, I see Bur
> Rabbit step back on de grave an' Simon were gone.[25]

The intensity of the dancing in the circle, to the music of Brer
Rabbit and Brer Mockingbird, was great, as indicated by the
pace of the music and the perspiration of the performers,
though snow covered the ground. From internal evidence
alone – and a large body of external data also suggest as much
– we know the dancers fairly whirled in counterclockwise
movement. To them dance was sacred, as in Suriname, where
"one of the most important expressions of worship is dancing." There the dancers "face the drums and dance toward
them, in recognition of the voice of the god within the instruments."[26] The Gold Coast myth, it appears, was elegantly
applied in Red Hill Churchyard, but descriptions of the ceremony there and elsewhere in North America make no mention
of dancers facing percussionists as a necessary aspect of ritual.
This is not surprising, for drums were rarely available to slaves.

Since the functions of the drum in Suriname and of the
violin in South Carolina slavery are the same, on the evidence
of the tale and the work of the Herskovitses, it is very tempting
to conclude that South Carolina slaves, not having access to
the drum, simply switched to the violin to express the threefold power. But a case can be made for another explanation
of why slaves in South Carolina, and almost certainly elsewhere, used the violin on so sacred an occasion. In this context, David Dalby's assertion that some understanding of "the
history and culture of the great medieval empire of Mali"

is crucial to an understanding of slave culture is particularly relevant.

> The civilization of Mali included a rich musical culture, based on an elaborate range of string, wind and percussion instruments and on a long professional training for its musicians. This musical culture has survived in West Africa for at least a thousand years and, by its influence on American music, has enabled the United States to achieve an independence from European musical traditions and to pioneer new forms. A bitter aspect of the American slave trade is the fact that highly trained musicians and poets from West Africa must frequently have found themselves in the power of slaveowners less cultured and well educated than themselves.[27]

Dalby's thesis takes on added significance when one looks at slave culture and discovers the extraordinary degree to which slaves, at gathering after gathering, relied on the fiddle. When one takes into account that the one-string violin was used in the Mali Empire, and is used today among the Songhai of Upper Volta, which is within the boundaries of the old empire, to summon the ancestral spirits, new light is cast on "Bur Rabbit in Red Hill Churchyard," revealing a vital Songhai component in the tale and among South Carolina slaves.[28] The presence of the old Mali Empire, then, is felt in a way that could scarcely be more important – in the ancestral ceremony directed by Brer Rabbit with his fiddle.

Among the ethnic groups of the empire, the violin was widespread, in contrast to the banjo, which was used to accompany the griot's declamation or recitation of stories. Where one had to be apprenticed to griots to learn to master the banjo – in Upper Volta and, possibly, elsewhere in West Africa – a non-professional could pick up and, after long practice, achieve mastery of the violin without being apprenticed. The violin was a democratic rather than an aristocratic instrument for the Songhai; this helps explain, together with its use elsewhere in West Africa before and through the centuries of the slave trade, its widespread use by American slaves. In fact, the violin was the most important instrument of slave musicians and important among northern slaves as well. It is small wonder that in "Bur Jonah's Goat" the storyteller says,

"Ef you was to take dat fiddle 'way from him [Brer Rabbit], he would perish 'way and die."[29]

Missionaries in Georgia attempted to eradicate the widespread use of the fiddle on the Hopeton plantation, where five hundred slaves, very large numbers of whom were children and some "old and superannuated," formed a slave community. Sir Charles Lyell, who visited the plantation in the 1840s, wrote about efforts of Methodists to rid slave culture of that instrument even though nothing raucous was associated with ceremonies in which it was played. So pervasive was the use of the fiddle at Hopeton that the Malian tradition of string instruments to which Dalby makes reference is the background against which Lyell's remarks should be placed.

> Of dancing and music negroes are passionately fond. On the Hopeton plantation above twenty violins have been silenced by the Methodist missionaries, yet it is notorious that the slaves were not given to drink or intemperance in their merry-makings.[30]

Even when we include the large numbers of children and the very old, we find the astonishing average, on Hopeton, of approximately one fiddler for every twenty slaves in a population of five hundred. When we exclude the young and old, our calculations show that about one in every ten slaves played the fiddle, which makes it difficult to conceive of any ceremony, especially burial rites, in which not even one fiddle was present. And since slaves from Upper Volta were represented on so large a plantation, there was probably a Songhai presence, with ancestral spirits and gods being called forth with the fiddle, as in Red Hill Churchyard, at least until the campaign against its use was launched. It is a study in contrasting cultures that missionaries thought the fiddle profane in religious ceremonies and the African thought it divine in that context.[31]

The ceremony Brer Rabbit directed in Red Hill Churchyard was one with which great numbers of Africans in North America could identify because it involved a burial rite common in enough particulars to West African ethnic groups as a whole. Whatever their differences in language, slaves from many different ethnic groups might easily, at such a ceremony, assume their places in the circle, dancing and singing around the deceased, whether in Virginia, South Carolina, North Carolina, Georgia, Louisiana, Pennsylvania, Maryland, the District of Columbia, or elsewhere. What is certain is that African customs in a more openly expressed form in the North were more likely to occur secretly and in the inscrutable language of the tale in the South. Since the fear of slave insurrections was much less there than in the South, slaves in Philadelphia, for example, were permitted to come together in large numbers for ceremonies.

> Many [in 1850] can still remember when the slaves were allowed the last days of the fairs for their jubilee, which they employed ("light hearted wretch!") in dancing the whole afternoon in the present Washington Square, then a funeral burying ground – the blacks joyful above, while the sleeping dead reposed below![32]

The burial ground provided an ideal setting, under the conditions of enslavement, for Africans from different ethnic groups to relate to one another, to find shared religious values that must have been an enormous source of satisfaction as they struggled to prevent their numbers from being smaller still as a result of ethnic allegiances. When customs vital to West Africa as a cultural complex were indulged, such as the relationship and obligations of the living to the ancestors, bonds among Africans of different ethnic groups, if before unknown to them, were recognized and strengthened in America despite differences in language and despite certain differences in burial ceremonies. Occasions for such discoveries were not infrequent, since slaves, permitted to participate in the last days of the fairs, decided that a collective ancestral rite would become an annual event. That meant scores of first-generation members of a particular ethnic group chose to participate in a ceremony practiced in Central Africa and all over West Africa as well. The choice of the graveyard for the setting did not prevent white onlookers from concluding that the slaves were carefree, because they did not understand that African dance was a form of worship essential to sacred ceremony or how painful it was for Africans to practice such a ceremony in an alien land, and as slaves. "In that field could be seen at once more than one thousand of both sexes, divided into numerous little squads, dancing, and singing, 'each in their own

115

tongue,' after the customs of their several nations in Africa."[33]

If they had been preserved, the lyrics of what was sung would tell us much about the impact of slavery on the consciousness of first-generation Africans and much about African religious ceremonies generally. But given the context of the songs, the overall meaning is clear enough: they were songs concerning the ancestors, songs some notes of which, like those of Brer Mockingbird in Red Hill Churchyard, conveyed the pain of being on the ground of the dead in an alien land far from the ancestral home. Under those conditions, the degree of musical improvisation must have been exceptional, even for a people noted for improvisational brilliance. Their annual movement to the burial ground in Philadelphia meant a continuing affirmation of their values, so they sang and danced in a circle "the whole afternoon," the ground beneath them being common ground.[34]

In the following section Stuckey turns to a more general analysis of slave religion, and especially of the role of spirituals in religious ritual. While not denying that the words of slave spirituals show Christian influences on slave culture, Stuckey argues that other historians have exaggerated this influence. Instead, he argues, when spirituals are seen in the total context of slave religious worship, they show that African culture was the main source of slave religion.

For decades before and generations following the American Revolution, Africans engaged in religious ceremonies in their quarters and in the woods unobserved by whites. From the time of the earliest importations of slaves to the outbreak of the Civil War, millions of slaves did the ring shout, unobserved, with no concern for white approval. But the possibility that whites might discover the guiding principles of African culture kept blacks on guard and led them, to an astonishing degree, to keep the essentials of their culture from view, thereby making it possible for them to continue to practice values proper to them. Such secretiveness was dictated by the realities of oppression and worked against whites acquiring knowledge of slave culture that might have been used to attempt to eradicate that culture. While Lydia Parrish fails to appreciate that political consideration, she effectively draws on

African tradition to explain her difficulty in securing certain types of cooperation:

> It took me three winters on St Simon's to hear a single slave song, three times as many winters to see the religious dance called the ring-shout, still more winters to unearth the Buzzard Lope and similar solo dances, and the game songs known as ring-play . . . The secretiveness of the Negro is, I believe, the fundamental reason for our ignorance of the race and its background, and this trait is in itself probably an African survival. Melville J. Herskovits . . . quotes a Dutch Guiana Bush Negro as saying: "Long ago our ancestors taught us that it is unwise for a man to tell anyone more than half of what he knows about anything." It is amusing to question Southerners as to the number of times they remember hearing Negroes volunteer information. Not one so far has recalled an instance in which something has been told that was not common knowledge.[35]

For the African, dance was primarily devotional, like a prayer, "the chief method of portraying and giving vent to the emotions, the dramatic instinct and religious fervour of the race."[36] That whites considered dance sinful resulted in cultural polarization of the sharpest kind since dance was to the African a means of establishing contact with the ancestors and with the gods. Because the emotions of slaves were so much a part of dance expression, the whole body moving to complex rhythms, what was often linked to the continuing cycle of life, to the divine, was thought to be debased. But a proper burial, not what whites thought, was what mattered, unless they were present on so sacred an occasion. A proper burial, for the great majority of slaves throughout slavery, was one in accordance with African tradition. "Wen one uh doze Africans die, it wuz bery sad," an old man recalled of slave days in Georgia. "Wen a man's countryman die, he sit right wid um all night. . . . You know . . . doze Africans ain got no Christianity. Dey, ain hab no regluh religion." After praying, before leaving the "settin' up," the countrymen "put deah han on duh frien and say good-bye."[37] The placing of hands on the dead was an African custom practiced in West Africa and elsewhere in the Americas, including Dutch Guiana, just as drumming was practiced in Africa and, when permitted, in slave America. But the drummer's tempo apparently varied from place to place in Africa, ranging from the rapidity of some tribes in the Congo area to the slow beat of the Africans who influenced some of the drumming in Georgia graveyards: "We beat duh drum agen at duh fewnal. We call it duh dead mahch. Jis a long slow beat. Boom-boom-boom. Beat duh drum. Den stop. Den beat it agen."[38] On such occasions, there was at times the singing of African lyrics but more often the new lyrics of the spirituals.

Spirituals were born as the religious vision of the larger society was caught, as by centripetal force, drawn to the innermost regions of black spiritual consciousness and applied to what blacks were experiencing in slavery. In an African ritual setting on one such occasion, a black man got on his knees, his head against the floor, and pivoted as members of the group around him moved in a circle, holding his head "down to the mire," singing "Jesus been down to de mire." The arms of those circling "reached out to give a push" and from overhead looked somewhat like spokes in a wheel – a continuation of a tradition centuries old in Sierra Leone and one maintained well over a century in America, which argues a significant Mende and Temne presence in slavery in Georgia. As descendants of Temnes and Mendes in America sang in this century, inspiration was drawn from awareness that Jesus knew despair. This confronting of tragedy was somehow strangely comforting, the throwing of one's whole being into the performance a possible source of the blues in the song sang – the sacred side of the blues, what they owe to the spirituals:

> You must bow low
> Jesus been down
>   to de mire
> Jesus been down
>   to de mire
> Jesus been down
>   to de mire
> You must bow low
>   to de mire
> Honor Jesus
>   to de mire

Lowrah lowrah
   to de mire
Lowrah lowrah
   to de mire
Lowrah lowrah
   to de mire
Jesus been down
   to de mire
You must bow low
   to de mire
low
   to de mire

"The refrain – repeated relentlessly – corresponds in its character and rhythmic beat to that of drums," the words so filled with emotion that, after a while, they dissolve into moans and cries.[39]

For all her merits as a student of folklore, Parrish, who observed that particular shout, never understood the depths of its spirituality. She considered the shout "a kind of religious dance," and this has been the going thesis for well over a century. Nevertheless, she concluded that "Sperrichels were most often sung at night on the plantations when the 'shout'" was held, a context that should have deepened the meaning of the shout for her, as the relationship between the shout and the spirituals deepens the meaning of the latter for us: "The people, young and old would gather in the praise house, or, if there was none, in one of the larger cabins, where the ceremonies were usually prolonged till after midnight, sometimes till 'day clean'." Thus, slave youths were introduced to the circle and to the singing of spirituals within it – all the while dancing in ways scholars acknowledge to be little different from black "secular" dance of today.[40]

Too often the spirituals are studied apart from their natural, ceremonial context. The tendency has been to treat them as a musical form unrelated to dance and certainly unrelated to particular configurations of dance and dance rhythm. Abstracted from slave ritual performance, including burial ceremonies, they appear to be under Christian influence to a disproportionate extent. Though the impact of Christianity on them is obvious and considerable, the spirituals take on an altogether new coloration when one looks at slave religion on the plantations where most slaves were found and where African religion, contrary to the accepted scholarly wisdom, was practiced. Because that was true, principles guiding African culture were found there, none in greater force than the practice of one determination or form leading to and containing vital elements of another. This is seen when one adds to the words of the spirituals the African rhythms that regulate all movement as the worshippers circle counterclockwise in the shout.

The relative simplicity of spirituals sung in the circle was noted by Higginson and others, among them James Weldon Johnson. But the possibility that those who sang them in a circle also sang them outside the circle appears not to have been considered. Given the complexity and irony of Negro–African culture and the reciprocity of forms that characterize black music in this country, it would follow that, as the contexts in which Higginson observed and discussed the spirituals changed, many of the slaves who sang them in the circle sang them in other contexts as well. Certainly Higginson gives us no reason to doubt it. It is not sufficient, then, to ascribe the simplicity of the spirituals when sung in the circle merely to their stage of development. Rather, it is more likely that the songs in the circle are simple because dance is so pronounced and indispensable a component of the ceremony. As a result, the lyrics are driven by complex percussive rhythms, and often give way to chants, whose repetition can have a hypnotic effect and contribute to the high religious purpose of possession.

That the spirituals were sung in the circle guaranteed the continuing focus on the ancestors and elders as the Christian faith answered to African religious imperatives. In that context and in that way, they were sung by the majority of the slaves who sang them as Higginson, a colonel in the Union Army, observed the shout on South Carolina plantations:

> Often in the starlit evening, I have returned from some lonely ride by the swift river . . . and, entering the camp, have silently approached some glimmering fire, round which the dusky figures moved in the rhythmical barbaric dance the negroes call a "shout," chanting, often harshly, but always in the most perfect time some monstrous

refrain. Writing down in the darkness, as I best could, – perhaps with my hand in the safe covert of my pocket, – the words of the song, I have afterwards carried it to my tent, like some captured bird or insect, and then, after examination, put it by.[41]

Unlike most students of the spirituals, who treat them as a musical form unrelated to dance, Higginson understood that the rhythms of dance regulated all movement and affected the singing of the lyrics. As the names of those participating in the ceremony were called out, the line between the living and the dead was blurred when the celebrants focused on the ancestors, all to "the measured clapping of hands" and "the clatter of many feet." "Hold Your Light," a favorite of the children as well, was sung:

> Hold your light, Brudder, Robert, –
>   Hold your light,
> Hold your light on Canaan's shore.
> What make ole Satan, for follow me so?
> Satan ain't got notin' for do wid me.
>   Hold your light
>   Hold your light
> Hold your light on Canaan's shore.[42]

A more resounding but plaintive spiritual was sung, and the participants added names, in turn, as the dust rose about them, the tempo quickening. The song conveyed a sense of the inevitability of death but no longing for it:

> Jordan River, I'm bound to go,
>   Bound to go, bound to go,
> Jordan River, I'm bound to go,
>   And bid 'em fare ye well.
> My Brudder Robert, I'm bound to go,
>   Bound to go . . .
> My Sister Lucy, I'm bound to go,
>   Bound to go . . . [43]

At times hand clapping and foot stomping took on a more sorrowful meaning, underscoring pain, urgency, and a longing not even the ring shout could satisfy:

121

> O, my mudder is gone! my mudder is gone!
> My mudder is gone into Heaven, my Lord!
> I can't stay behind!
> Dere's room in dar, room in dar,
> Room in dar, in de heaven, my Lord
> I can't stay behind!
> Can't stay behind, my dear,
> I can't stay behind!
>
> O, my fader is gone! my fader is gone
> My fader is gone into Heaven, my Lord!
> I can't stay behind!
> Dere's room in dar, room in dar,
> Room in dar, in de heaven, my Lord!
> I can't stay behind!
> Can't stay behind, my dear,
> I can't stay behind![44]

The repetition of stanzas as the dancers circled around and around with ever greater acceleration reinforced and deepened the spirit of familiar attachment, drawing within the ancestral orbit slaves who may not have known either a father or a mother, their involvement being an extension of that of others, the circle symbolizing the unbroken unity of the community. Familiar feeling in the broad sense of clan and in the personal sense of one's own parents was a dominant, irresistible theme of slave consciousness when "Room in There" was sung. When it was, "every man within hearing, from oldest to youngest, would be wriggling and shuffling as if through some magic piper's bewitchment; for even those who at first affected contemptuous indifference would be drawn into the vortex." Such a response, from the oldest to the youngest, could not easily have been evoked by an appropriation from another culture; rather, the magical pull was an expression of traditional values of a people, those that moved the oldest to engage in sacred dance and the young to join them in the circle. All within hearing of the shout joined in the last chorus of the song:

> I'se been on de road into heaven, my Lord
> I can't stay behind!
> O, room in dar, room in dar,

122

Room in dar, in de heaven, my Lord!
I can't stay behind![45]

While the clapping of hands and dance were clear manifestations of the ancestral context of the songs, the monotonous
refrains, characteristic of ring shout spirituals, had the effect
of reinforcing in the consciousness of the participants the concerns of the song and the ceremony generally, thereby building
emotional and physical tension. The wider African context, not
the words alone, should be kept in mind when interpreting, as
slaves moved in a circle, their meaning when singing:

> Nobody knows de trubble I sees,
> Nobody knows de trubble I sees,
> Nobody knows de trubble I sees,
> Nobody knows but Jesus.[46]

And

> I know moon-rise, I know star-rise,
> Lay dis body down.
> I walk in de moonlight, I walk in de starlight,
> To lay dis body down,
> I'll walk in de graveyard, I'll walk through de
> graveyard,
> To lay dis body down.
> I'll lie in de grave and stretch out my arms;
> Lay dis body down.
> I go to de judgment in de evening' of de day,
> When I lay dis body down;
> And my soul and your soul will meet in de day
> When I lay dis body down.

Though Higginson read the song brilliantly in noting that in
"I'll lie in de grave and stretch out my arms" man's desire for
peace had never been "uttered more plaintively," death and
reunion with the ancestors – "And my soul and your soul will
meet in de day" – a process endlessly renewed, was an aspect
of that peace for most Africans in American slavery.[47] The
achieving of spiritual peace involved a complex ritual essential
for harmony between the living and the dead, command of a
symbolic world in which the circle steadily appears.

Although spirituals with poetry of a superior cast, such as "I

123

Know Moonrise," were in fact better suited for being sung outside the ring, to the swaying of bodies, slaves who sang spirituals in the ring shout apparently were the ones who, in the main, sang them outside the ring, for Higginson makes no distinction between them and other blacks. Marshall Stearns writes, "If we start with a more-or-less African example such as the ring-shout, we can see that as the rhythm dwindled, the melody lengthened and harmony developed." In other words, the ring shout itself may well have provided the creative breakthrough that led to spirituals being sung outside the ring:

> This process is enormously complicated by the West African tradition of improvisation, augmented by the free style of the folk hymn – no one melody is sacred; it can always be changed by spontaneous embellishments. Thus, although many spirituals are written down and ring-shouts generally are not, it is conceivable that the former's sustained melody could have emerged momentarily from a ring-shout. The evolution is fluid, proceeding at different speeds in different mixtures, with much depending upon the performer.[48]

While one differs with Eugene Genovese regarding the extent to which slaves were influenced by Christianity, his discussion of slave religion contains a profound insight: "The black variant of Christianity laid the foundations of proto-nationalist consciousness and at the same time stretched a universalist offer of forgiveness and ultimate reconciliation to white America."[49] In arguing that protonationalist consciousness was achieved, Genovese sensed a greater degree of autonomy in the slave community than scholars before him had found. Still, he underestimated the degree of nationalist consciousness, for slave consciousness was grounded in a continuing awareness of the fundamentals of African faith. But there is no question of the force of his argument that Christianity enabled the slave to stretch "a universalist offer of forgiveness and ultimate reconciliation" to whites – an achievement that began, if Stearns is right, in the ring shout during moments of sustained melody. Considering their rich experiences with multiple ethnic groups, it is fitting that Africans attempted to make Christianity real in the lives of others – in effect, to give it universal appeal.

NOTES

The Editor gratefully acknowledges permission to reprint these excerpts from *Slave Culture: Nationalist Theory & The Foundations of Black America*, by Sterling Stuckey. New York: Oxford University Press, 1987. Copyright © 1987 by Sterling Stuckey. Reprinted by permission of Oxford University Press Inc., and the author.

1 Peter Wood, who makes interesting use of African ethnicity in relation to work and resistance, notes of the colonists, "Most white colonists would have marvelled at the ignorance of their descendants, who asserted blindly that all Africans looked the same." Peter Wood (1974) *Black Majority: Negroes in Colonial South Carolina from 1670 through the Stono Rebellion* (New York), 179. . . . In general, slave masters in the nineteenth century paid little attention to African ethnicity, which was of immense value in the process of Pan-Africanization – of Africans, despite ethnic differences, becoming a single people – since masters did not attempt to maintain ethnic barriers. The most extended treatment of the slave masters' perceptions of ethnicity in the colonial period is found in Daniel C. Littlefield (1981) *Rice and Slaves* (Baton Rouge, La.,) chap. 1. For the most thorough treatment of ethnicity and the Atlantic slave trade, see Phillip Curtin (1969) *The Atlantic Slave Trade* (Madison, Wisc.).

2 Robert F. Thompson estimates that 30 per cent of the Africans brought to North America during the slave trade were brought from the Congo–Angola region of Africa. . . . Robert F. Thompson (1981) *The Four Moments of the Sun* (Washington, D.C.), 148. [Omitted here is a discussion of some of the complexities in discerning specific ethnic influences.]

3 P. Amaury Talbot (1926) *The Peoples of Southern Nigeria* (London), 804. . . .

4 Ibid., 803.

5 Thompson, *Four Moments*, 54, 28.

6 Parrish's observation that "the solo ring performance is apparently the only form in use" in North Carolina and Virginia and that "the ring shout seems to be unknown" is probably wide of the mark, as we shall see. Lydia Parrish (1942) *Slave Songs of the Georgia Sea Islands* (New York), 54; Melville J. Herskovits (1938) *Dahomey* (New York), 1: 216.

7 Herskovits, *Dahomey*, 67–8.

8 Thompson, *Four Moments*, 28.

9 Ibid.

10 Suzzane Blier (1981) "The dance of death," *Res* 2: 117.

11 Interview with Conteh-Morgan, Spring 1984. . . . [Cf.] Thomas Wentworth Higginson (1869) *Army Life in a Black Regiment* (reprinted New York, 1984), 36–8.

12 Interview with Conteh-Morgan, Spring, 1984.

13 Ibid.

14 Melville J. Herskovits (1941) *The Myth of the Negro Past* (Boston), 106–7.
15 Marshall Stearns (1956) *The Story of Jazz* (New York), 12–13. . . . [Cf.] John A. Lomax and Alan Lomax (1947) *Folk Song U.S.A.* (New York), 335 . . . and . . . Harold Courlander (1963) *Negro Folk Music, U.S.A.* (New York), 194.
16 "Bur Rabbit in Red Hill Churchyard," in E. C. L. Adams (1928) *Nigger to Nigger* (New York), 171.
17 For Brer Rabbit and headless horsemen, see "The dance of the little animals," in Adams, *Nigger to Nigger*, 178.
18 Adams,"Churchyard," 171.
19 Ibid.
20 Ibid., 172.
21 Ibid.
22 Ibid.
23 Melville and Frances Herskovits (1936) *Suriname Folklore* (New York), 520.
24 Adams, "Churchyard," 172–3.
25 Ibid., 173.
26 Herskovits, *Suriname Folklore*, 521. [Omitted here is a discussion of African conceptions of God.]
27 David Dalby (1970) "Jazz, jitter and jam," *New York Times*, 10 November, op-ed. page.
28 I wish to thank the anthropologist Paul Riesman for bringing Songhai burial ceremonies, and the place of the violin in them, to my attention. Interview with Riesman, Spring 1982.
29 Adams, "Bur Jonah's goat," *Nigger to Nigger*, 174. Dalby's thesis regarding Malian influences on slaves in America is supported by linguistic studies of Lorenzo Turner, who notes the prominence of Malian linguistic influences among Gullah-speaking blacks in the Sea Islands of South Carolina and Georgia, where Wolof, Malinke, Mandinka, and Bambara ethnic groups were represented in antebellum America.
30 Sir Charles Lyell (1849) *A Second Visit to the United States of America* (New York), 262–9.
31 On the Hopeton plantation, moreover, there was a distinct preference among slaves, during Christian baptism, for "total immersion," a widespread practice in Central and West Africa. On such occasions, the "principal charm" for slave women was "decking themselves out in white robes." Since in Georgia the Episcopal bishop, one Dr Elliott, "found that the negroes in general had no faith in the efficacy of baptism except by complete immersion, he performed the ceremony as they desired." Lyell, *Second Visit*, 269.
32 John Fanning Watson (1850) *Annals of Philadelphia* (Philadelphia), 2: 265. It is almost certain that slaves in the Philadelphia graveyard were doing the ring shout, for as late as the 1870s the shout was pervasive and powerful among blacks in that city. Blassingame makes mention of the ring shout in treating slave culture, and Raboteau gives more than passing attention to that ritual. Geno-

vese perceptively notes that the dance of the shout is the foundation of jazz dance, and Levine presents the shout over several pages in his work. While these scholars, all important contributors to scholarship on slave culture, were by no means unmindful of the importance of the shout, they did not probe its significance in African ancestral terms. See John W. Blassingame (1972) *The Slave Community* (New York), 65–6; Albert J. Raboteau (1978 *Slave Religion* (New York), 66–73, 339–40; Eugene D. Genovese (1974) *Roll, Jordan, Roll* (New York), 233–4; Lawrence W. Levine (1977) *Black Culture and Black Consciousness* (New York), 37–8, 165–6; . . . Robert L. Hall, "Africanisms in Florida: Some Aspects of Afro–American Religion," (unpub. essay); Charles Joyner (1984) *Down By the Riverside* (Urbana, Ill.), 160–1.

33 Watson, *Philadelphia*, 265. [Omitted here is discussion of African religious practices that did not "survive the slave experience."]

34 Watson, *Philadelphia*, 265.

35 Parrish, *Slave Songs*, 20.

36 Talbot, *Southern Nigeria*, 802. . . . For a discussion of the uses of dance and song in urging African men to acts of valor in battle, see Joshua Leslie and Sterling Stuckey (1982) "The death of Benito Cereno: a reading of Herman Melville on slavery," *Journal of Negro History* 67: 290. . . .

37 "In the Euro-Christian tradition," writes Courlander, "dancing in church is generally regarded as a profane act." He argues mistakenly, however, that the ring shout reconciled this objection, in that the shouters avoided crossing their legs and thereby stopped short of dance – and hence the compromise. For one thing, neither Courlander nor anyone else has demonstrated that the crossing of legs was ever a part, essential or otherwise, of the shout. See Courlander, *Negro Folk Music*, 195.

38 Georgia Writers Project (1940) *Drums and Shadows* (reprinted Westport, Conn., 1973), 107.

39 Parrish, *Slave Songs* 71. At Possum Point in the Sea Islands, blacks

alluz [always] does [one] dance. We calls it "Come Down tuh duh Myuh." We dance roun and shake duh han an fiddle duh foot. One ub us kneel down in duh middle uh duh succle. Den we all call out an rise an shout roun, and we all fling duh foot agen.

Georgia Writers' Project, *Drums and Shadows*, 141.

40 Jean and Marshall Stearns (1964) *Jazz Dance* (New York), 31, 32.

41 Higginson, *Black Regiment*, 188.

42 Ibid., 187–8.

43 Ibid., 188.

44 Ibid., 189–90.

45 Ibid., 190.

46 Dena Epstein (1977) *Sinful Tunes and Spirituals* (New York), 281.

47 Higginson, *Black Regiment*, 199.

48 Stearns, *Story of Jazz*, 130.

49 Genovese, *Roll, Jordan, Roll*, 278.

5

THE MASK OF OBEDIENCE
Male slave psychology in the Old South
Bertram Wyatt-Brown

In his Southern Honor: Ethics and Behavior in the Old South *(1982), Bertram Wyatt-Brown drew on anthropological theory to explore the origins and nature of the Old South's culture. Like Genovese, he viewed that culture as premodern in many ways. Unlike Genovese, he argued that the roots of the southern culture lay in a concept of "honor" that originated in the folk cultures of early Europe, rather than in the master–slave relationship itself.*

In this essay, Wyatt-Brown again draws on anthropological studies of culture to explore the pyschology of slavery. In some ways, he is returning in this essay to one of the central questions posed by Stanley Elkins in his book, Slavery.* *Elkins had suggested that the brutality of slavery had caused severe psychological damage to many slaves, in effect reducing them to childish "Sambo" personalities. More recent studies of slavery have argued that slaves created a partly autonomous culture that enabled them to resist such psychological damage.*

Here Wyatt-Brown returns to the question of slave psychology. He argues that the personality and psychology of slaves needs to be understood in the context of African cultures that, like southern culture, itself, placed great value on "honor," and thought of the loss of honor as shameful. While not agreeing fully with Elkins, Wyatt-Brown suggests that the shame felt by slaves caused more damage to individual slaves and their communities than some historians have allowed.

Oppression driveth the wise man mad,
Benjamin Drew, The Refugee[1]

In August 1788, Thomas Foster, a dirt farmer of Spanish

---

* See the Introduction for comments on Elkins.

Natchez, purchased for $930 two slaves – "dos negros brutos," the deed said, meaning that they were recent imports from Africa. One of the slaves was named Samba, "second son" in the Fullah language of his native locale in the Futa Jallon country of modern Guinea. The other captive had a much more unusual name and finer pedigree: Abd-al-Rahman Ibrahima. He was the son of Sori, the *alimami*, or theocratic ruler, of the Fulani tribal group, whose capital was Timbo, an inland center that traded with distant Timbuktu, where Ibrahima had received Islamic training.[2] Some months earlier, at the head of a cavalry detachment in his father's army, Ibrahima had been assigned to punish coastal tribesmen interfering with Fulani trade. He had been ambushed, captured, and sold to *slattees*, or native African slave traders.[3]

Through some means, Ibrahima conveyed to Foster the possibilities of ransom for himself in cattle and other valuables, perhaps including slaves, of which there was a great supply in Futa Jallon. But Foster had more immediate prospects in mind. The master dubbed his new prize "Prince" and at once had Ibrahima's long plaits of hair cut, although it took several men to restrain him. Intentionally or not, Foster had deeply shamed his black antagonist. In Ibrahima's eyes, he, a Fulani warrior, had sunk to the level of a tribal youngster.[4]

Other and worse humiliations followed when Ibrahima refused to work. The Fulani were pastoral folk among whom even the lowliest herdsman looked on manual labor with disdain. Agricultural work was the task of the Jalunke, many of whom the Fulani had conquered and enslaved.[5] After one of several whippings, Ibrahima ran off to the woods. Like most runaways, African or Creole, he probably did not stray too far from the Fosters' five-acre clearing. Weeks passed, and Ibrahima realized the hopelessness of his situation. Since suicide was a serious violation of the Koran, he was left to assume that Allah had intended his predicament. According to a story long remembered in Natchez, he appeared in the doorway when Thomas Foster's wife Sarah was alone. Looking up, she saw the tall and ragged frame of the missing slave, eyes fierce and staring. But rather than recoil in terror, she smiled, according to the story, and offered her hand in greeting. Ibrahima took it, then knelt on the floor and placed her foot on his neck.[6]

Ibrahima's experience with bondage offers us clues about male slave psychology. The discussion is best limited, it should be added, to male slaves because they were considered the most troublesome, and therefore on them fell the greater demands for signals of full compliance. For newly acquired Africans, the requirement of docility and abject obedience, masters believed, had to replace traits associated with manly independence and self-direction. For those males born in slavery, dangerous signs of resentment or resistance were bound to meet prompt reprisal. In the struggle for control, masters ordinarily had less reason to fear open rebellion from their female property: the women could be coerced with threats against their men or their young. Slaveholders expected that the women would fall into line if the men were subdued and that mothers would raise their children with an understanding of the system and their circumscribed roles in it.

Few anecdotes – or even legends – explain how newly arrived Africans reacted to this regimen, which commanded not only their labor but also their change of behavior, even personality. We are accustomed to think in terms of stereotypical and anonymous figures like Samba, the other slave that the New Orleans trader had sold to Foster. Yet there was a connection between the Timbo prince's bad luck and what has come to be called "samboism," the expression of complete servility.[7] In fact, Ibrahima's gesture of submission can symbolize for us that process of learning the demands of servitude as well as what servitude meant for the millions once in bondage. Although they learned subservience, Ibrahima and countless other blacks retained independent judgment. As Erik Erikson has pointed out, "it takes a well established identity to tolerate radical change."[8] The Fulani warrior had that kind of resiliency, pride and dignity. His religion and former place in African society prepared him to make the best of things without losing his sense of who he was.

More important to our purposes, community life in American slave culture, as in all societies, can be rendered unstable with differing effects on individual members, as circumstance, temperament, and the general situation shape their responses. Under oppressive conditions, which traits are most affected may be subject to debate, but the issue of damage itself must be faced. We simply cannot continue expatiating on the riches of black culture without also examining the social and psychological tensions that slavery entailed.

Three approaches can help explain male slave psychology: the behaviorist, the Freudian, and the cultural. None of them can be wholly separated from the others. The first involves role-playing, which can be oversimplified as a superficial performance without internal effect on the actor. A more sophisticated perception suggests that role-playing does involve inner feelings. Pressure to conform to bondage, to recite the script as given, can lead to self-deprecation or even self-hatred. The problem is not confined to slaves alone. In the eyes of others, "deviants" of one description or another must meet the obligations of their assigned stereotypes. According to Erving Goffman, the response of the victim to such requirements may be "hostile bravado," "defensive cowering," inarticulateness, or some other ineffectual reaction. Eugene Genovese found the behavioral model inadequate in explaining slave behavior, but role-playing is itself part of one's identity.[9] If we are brave or timid, confident or self-doubting, these traits will be registered by others. As Robert Park pointed out, "It is probably no mere historical accident that the word person, in its first meaning, is a mask." In all social circumstances, everyone plays a part. By these roles "we know each other," Park observed; "it is in these roles that we know ourselves."[10]

The second approach, the Freudian, has been somewhat discredited, owing to the disfavor into which Stanley Elkin's *Slavery* – and Sigmund Freud himself – has fallen. The pioneer scholar of slave psychology had adopted Harry Stack Sullivan's concept of the "significant other." As Elkins applied it, the Sullivanian theme was a variation on Freud's oedipal theory, which the historian used to describe the totalitarian relationship of white master and black slave. According to this analysis, the "sambo" personality was derived from that loveless, brutal connection, one in which neither black culture, black family life, nor white institutions of church and state played any major mitigating role.[11] Yet, for all its defects, which need not be recited here, Elkins's thesis was more Freudian than

Eugene Genovese and Elizabeth Fox-Genovese have characterized it and is the stronger for that foundation.[12] Clearly, the
slave in relationship with the master does not literally undergo
the child's evolution from "object-choice" to identification with
the master's superego as Freud described the process. Yet, in
slavery, the power as well as the authority to demand dependency and total obedience was analogous to the impact of
father on child, as the proslavery, "patriarchal" ideology
emphasized.[13] Elkins recognized that subservience carried
hidden psychic costs, which, even at the height of the controversy over *Slavery*, his more discerning critics acknowledged
as well.[14] Moreover, Elkins introduced a topic that has now
almost receded from historiographical consciousness, a circumstance that does injustice to the complexity of the matter.[15]
As Moses I. Finley, the Oxford University classicist, wisely
observed, "Nothing is more elusive than the psychology of
the slave."[16]

A third approach combines elements of the first two but in
addition stresses the cultural aspects of slave psychology. The
focus is less on the individual psyche and more on the social
character of the slave personality itself. As Bernard Meltzer
reminded us, "The mind is social in both origin and function.
It arises in the social process of communication. Through
association with the members of his groups, the individual
comes to internalize the definitions transmitted to him."[17]
Moreover, such a characterization is particularly applicable to
the small-scale, face-to-face community settings in which slaves
and masters were placed. Under those circumstances, there
was less room for the kind of individualism that modern
societies encourage, with regard not only to the slave but also
the master as well. The combining of behavioral, psychoanalytic, and cultural factors provides a much sturdier basis for
understanding slave behavior and motivation than the adoption of one alone. In one of the few recent studies of the
topic, Genovese and Fox-Genovese recognized the value of
this strategy:

> Historians need some sensitivity to personality structure
> and unconscious mental processes as well as to material
> conditions in order to understand the cultural patterns to
> which the newly enslaved clung, the ways in which they

compromised with their enslavement, and the cultural order they forged for themselves.[18]

Africans transported to the western world were already acquainted with the dictates of absolute rule and absolute servility, the latter a condition that encouraged a resignation severely inhibiting thoughts of rebellion. Slave rebellions were as rare in Africa as they were in North America, perhaps because Americans combined a familial bondage – the African mode – with commercial cropping on relatively small estates. The purely commercial, impersonal, and large-scale plantations in the West Indies, by contrast, resulted in much greater degrees of unrest.[19]

The African past and the servile present that Ibrahima symbolizes had in common a cultural pattern both parties understood: the ethic of honor and shame. Indeed, the culture from which Ibrahima – and so many of the blacks enslaved in early America – came resembled much more the honor–shame paradigm I have proposed for the white South than the conscience–guilt model of the northern section. But the power exercised over the slaves complicated the situation. Slaves were forced by circumstance to adopt the amoral posture of shamelessness, a pose intended to avoid the excesses of their victimization but that resulted in personal and social instability for them.[20] Three major types of servility can be distinguished. The first is exemplified by Ibrahima – ritualized compliance in which self-regard is retained. The second is the socialization of subordination, a natural acceptance of circumstance that involves the incorporation of shame. The third type of subordination is the adoption of "samboism," as it may be called, or shamelessness. None of the forms of subservience is exclusive, for each merges into another with as much variation and contradictoriness as might be found in any individual. Samboism was a disengagement from, a denial of, the conventional ethic, though a part of the social order that both whites and blacks recognized. As a strategy for dealing with whites, samboism did not in itself signify mental aberration or perversion. It did, however, involve character disorder, an insensitivity to others, and a dangerous selfishness. The untroubled sambos served masters and themselves, sowing suspicion in the quarters and thus adding to the troubles of all. In other words, the slave who played sambo did not suffer much psychic injury, because, lacking a sense of morality at the time of taking the role, he lacked conflict. It was instead slaves of some sensitivity who had the real dilemma: how to maintain dignity in the face of shamelessness by masters and even by fellow slaves. In fact, both shame, as accepted by the slave, and shamelessness, as sometimes adopted, were involved in community but not necessarily personal instability. In poorly run or cruelly mismanaged plantation households, however, emotional confusion, misdirected violence or scapegoating out of repressed anger, severe or mild depression, self-contempt, and collective paranoia and mistrust could easily arise.

First, let us review the chief aspects of the honor–shame culture. It differs from the conscience–guilt style of conduct – the introspective, democratic, and individualized patterns that we like to think guide our own lives. "Whereas," wrote Gerhard Piers, "guilt is generated whenever a boundary . . . is touched or transgressed, shame occurs when a goal . . . is not being reached. It thus indicates a real 'short-coming.' Guilt anxiety accompanies transgression."[21] On the other hand, shame involves a total failure of the individual: the incapacity to do, think, and feel the "right" way after recognizing the low opinion and disrespect in which one is held by others, who have respect and power. The excitation of shame involves a sense of defenselessness against the opinion and possibly the physical threats of others who claim superiority. Still more serious, a person shamed also suffers, as Norbert Elias, the German sociologist, pointed out, an internal conflict "with the part of himself that represents this social opinion. It is a conflict within his own personality; he recognizes himself as inferior."[22] In the case of the male slave, shame operates to affect his relations with other slaves whose good opinion he wishes to have in order to enhance his own self-esteem. To some extent, shame also conditions him to seek the good will of his master, so that the master is less likely to shame him in front of his fellow slaves and the white world as well.

Just as shame and guilt are distinct, so too are honor and conscience. Here, honor refers to the expression of power through the prism of reputation and rank based on such factors as gender, skin color, age, wealth, and lineage, rather than on meritocratic criteria. Those who deviate from the accepted moral standards appropriate to their rank or who, by their race, color, or lowly occupation, are rejected by the group are subject to the sanctions of shame.[23] Honor distinguishes between kin and alien, friend and enemy, in very obvious terms. Group and personal esteem is tied to family and to friendship as well as to vengeance against betrayers of one or both. It follows that kinlessness and friendlessness are the marks of shame and disgrace in all honor cultures. For Africans like Ibrahima, the great fear was "unhappy solitude," the dread of being alone. The same was also characteristic of white southern life.[24]

Deference to illegitimate authority could not be countenanced by a man of honor. That was a principle that Ibrahima had come to live by. But, if enslavement was one's fate, the Fulani tribesman believed resignation to be the only response possible because divine forces had ordained it. The gesture that Ibrahima employed was the traditional emblem of unconditional surrender in West Africa. Orlando Patterson has called enslavement "social death," a literal reprieve from actual death.[25] By formalizing his subjection in this way, however, Ibrahima was not merely prolonging his life. He was helping to smooth out the hills and valleys of his emotions into a level plain. Rituals serve to inhibit and control wild feelings of total despair. Similar if less dramatic rituals of slave deference served that function for other slaves. Since honor was something that all whites shared in contrast to the shame of all blacks, acts of homage lent – or were intended to lend – predictability to a situation that offered no permanent security.

For Ibrahima, the act of subjection was the beginning of unlearning his old self and teaching himself to present a new face of conformity. But he determined not to confess to dishonor, not to lose self-control. The Fulani people from which he came were well versed in the connection between male honor and the ideal of emotional restraint. To lose control was to forfeit honor and authority, to acknowledge unmanliness. No doubt, his success in maintaining dignity prompted his master to recognize his leadership qualities. Ibrahima became Thomas Foster's chief driver, to whom other slaves, some of them also from Futa Jallon, had to defer.

The second category of subservience, the inculcation of shame, can also be illustrated by reference to the Fulani experience in Africa. In the Fulani areas, the condition of slavery was one that anthropologist Paul Riesman argued "most clearly expressed everything that is the opposite of Fulani." Slaves and captives belonging to that people were labeled "black, fat, coarse, naive, irresponsible, uncultivated, shameless, dominated by their needs and their emotions."[26] Slavery was a status given to strangers who were captured or bought; they became and remained kinless and subordinate, a traumatic experience in a society based on lineage and kinship networks.

More to our purposes are the slaves born into that condition in another Fulani corner of West Africa today. Anthropologist Bernd Baldus has recently studied the slave systems of Fulani herdsmen in the Borgu region of northern Benin. The Batomba are agriculturalists and have lived side by side with the Fulani since Fulani migrations began in the eighteenth century. Like other West Africans, the Batomba have long believed that, if a child's teeth appeared first in the upper jaw, fearful disaster would afflict the kinspeople and tribe. Parents underwent rites of purification, but the affected babies were killed. After the Fulani had settled, the Batomba gave or sold the infants as slaves to their new pastoral neighbors, whose Islamic beliefs did not include the dental taboo.

Called *machube* (singular: *machudo*), the stigmatized slaves and their descendants thereafter stood lower than those subject to three other forms of servitude in the area. As a result, when slaves of Borgu were freed under French colonial rule eighty-odd years ago, the *machube* continued in bondage more or less by force of custom alone. (Except briefly and ineffectively at the time of official abolition, they have not risen up against their masters.) Today, the Fulani use neither physical nor legal means of coercion to enforce their will. When Baldus recently interviewed the slaves, he found that they had internalized their lowly status, ranking themselves below the Fulani and Batomba. Baldus discovered that the *machube* blamed themselves, not their superiors, for their plight. Their sense of humiliation was so powerful that, much abashed, they hesitated to account for their bondage until the anthropologist explained that he already knew. Somehow, the *machube* were convinced that the Fulani provided them with special status. Whereas a Fulani master assumes authority as a right, a *machudo* accepts slavery out of a mixture of awe for Fulani magic and a sense of gratitude. Said one:

> I work for the Pullo [another term for Fulani] because he has taken me as a child from the Batomba. He has raised me, washed me, he has given me milk. . . . For this reason, as a sign of recognition, one carries out all his commands.[27]

This mode of adaptation to an oppressive system very much resembles what Anna Freud called "identification with the aggressor" as a "potent" means for surviving danger.[28] According to Robert A. LeVine, an African anthropologist with particular interest in the Fulani and Hausa peoples of Nigeria, the incorporation of an individual's status into patterns of childrearing requires a generation or two. Eventually, though, parents learn to shape their children's playing and acting to ensure a match between how the children perceive themselves and the social and occupational positions they are to take up in maturity. Those who adopt the strategy of imitative subserviency are by no means irrational or "childish" in some pejorative sense. In fact, in a patron–client society such as that from which Ibrahima had come, "social incentives" tend to favor "the subservient follower" who understands human relations over the less politically minded, "independent entrepreneur or occupational achiever."[29] Nor are their actions altogether selfish, as the whole group may benefit from a greater sense of security.

Cosmic ideas also reinforce *machudo* docility. The slaves adopt a fatalism similar to Ibrahima's Islamic faith of centuries ago but more intense. They find safety, protection, and even ultimate salvation by doing exactly as their forebears had done and Allah commanded. "It has always been that way" and "we have found it this way from the beginning" were typical *machube* comments to explain their situation. Also, they responded with such aphorisms as, "If you have a cock, then you do with the cock what you want, don't you?"[30] This identification with the owner's perspective rather than their own suggests the mimetic feature of dependence: the desire to imitate the master's way. By this means, something of the status of the Fulani master is supposed to be accessible to the slaves. They want "to look like a Pullo," dress like him, talk like him, swagger like him. In error-ridden and inappropriate ways, they adopt some of his exclusive customs despite the mockeries and derision of the Batomba and Fulani. The point is not to win favor from the masters. Instead, an acceptance of the master's power involves adaptation to his ways. As one former slave in America lamented, "The nigger during slavery was like the sheep. We have always had to follow the white folks and do what we saw them do."[31] Like the *machube*, American slaves imitated in order to raise their own low self-esteem and create a distance between themselves and whites whose position in society was equally low. When American slaves belonged to "quality folks," they often disdained "po' white trash."

This kind of behavior is part of the cultural order. Conventions of shame come out of the group's accepted wisdom, arising from necessity, not voluntary adoption. Just as whites in the Old South assumed their status over blacks and the sanctions and alleged superior worth that a higher position conferred, so slaves, as a means of day-to-day survival, accepted their position, only questioning it, consciously resenting it, when crises arose. Eugene Genovese claimed that such slaves had adopted "a paternalistic pattern of thought."[32] Frederick Douglass, with reference to the country slaves among whom he grew up, recognized the effects of ignorance and vulnerability. Alternatives to servitude were unimaginable because "life, to them, had been rough and thorny, as well as dark." Douglass, on the other hand, had experienced relative freedom as a slave in Baltimore, a circumstance that broadened his awareness of options and heightened his revulsion against bondage itself.[33]

Internalization of the master's values was often so complete that slaves ignored opportunities to escape. Josiah Henson, a slave who eventually escaped to freedom, lamented that in his youth he, like other country blacks, had long assumed the legitimacy of his own bondage. Moving his property prior to a sheriff's sale, his master had assigned Henson to guide some eighteen slaves from Virginia to Kentucky. "My pride was aroused in view of the importance of my responsibility, and heart and soul I became identified with my master's project of running off his negroes." Even though they floated past the wharves of Cincinnati, where crowds of free blacks urged them to flee, Henson suppressed excited talk of freedom. As he sadly recalled, he "had a sentiment of honor on the subject." Accustomed to obedience and "too degraded and ignorant of the advantages of liberty to know what they were forfeiting," the crew heeded his orders, and the barge journeyed southward.[34] The incident was tragic, as Henson later realized in anguish, but most understandable. Plantation blacks who had little experience with autonomy were seldom quick to repudiate a humble conservatism that had long served as a means of survival.

To return momentarily to the African experience with bondage, Baldus argued that our western notions of corrective conflict, whereby the oppressed inevitably rise up in moral indignation as if by scientific or Marxian law, may simply not apply to the forms of socialization found in the northern Benin culture.[35] Other evidence from Africa supports his generalization. Observing "a prescribed code of conduct," T. J. Alldridge, an English trader, recounted how Mende slaves were accustomed to "cringe up and place their two hands one on each side of their master's hand and draw them back slowly . . . while the head is bowed." Similarly, on one occasion, a recently imported African from Futa Jallon, possibly an enslaved Jalunke (a non-Fulani black), met and recognized Ibrahima in Natchez. "Abduhl Rahahman [Ibrahima]!" he cried in wonder and fear. At once, he prostrated himself on the ground before him.[36]

Although American bondage was different in purpose and context from that of the Borgu tribes, Baldus's insights are pertinent to understanding servility in the Old South. Long-acculturated American slaves, whose concepts of liberty were far more sophisticated than those of slaves serving the Fulani, held to a peasant caution, with its own sanctions and rituals of allegiance, as part of their cultural heritage. Even after emancipation, as Leon Litwack has observed, some country blacks found it hard to break old habits of deference – much to the gratification of previous masters. South Carolinian Louis Manigault, Litwack recorded, was pleased that former slaves were still "showing respect by taking off their caps."[37] That attitude of mind was not just a casual matter: it was handed down from parent to child to prevent disaster. The trickster stories, which instructed as well as entertained, explained not only how shrewd and manipulative behavior could outsmart the powerful foe but also how, sometimes, the trickster's defiance led to trouble, defeat, even death. Recalling a ghost story from slavery days based on a real incident, ex-slave Silas Jackson, ninety years old, told how a slave, overheard praying for freedom, was killed by his master. "After that down in the swamp," he said, "you could hear the man who prayed in his cabin praying."[38] As such tales and interpretations of events indicated, children of oppression had to learn the hard ways of the world. Said another old-timer, interviewed in the 1930s, "I tells the young fry to give honor to the white folks and my [black] preacher tell 'em to obey the white folks, that they are our best friends, they is our dependence."[39]

It would be inappropriate to claim a universality of response from either such American examples or from the *machudo's* experience. This form of slavery is unusual in its sole reliance on self-blame and on perpetual subjection. Undoubtedly, the American slave had access to different and more liberating values than did the *machube*. Even in Africa, other forms of slavery flourished along different lines and provided for the slaves' more secure incorporation into the local society. Sometimes, descendants were allowed to marry into the non-slave community. When told on one occasion that African and American slavery were much alike, Ibrahima disagreed, "No, no, I tell you, [a] man own slaves [at Timbo] – he join the religion – he very good. He [master] make he slaves work till noon, go to church, then till he sun go down, they work for themselves." Alas, Ibrahima exaggerated the benignity of his homeland institution, just as white masters did in America. As timocratic or honor-guided societies, the Fulani and other slaveholding tribes looked on slavery as a means to procure "basic needs." Likewise, the southern ethic of honor upheld slavery just as slavery served honor.[40] None the less, the African experience of bondage involved only the issue of caste or status, not race as well.

The first two forms of servility, the ceremonial type that Ibrahima epitomized and the more common pattern of cultural response to subordination are somewhat different in character. The first involved less internalization than the second. Both, however, entailed outward demonstrations of fidelity beyond simply work faithfully performed. (Masters, for instance, liked to hear their slaves singing in the fields; silence was too ominous.) In keeping with that expectation, Ibrahima became what one of the Fosters' Pine Ridge neighbors described as "a faithful, loyal servant." To please his American-born wife and Sarah Foster, his owner's wife, Ibrahima even attended Baptist services on a regular basis after 1818, although he did not entirely forgo his Muslim religious practices.[41] Drab and demeaning though the role was, servility and its rituals were for him raiment to cover nakedness and vulnerability. By such means, one suspects, as his master's driver, he remained an aristocrat, never forgetting *pulaaku*, that is, the quality of character that identified the Fulani warrior as virtuous and honor-proud. He expressed his feelings by never smiling, or so one white acquaintance who observed him for years reported. The withholding could well have signified his submission to Allah's will, not to man alone.[42] Ibrahima's style represented the requisite obedience that all slaves had to display in the daily presence of whites, a demeaning ritual but not one that required internalized self-abasement. The second form of servility, a pattern that began with childhood and formed part of the social order of the slaves themselves, was more deeply ingrained and did require a degree of low esteem.

The third ingredient in the framework of male subservience is the traditional sambo himself – one not so habitually deferential as the *machudo* example nor so reserved and dignified as Ibrahima. Elkins erred in defining this character as a whole personality. Sambo was in fact a guise, adopted and cast aside as needed. When a slave took the role – some resorting to it more often than others – he made use of the third proposition in the system of honor and shame, namely, shamelessness.[43] As Elkins correctly argued, naked power, unchecked by any custom or institutional restraint, morally but not necessarily emotionally deforms both victimizer and victim. In other words, repudiation of ordinary and mediated ethics on the master's part could have induced an excessive servility and sense of unworthiness on the part of the slave. As Anthony F. C. Wallace has noted, "shame – awareness of incompetence in any sphere, whether growing from self-observation or information from others – may arouse so much anxiety as to inhibit further the person's competence."[44] Such individuals were probably rare in the slave quarters, because most could find some skill or expertise to counteract the contempt of the whites.

Even though Elkins failed to recognize the different responses that slavery could elicit, he was essentially right that Sambo behavior was authentic – but as ritual behavior, similar to but not identical with Ibrahima's alleged gesture. A reminder of how well this model of servility could be acted out appears in the diary of that remarkable South Carolinian, Mary Chesnut, at the close of the war:

> We had a wonderful scene here last Sunday – an old African – who heard he was free & did not at his helpless old age relish the idea. So he wept & prayed, kissed hands, rolled over on the floor until the boards of the piazza were drenched with his tears. He seemed to worship his master & evidently regarded the white race as some superior order of beings, he prostrated himself so humbly.

The whites rewarded his gratifying performance with a blanket and other throwaways.[45] The observers knew how insincere the beggar was, and all parties involved appreciated his immunity from moral responsibility in adopting the role.

The samboism of the roguish, coarse, and deceitful slave describes only one role slaves might play, but in all honor–shame societies in which slavery is a key institution, one finds the same ritualized and highly expressive practice: in Muscovite Russia, Greece, and Rome, in Brazil, the West Indies, in fact, nearly everywhere save parts of Asia. In all such societies, the slave was perceived as childlike and womanlike in character, only more so – violent (when spoiled) but usually passive, even affectionate.[46]

The necessity for adopting the trickster role lay in the unpredictability of the master's behavior, a point that Elkins convincingly made. The slaveholder could be shameless in rule and the slave shameless in protestations of dependency, driven by the emotions of the moment in a childish way. The survivor was the conscienceless "chameleon" who adopted the coloration that the totalitarian slave regime – or the master's whim – imposed. An example from contemporary society appears in Nien Cheng's *Life and Death in Shanghai*. In Communist China "chameleon" is the term used for those able to adjust quickly to authoritarian changes of policy.[47] Both southern slaveowner and servant could act with a lack of decorous inhibition and yet not be mentally "damaged" or neurotic.[48]

In premodern societies, men and women lived in a very public style over which collective opinion reigned supreme.[49] Among the classical Greeks, explained Kenneth Dover, to "be regarded as" virtuous was the moral equivalent of our more individualistic desire to *be* virtuous.[50] "I *wish* to be thought servile," says the sambo, in effect; not, "I *am* servile." But the shameless individual has no need to appear virtuous at all. As Orlando Patterson's study points out, those outside the circle of honor "aspire to no honor" and therefore "cannot be [made to feel] humiliated." In that freedom from the restraints and rules of dignity, the male slave exercised a certain level of autonomy in response to the willful and uncontrolled power of his owner. Probably the most eloquent form of shameless-ness as a device for self-protection and enhancement was the wildly articulate lie. Mention has been made of the conscience-less trickster, Brer Rabbit and others, in black tales for children and even adults. According to the stories' common moral lesson, the mouth and brain, not the arm and weapon, were the best protections available to the slave. As Charles Joyner observed, many of the tales provided a fantastic story of tri-umph in which the wolf (master) is not only outdone by the weaker animal (slave) but also thoroughly humiliated. In these little narratives, victory for the slave lies in cunning and highly competitive action but, as earlier remarked, sometimes the trickster is himself outwitted. The moral lesson was double: subterfuge was necessary to win against the stronger party but it was equally imperative to avoid being foolish and embar-rassed oneself. Thus even thievery from the master, particu-larly appropriation of food, served as an implicit rejection of master's honor and slave's dependency on one level and a practical answer to hunger on another – without the insupport-able risk that conspiracy to rebel involved.[51]

Not surprisingly, black manhood was connected with the capacity to think, talk, and act quickly. More significant than the moral lessons of folktales, role-playing – "playing the dozens" as it is now called – taught by doing. In this children's game, one boy insulted another's family so that the second boy felt obliged "to defend his honor" (and that of his family).

The challenges and replies escalate, while the group eggs on the participants with laughter and groans. The game served a number of functions – as group sport, as an outlet for aggression that could not be directed towards whites, as a way to pick leaders for verbal agility, but also, most important of all, as a device for making the repression of deep feelings habitual. A black psychologist explained it as the participants' experiment in keeping "cool and think[ing] fast under pressure, without saying what was really on their minds." Even if only half believed, an elaborate alibi could reduce the chance of white revenge. Yet this kind of activity was amoral – shameless – defiantly so, since the honor–shame nexus left no room for individual expression except in the form of the dramatically deceptive self.[52]

Like honor and shame, sporting insult of this kind was another example of Afro–American cultural transference with modifications designed to meet new circumstances. In Ibrahima's homeland, games of verbal abuse today enable elders to discipline children and to vent tensions against others in a ritualized context, but the major objective remains teaching and learning how to show restraint under provocation. Fear paralyzes the tongue, so worthiness to belong among peers can be achieved through the exchanged tauntings. One Africanist called it "familiarity with a vengeance."[53]

An early and instructive example of how the male hid personal feelings and articulated servile responses to authorities can be found in recorded testimony before the governor's council in South Carolina, 1749. A group of slaves, most of whom belonged to James Akin, a Cooper River planter, had to testify before the council about an insurrectionary plot hatched by a former overseer on one of Akin's plantations a year or two before. The slaves' confessions before the dignitaries not only identified black conspirators on their own and other plantations but also named some white transients as guilty of complicity. The whole group, they claimed, was preparing to canoe downriver to Charleston, burn the city, blow up the magazine, and seize a ship to sail for Spanish St Augustine.[54] Other planters, including Akin's brother Thomas, eventually informed the council members that no such plot ever existed but was a concoction of Akin himself. Upon reexamination before the royal governor, one imprisoned slave named Cyrus recanted. He explained that, prior to their first appearance before the council, Agrippa, another alleged conspirator, had told him and Scipio to leave the talking to him, as he "knew how to go before Gentlemen . . . had waited before on his Master in the Council Chamber, and was used to it." But, Agrippa had warned, keep Kent quiet because he "was a Fool and did not know how to Talk before White People." Indeed, Cyrus continued, if Agrippa had not "stood by and Pinched him, he would have told all & blown them." Scipio also said that Kent had been deeply afraid and that Scipio had "hunched him to make him speak as he ought to" before the governor. Some slaves could dissemble, as the testimony shows, especially those who had frequent contact with the master class. Others were unable to do so and were thought in the slave quarters to be "fools."

When it became obvious during the hearings at Charleston that truth would prove more advantageous than falsehood, again the shameless sambo type seemed the most articulate and credible. George, another slave, began his confession by saying:

> "Sir I am in your presence, my Master tells me that you are head of the Country. It is true I am not a white Man but I have a soul as well as others, and I believe there is a Heaven and a Devil."

He claimed to be afraid that "God Almighty" would punish him if he continued to lie, and he was "glad he was sent for, that he might tell all."[55] The ease with which the stories changed to fit the exigencies of the situation, the care with which the slaves shielded themselves from blaming any white, especially their master, the contrast between the articulate sambos and the frightened mutes like Kent, and the unreliability that coercion had forced all of them to exhibit showed how smoothly slaves could function in the honor–shame context.

None the less, the system of southern oppression was bound to have unhappy consequences for slave community and personal well-being. Black personality under bondage was partly dependent on the social climate that masters provided. Bitterness, hatred, or even the sense of security could be determined by a master's disposition.[56] In so far as black honor under bondage is concerned, the true psychological limitation of slavery lay not in acceptance of honor–shame strictures but rather in the absence of rules and structure – anarchy, sometimes legalized anarchy. Plantation chaos and cruelty could place an emotional strain on the slave that is hard for us even to imagine. In other words, Ibrahima's maintenance of high character depended in part on the reliability of his master. Had Thomas Foster been monstrous, his princely driver's actions might have been different.

Thus a range of different degrees of deference and inner acceptance existed, with each slave adopting or, at times, rejecting servility as the plantation environment, personal temperament, mood, and even unconscious motive allowed. A small number may well have fitted Elkins's unhappy description and lived lives of self-deprecation and deception. At the other, more inspired, extreme of samboism, some slaves took positive delight in the jesting, roguish performance. Almost all varieties of servility involved some degree of shamelessness, for that signaled an inner contempt for the values of honor on which the master rested his authority. But, in dealing with each other as opposed to the requirements of slavery, slaves avoided extremes for the most part. Some gave out contradictory or ambivalent signals. Such, for instance, was "Runaway Dennis," a slave belonging to Katherine Du Pre Lumpkin's grandfather in middle Georgia. Dennis so constantly quarreled with fellow slaves that they " 'fought shy' of him" but protected him as well, she recalled from family retellings. When called to account by the black driver, the overseer, or the owner, Dennis would vanish. None of the slaves ever betrayed his whereabouts. He "shamefacedly" reappeared only when word reached him through the quarters that he had been promised amnesty, usually through the intercession of Lumpkin's grandmother, whom he revered. For a short time, Dennis was once more a model of conscientiousness and servile compliance. After freedom, the unreconstructed former slave remained as "friendless' in the black community as he had been during slavery but showed his loyalty to Lumpkin by voting Democratic.[57]

Konstantin Stanislavsky, the famous acting instructor, would have appreciated such attention to proper slavish behavior –

the shuffling feet, hunched shoulders, downcast eyes, aimless gesturings of hand and body, along with the shrewd or self-deprecating remark to entertain overseer or master. As Stanislavsky noted, "an actor lives, weeps, laughs on stage, but as he weeps and laughs he observes his own tears and mirth."[58] This "double existence" could make "art" out of samboism. Unfortunately, the black slave, unlike the actor, had only one role to play before whites. No doubt that limitation had much to do with the rejection of shame that was part of the sambo role itself. "He who is ashamed," wrote Erikson, "would like to force the world not to look at him, not to notice his exposure." But, he continued, "too much shaming does not lead to genuine propriety but to a secret determination to try to get away with things, unseen – if, indeed it does not result in defiant shamelessness."[59] Thievery, the breaking of tools, and other "subversions" by slaves should be seen in this light, not as rebellion but as a covert means of gaining advantage and, also, staining the vaunted honor of the master. "I was never acquainted with a slave who believed, that he violated any rule of morality by appropriating to himself any thing that belonged to his master, if it was necessary for his comfort," declared Charles Ball, a fugitive slave.[60] Caught like a child in the grip of a demanding, arbitrary father, the slave might react in open shamelessness. Richard Wright in *Black Boy*, describes first hand how an elevator operator named Shorty, playing the slavish clown, maneuvered a Memphis white man into giving him a quarter in exchange for a kick in the rear. Wright was disgusted with the triumphant Shorty. " 'But a quarter can't pay you for what he did to you.' 'Listen, nigger,' he said to me, 'my ass is tough and quarters is scarce.' " Anything goes so long as it means survival, as Elkins asserted. Ethically, however, the southern black lived in two worlds.[61] To please those in one sphere could well mean loss of respect in another. Since ultimate power lay with the master, the temptation to rely on his largess and good favor was understandable.

To escape the dictates of shame and humiliation, then, male slaves had to repress emotions and maintain confident behavior under pressure. But, even so, the unpredictability of masters, the difficulty of avoiding white surveillance, the powerlessness of any slave in jeopardy could result in self-devaluation and especially doubt, what Erikson called "the brother of shame."[62] Ball explained these feelings in the case of his own family under slavery. Helpless to prevent the sale of his wife, Ball's father, once a man "of a gay social temper," turned "gloomy and morose . . . and spent nearly all his leisure time with my grandfather, who claimed kindred with some royal family in Africa." To avoid sale himself, Ball's father had to run away, and only the grandfather remained to raise the boy, doing his best to endow Ball with a sense of selfhood based, like Ibrahima's, on the family lineage.[63]

The male slave's abuse of women – sexual violence, desertion, insult – recapitulated white men's assaults on the black male ego, even as it arose from feelings of personal dissatisfaction.[64] These emotions of rage, depression, and stony resentment – often inwardly directed and involving alcoholism – are constantly emphasized in modern black autobiography and fiction, sources that put in artistic form some realities of black alienation.[65] The situation was the classic issue of neurotic conflict as Karen Horney portrayed it in *Neurosis and Human Growth*.[66] Although condemned for his unrealistic portrait of the historical Nat Turner, William Styron presented a picture of anarchic cruelty as the basis for such reactions, cruelty that blacks adopted in whole or in part to protect selfhood.[67] The very pecking order of the plantation – mirror image in the slave quarters of the patriarchal, male-dominated, honor-obsessed rankings of the white society – encouraged shamelessness, disesteem of others, and self-abnegation. Household servants were contemptuous of field hands, drivers of their underlings, lowly male slaves of the women, and women of the inferior members of their own sex. Accepting white standards of physical beauty, slaves often expressed a preference for light skin.

Deep mistrust and rivalry rent the harmony of the slave quarters. Such problems had potentially tragic consequences. The darker side of "shamelessness," for instance, was that busy sambos made untrustworthy companions. They might have been and probably were emotionally undamaged. The male slave who acted the part but felt it contrary to his nature was a likely victim of his own rage and conflict. But an imperviousness to moral controls made the effective trickster dangerous to the stability of the slave community. In a novel, W. E. B. Du Bois created one such figure named Johnson, whom a Colonel Cresswell called " 'a faithful nigger.' He was one of those constitutionally timed creatures," the narrator said, "into whom the servility of his fathers had sunk so deep that it had become second nature," but to the other Negroes, "he was a 'white folks' nigger,' to be despised and feared."[68] According to a recent study, Du Bois believed that the psychic damage of slavery was "an intense self-hatred" that made "racial solidarity an alien concept." Distrust and insecurity among blacks themselves multiplied as a result.[69] Of course, it is possible that sambo-like behavior – playing dumb or unconcerned – could well mask other designs or fool the white onlooker – to the satisfaction of the performer and his colleagues.[70] None the less, one wonders how much effort, time, and emotional stress had to be directed toward self-protection alone, leaving less energy for more creative pursuits and self-development. What saved the situation from complete demoralization was the strength of family ties in a wide, extended-family kinship network characteristic of both North American black and African culture. Although circumstances differed on both continents, sources of security outside the family were not available. In the American South, it did not pay to trust others in the quarters under such circumstances.[71] Du Bois observed that blacks responded to the disruptive, unreliable world around them with a "double-consciousness," that is, a "sense of always looking at one's self through the eyes of others, of measuring one's soul by the tape of a world that looks on in amused contempt and pity." How different from the studied and voluntary doubleness of the stage actor.[72]

Equally damaging was the sheer physical punishment that masters could inflict. The point is so obvious that I hesitate to belabor it, but even the most knowledgeable historians of slavery have underestimated its frequency and psychological effects.[73] The prospect of 150 lashes would make almost anyone a cringing coward. In fact, slaves exercised remarkable control. Their fortitude certainly had African roots. In some tribes, thrashing ceremonies, called in northern Nigeria the *sheriya*, tested stoic manhood. In any event, the physical effects could be very severe under law rather than simply under the arbitrary passion of an irate master. Corydon Fuller, a pious young bookseller traveling through Louisiana, recorded that, in Claiborne Parish, Louisiana, 1858, a slave who had inadvertently struck his mistress in the face with a bridle was sentenced to *"one thousand* lashes to be inflicted 100 each day for ten days. Many think he will die."[74] Such punishments were scarcely everyday occurrences, but neither were they rare.[75]

From the psychological point of view, whippings had three major effects. They degraded the victim, shut down more normal communications, but, most important of all, compelled the victim to repress the inevitable anger felt toward those responsible for the pain and disgrace. As a result, even the merest hint of violence obliged the victim to retreat into as compliant a pose as could be managed. Edward Wilmot Blyden, an early nationalist and advocate for Liberian settlement, declared, "We have been taught a cringing servility. We have been drilled into contentment with the most undignified circumstances."[76] White oppression stirred both compliance and fierce resentment, as Genovese explained in *Roll, Jordan, Roll.*

In addition, less physically injurious cruelties abounded. We need not mention the threat of sale and separation from family and community, a sudden and often unpredictable event with sorrows hard to imagine. Also, masters sometimes used shaming rites, ones that could enlist the other slaves into enjoying the spectacle, thereby doubling the misery while keeping the slaves disunited. Bennet Barrow, a slaveholder of Louisiana, once threatened to put an offending slave on a scaffold in the yard, wearing a red flannel cap. In another example, a slave with an insatiable craving had stolen an enormous seed pumpkin from his master's patch. The other slaves told on him, and the master easily recovered the unconcealable object. He made the slave eat a "big bowl of pumpkin sauce." The old slave who recalled the incident declared, "it am funny to see that colored gentleman with pumpkin smear on he face and tears running down he face. After that us children call him Master Pumpkin, and Master have no more trouble with stealing he seed pumpkins."[77]

With all the psychological, social, political, military, economic, and educational advantages that whites wielded, slaves could scarcely avoid feelings of oppression – and therefore of repression in a part of their social personality. To be sure, an essential self remained inviolable. Behind the mask of docility, the male slave was still himself and gave the lie to southern claims of "knowing" their blacks. As W. J. Cash pointed out, "even the most unreflecting must sometimes feel suddenly, in dealing with him, that they were looking at a blank wall, that behind that grinning face a veil was drawn which no white man might certainly know he had penetrated."[78] And yet the cost of building that impenetrable wall was high: repressing the hatred of the oppressors, bearing the slave's own powerlessness and the slavishness of other blacks. Male honor was richly prized in the slave quarters, and a defense of it established rank among fellow slaves. But slave honor was confined to the slave quarters, a restriction that may have made them all the more brutal out of frustration. Judge Nash of the North Carolina Supreme Court once declared that the slaves "sometimes kill each other in heat of blood, being sensible to the dishonor in their own caste of crouching in submission to one of themselves." Such behavior betokened a self-despising that sought a scapegoat in another person. For instance, Dan Josiah Lockhart, a fugitive in Canada, but once a plantation driver, admitted, "I was harder on the servants than [my master] wanted I should be." From his account, he was clearly taking out his resentment against his owner for selling his wife to a farmer an unreachable eight miles away.[79]

Another sign of self-hatred can be located in the examples of sabotage or apparent plantation "accidents" that historians have largely attributed to motives of subversion rather than to racist ideas of black "laziness" and irresponsibility. For instance, James Redpath, a journalist with strong antislavery convictions, reported that, on a trip through the South, he had witnessed a slave drayman lashing the horses' legs unmercifully as they hauled uphill a two-ton load of plaster. "This is a fair specimen of the style in which Negroes treat stock," he remarked. Frederick Law Olmsted offered similar testimony. Planters, he said, used mules more often than horses because "horses cannot bear the treatment they always must get from negroes" whereas "mules will bear the cudgeling."[80] To take out disappointments on a hoe or horse would, then, be less politically calculated than an impulsive expression of anger against personal miseries in the quarters as well as in the slave system itself. We are unlikely ever to know.

Likewise, historians understand little about how mothers reared their slave children. One suspects that at some point early affection had to give way to stern and perhaps arbitrary discipline – a cuffing without explanation – to turn the child toward automatic obedience and toward staying out of trouble with the white man. Male children more than female would have to be so trained. Wright implied in *Black Boy* his autobiographical novel, that the reason why his mother, grandmother, and other family elders cuffed, slapped, and beat him was not only a venting of their own miseries against a smaller creature but also an expression of a desperate love for him: without such treatment to curb his uncalculating independence, he would surely one day become, they thought, a white mob's victim.[81] "How many mothers and fathers had to punish severely children they loved so as to instill in them the do's and don'ts of a hideous power system in which a mistake could cost lives?" asked Genovese.[82]

Evidence of similar patterns in the experience of the Fulani slaves provides further insight. Bernd Baldus noted that the Fulani and Batomba superiors consider the *machudo* slave "uncivilized" or "wild." The *machube* are demoralized to the point of extreme aggressiveness toward each other. They never assault the mocking rulers but instead fall on one another in often fierce violence. "Mistrust" and lack of internalized controls are "pervasive, covering even close social ties among neighbors, friends, or family members." The experience of the *machube* was different from that of American slaves, who had the benefit of a Christian humanitarianism and more sophisticated attitudes with which to forge the bonds of a community. But such unhappy conditions could well have existed on those plantations where masters sought to destroy any sense of black collectivity.[83]

In the last few years, the darker side of slave life has regained scholars' notice, but generally historians place the emphasis on the remarkable endurance and even joyousness that slaves extracted from harsh conditions. Significant and valid though the brighter view is, the costs of honor, shame, and shamelessness should not be ignored.[84] If repression and its manifestations in inappropriate ways was one of the chief emotional problems of bondage, another was the related problem of communal mistrust and its effect on the social personality of the slave.

Nat Turner's recurrent nightmare in William Styron's novel

about the great Virginia slave revolt involves Nat seeing himself floating down a river and on a hill stands a white temple, familiar but closed to him. As he drifts by, all Nat can do is worship from afar the power of the whites' world that the edifice represents. The river takes him nowhere, just as the real Nat Turner's rebellion, for all its celebration in recent times, was futile.[85] Ibrahima also dreamed of water and familiar, distant places. After a lifetime of helping to build his master's estate into one of the great fortunes of Mississippi, Ibrahima hoped to die in his native land. His aged master, Thomas Foster, at last was willing to release him. But Ibrahima died at Monrovia, the home for freed slaves on the African coast, far from Timbo, with only his African kin to honor his memory.[86]

NOTES

The Editor gratefully acknowledges permission to reprint material from "The mask of obedience: male slave psychology in the Old South," by Bertram Wyatt-Brown. *American Historical Review* 93 (December 1988): 1228–52. Copyright © 1988 by Bertram-Wyatt Brown. Used by permission of the author.

A shorter version of this article was presented as the Commonwealth Fund Lecture at University College, London, on 2 February 1985. I wish to acknowledge the useful commentaries of the following participants at the seminar: Howard Temperley, most especially, and also Hugh Brogan, Peter J. Parish, Owen Dudley Edwards, and Betty Wood. Also I thank these American critics for their helpful reviews of the document: Lawrence J. Friedman, Stanley L. Engerman, Timothy Huebner, and, above all, Anita Rutman. A fellowship from the National Endowment for the Humanities is also acknowledged.

1 Benjamin Drew (1855) *The Refugee: A North-Side View of Slavery* (reprinted Reading, Pa., 1969), 4.

2 There are a number of terms by which the Fulanai are known, but for the sake of clarity I use only this form in singular, plural, noun, and adjectival position.

3 This account is based on Terry Alford (1977) *Prince among Slaves* (New York), esp. 3–38. See also Charles S. Sydnor, (1937) "The biography of a slave," *South Atlantic Quarterly* 36 (January): 59–73; "The unfortunate Moor," *African Repository* 3 (February 1828): 364–7; and Thomas H. Gallaudet (1828) *A Statement with Regard to the Moorish Prince, Abduhl Rahhahman* (New York), 3–4. There are inaccuracies, however, in these accounts, so Alford's careful researches are to be preferred. See also Paul E. Lovejoy (1983) *Transformation in Slavery: A History of Slavery in West Africa* (Cambridge), 114–15; and entries for 9–12 March 1794, in "Journal of James Watt

in his expedition to and from Teembo in 1794 copied from the author's own hand," MSS Afr. 22, Rhodes House Library, Oxford University.

4 Alford, *Prince among Slaves*, 23, 44.

5 In Futa Jallon, Ibrahima's region, slaves constituted a majority of the population. See Paul E. Lovejoy (1979) "The characteristics of plantations in the nineteenth-century Sokoto Caliphate (Islamic West Africa)," *AHR* 84 (December): 1273.

6 Alford, *Prince among Slaves*, 45–7; and Steve Power (1897) *The Memento: Old and New Natchez 1700 to 1897* (Natchez. Miss.), 13–14.

7 Joseph Boskin (1986) *Sambo: The Rise and Demise of an American Jester* (New York), 17–41.

8 Erik H. Erikson (1964) *Insight and Responsibility: Lectures on the Ethical Implications of Psychoanalytic Insight* (New York), 96.

9 Erving Goffman (1963) *Stigma: Notes on the Management of Spoiled Identity* (reprinted New York, 1974), 17; Eugene D. Genovese (1978) "Toward a psychology of slavery: an assessment of the contribution of *The Slave Community*," in Al-Tony Gilmore (ed.) *Revisiting Blassingame's "The Slave Community": The Scholars Respond* (Westport, Conn.), 27–41.

10 Robert Ezra Park (1950) *Race and Culture* (Glencoe, Ill.), 249.

11 Stanley Elkins (1959) *Slavery: A Problem in American Institutional and Intellectual Life* (Chicago); "Slavery and ideology," in Ann J. Lane (ed.) (1971) *The Debate over "Slavery": Stanley Elkins and His Critics* (Urbana, Ill.), 325–78; "The slavery debate," *Commentary* 60 (December 1975): 40–54.

12 Elizabeth Fox-Genovese and Eugene D. Genovese (1983) *Fruits of Merchant Capital: Slavery and Bourgeois Property in the Rise and Expansion of Capitalism* (New York), 91–135, esp. 102–5, 117–25.

13 See especially Sidney Axelrad and Lottie M. Maury (1951) "Identification as a mechanism of adaptation," in George B. Wilbur and Warner Muensterberger (eds) *Psychoanalysis and Culture: Essays in Honor of Gèza Róheim* (New York), 168–84. Sigmund Freud (1933) *New Introductory Lectures on Psychoanalysis* (New York) is briefly and lucidly explained in Peter Gay (1988) *Freud: A Life for Our Time* (New York), 415–16.

14 See Kenneth M. Stampp (1979) "Rebels and sambos," in Allen Weinstein, Frank O. Gatell, and David Sarasohn (eds) *American Negro Slavery* (New York), 240, 252 n.39 and n.40, 241; James P. Comer (1972) *Beyond Black and White* (New York), 174–5.

15 Compare Sterling Stuckey (1987) *Slave Culture: Nationalist Theory and the Foundations of Black America* (New York); Boskin, *Sambo*, 17–41; Mary Frances Berry and John Blassingame (1982) *Long Memory: The Black Experience in America* (New York), 11; Robert Fogel and Stanley L. Engerman (1974) *Time on the Cross: The Economics of American Negro Slavery*, 2 vols (Boston), 1: 228–32. For a more realistic appraisal of bondage and black reaction, see Willie Lee Rose (1982) *Slavery and Freedom*, ed. by William F. Freehling (New York), 164–76.

16 Moses I. Finley (1983) *Economy and Society in Ancient Greece*, ed. by Brent D. Shaw and Richard P. Shaller (New York), 108.

17 Bernard N. Meltzer (1972) "Mead's social psychology," in Jerome G. Main and Bernard N. Meltzer (eds) *Symbolic Interaction: A Reader in Social Psychology* (Boston), 13.

18 Fox-Genovese and Genovese, *Fruits of Merchant Capital*, 109.

19 James L. Watson (1980) "Slavery as an institution: open and closed systems," in Watson (ed.) *Asian and African Systems of Slavery* (Berkeley, Calif.), 3–13; Allan G. B. Fisher and Humphrey J. Fisher (1971) *Slavery and Muslim Society in Africa: The Institution in Saharan and Sudanic Africa and the Trans-Saharan Trade* (New York), 109.

20 See Bertram Wyatt-Brown (1982) *Southern Honor: Ethics and Behavior in the Old South* (New York); Orlando Patterson (1982) *Slavery and Social Death: A Comparative Study* (Cambridge, Mass.).

21 Gerhard Piers quoted in Helen M. Lynd (1958) *On Shame and the Search for Identity* (New York), 51.

22 Norbert Elias (1939) *The Civilizing Process*, vol. 2, *Power and Civility*, trans. by Edmund Jephcott (reprinted New York, 1982), 292–3.

23 See Julian Pitt-Rivers (1968) "Honor," in David L. Sills (ed.) *International Encyclopedia of the Social Sciences* (New York), 6, 503–11.

24 Paul Riesman (1974) *Freedom in Fulani Social Life: An Introspective Ethnography*, trans. by Martha Fuller (1974 French edn: Chicago, 1977), 67.

25 Riesman, *Freedom in Fulani Social Life*, 66, 68–9; Paul Riesman (1975) "The art of life in a West African community: formality and spontaneity in Fulani interpersonal relationships," *Journal of African Studies*, 2 (Spring): 39–63: Allan Hoben (1970) "Social stratification in traditional Amhara society," in Arthur Tuden and Leonard Plotnicov (eds) *Social Stratification in Africa* (New York), 195; O. Patterson, *Slavery and Social Death*; Alford, *Prince among Slaves*, 47.

26 See Riesman, *Freedom in Fulani Social Life*, 117, 135. Although slavery was practiced by many tribes from whom transatlantic slaves were drawn – Wolof, Yoruba, Azande, Ibo, Congolese, and Angolan – there were great variations in household incorporation, intermarriage, and means to emancipation.

27 Bernd Baldus (1977) "Responses to dependence in a servile group: the Machube of Northern Benin," in Suzanne Miers and Igor Kopytoff (eds) *Slavery in Africa: Historical and Anthropological Perspectives* (Madison, Wis.), 446; also 435–58.

28 Anna Freud (1947) *The Ego and the Mechanisms of Defense* (New York), 117.

29 Robert A. LeVine (1966) *Dreams and Deeds: Achievement Motivation in Nigeria* (Chicago), 41; also 19–22.

30 Baldus, "Responses to dependence," 446, 447; also 446–58. The *machube* were Islamic in conviction as were their masters, a common identification of faith, as Max Weber first theorized regarding the nature of slave religious belief. So too does Weber's hypothesis apply in North American slavery. See Weber as dis-

cussed in John C. Gager (1975) *Kingdom and Community: The Social World of Early Christianity* (Englewood Cliffs, N.J.), 105–6.

31 B. A. Botkin (ed.) (1945) *Lay My Burden Down: A Folk History of Slavery* (Chicago), 14–15.

32 Eugene D. Genovese (1974) *Roll, Jordan, Roll: The World the Slaves Made* (New York), 143–4.

33 Frederick Douglass, (1855) *My Bondage and My Freedom*, ed. by William L. Andrews (reprinted Urbana, Ill.), 111. For examples of black identity arising from skills and social status, see the account of John Drayton, lumberjack, in Botkin, *Lay My Burden Down*, 11–12; and of May, harpoonist, in Louis D. Rubin, Jr., (1975) *William Elliott Shoots a Bear: Essays on the Southern Literary Tradition* (Baton Rouge, La.), 1–27.

34 Josiah Henson (1858) *Father Henson's Story of His Own Life* (reprinted Williamstown, Mass., 1973), 48, 53.

35 Baldus, "Responses to dependence," 448; also 448–56.

36 Alldridge quoted in John J. Grace, "Slavery and emancipation among the Mende in Sierra Leone, 1896–1928," in Miers and Kopytoff, *Slavery in Africa*, 419; Alford, *Prince among Slaves*, 61. Jacob Stroyer, a former slave of South Carolina, recalled that "the [slave] boys were required to bend the body forward with the head down and rest the body on the left foot, and scrape the right foot backwards on the ground while uttering the words, 'howdy Massa and Missie.'" Stroyer quoted in Thomas L. Webber (1978) *Deep Like the Rivers: Education in the Slave Quarter Community 1831–1865* (New York), 33.

37 Leon Litwack (1979) *Been in the Storm So Long: The Aftermath of Slavery* (New York), 253.

38 Quoted in Norman R. Yetman (ed.) (1970) *Life under the "Peculiar Institution": Selections from the Slave Narrative Collection* (New York), 177.

39 Botkin, *Lay My Burden Down*, 35. Dependence of this kind by no means implies servile gratitude a sentiment arising from a balance of felt indebtedness and sense of independence. In a clientage or slave system in Africa, America, or anywhere, dependency leads directly to hostility when trust, ability, or exigency to protect the client is snapped, a situation that occurred on a massive scale with Civil War emancipation. So-called slave ingratitude and hostility to former, often "kind" masters, especially by domestics and others well treated, grew from resentment of slavery (enforced dependence) from justifiable bitterness at abandonment, and from contempt for the once "superior" whites' loss of honor and power. Given the honor–shame ethos of bondage, white expectations of slave gratitude were ridiculous. See O. Mannoni (1950) *Prospero and Caliban: The Psychology of Colonization*, trans. by Pamela Powesland (New York), 44–8: see also Daniel E. Sutherland (1981) "A special kind of problem: the response of household slaves and their masters to freedom," *Southern Studies* 20 (Summer): 151–66, which provides examples.

40 Alford, *Prince among Slaves*, 49, but see also 208 (note for p. 8);

John Grace (1975) *Domestic Slavery in West Africa with Particular Reference to the Sierra Leone Protectorate, 1896–1927* (New York), 10; also 1–19. "Introduction," in Miers and Kopytoff, *Slavery in Africa*, 3–81, shows the diversity of African slavery but stresses the severe marginality of the slaves' status. Watson. "Slavery as an institution," 3–15, criticizes Miers and Kopytoff for underplaying the "closed" types and the "property" aspect of slavery in all societies. See also M. G. Smith (1954) "Slavery and emancipation in two societies," *Social and Economic Studies* 3 (December): 243.

41 Alford, *Prince among Slaves*, 48; also 17, 79–81. See also "Letter from a Gentleman of Natchez to a Lady of Cincinnati . . . April 7th, 1828," in *National Intelligencer* (Washington), 8 May 1828: *African Repository* 3 (February 1828): 364–7; *African Repository* 4 (May 1828): 77; (October 1828): 243; (February 1829): 379; John W. Blassingame (ed.) (1977) *Slave Testimony: Two Centuries of Letters, Speeches, Interviews, and Autobiographies* (Baton Rouge, La.), 682–6. In Blassingame, *Slave Testimony*, 470–4, Omar Ibn Said, another formerly highly placed Fulani, enslaved in North Carolina, refused inquiries about returning to his homeland; he also submitted to Christian convictions after years of serving Allah in America.

42 In 1828, Ibrahima claimed to be a loyal Muslim but "anxious" to have a Bible in Arabic. See *National Intelligencer* (Washington), 8 May 1828; Alford, *Prince among Slaves*, 57. Gallaudet, *Statement with Regard to the Moorish Prince*, 3, asserted that Ibrahima's "wife, and eldest son have been baptized, and are in connexion with the Baptist Church." Paul Riesman, as quoted by Patterson, noted that, like "chivalry," *pulaaku* signifies "at once certain moral qualities and a group of men possessing these qualities"; O. Patterson, *Slavery and Social Death*, 84.

43 Julian Pitt-Rivers (1966) "Honour and social status," in J. G. Peristiany (ed.) *Honour and Shame: The Values of Mediterranean Society* (Chicago), 40–3; Charles Joyner (1986) "The trickster and the fool: folktales and identity among southern plantation slaves," *Plantation Society* 2 (December): 149–56.

44 Anthony F. C. Wallace (1961) *Culture and Personality* (reprinted New York, 1966), 182–3.

45 C. Vann Woodward and Elizabeth Muhlenfeld (eds) (1984) *The Private Mary Chestnut: The Unpublished Civil War Diaries* (New York), 4 June 1865, 256.

46 See W. Thomas MacCary (1969) "Menander's slaves: the names, roles, and masks," *Transactions and Proceedings of the American Philological Association* 100: 277–94; Philip Whaley Harsh (1955) "The intriguing slave in Greek comedy," *Transactions and Proceedings of the American Philological Association* 86: 135–42; George E. Duckworth (1952), *The Nature of Roman Comedy* (Princeton, N.J.), 249–50. On slave tricksters in other slave societies, see Nerys W. Patterson (1981–2) "Honour and shame in medieval Welsh society: a study of the role of burlesque in the Welsh laws," *Studia Celtica* 16–17: 73–103; esp. 91–3; Keith Hopkins (1978) *Conquerors and Slaves* (Cam-

bridge), 121; Richard Hellie (1982) *Slavery in Russia, 1400–1725* (Chicago), 313–17; Lionel Caplan, "Power and status in South Asian slavery," in Watson, *African and Asian Systems of Slavery*, 169–94; James H. Vaughan, "Mafakur: a limbic institution of the Margi (Nigeria)," in Miers and Kopytoff, *Slavery in Africa*, 95–6.

47 Nien Cheng (1986) *Life and Death in Shanghai* (New York), 363.

48 Ebeneezer Hazard, a New Englander visiting Georgia in 1778, remarked, "The *Country Gentlemen* are . . . accustomed to tyrannize from their Infancy, they carry with them a Disposition to treat all Mankind in the same manner they have been used to treat their Negroes. If a man has not as many Slaves as they, he is esteemed by them their Inferior, even though he vastly exceeds them in every other Respect." Entry for 25 February 1778, in Fred Shelley (ed.) (1957) "The Journal of Ebeneezer Hazard in Georgia, 1778," *Georgia Historical Quarterly* 41 (September): 318–19 (citation kindly supplied by George Crawford). See also Solomon Northup, in Gilbert Osofsky (ed.) (1969) *Puttin' on Ole Massa: The Slave Narratives of Henry Bibb, William Wells Brown, and Solomon Northup* (New York), 338.

49 Norbert Elias (1939) *The Civilizing Process*, vol. 1, *The History of Manners*, trans. by Edmund Jephcott (reprinted Oxford, 1978).

50 Kenneth James Dover (1974) *Greek Popular Morality in the Time of Plato and Aristotle* (Berkeley, Calif.), 226.

51 O. Patterson, *Slavery and Social Death*, 79, quoting from Julian Pitt-Rivers. See Pitt-Rivers, "Honour and social status," 19–78; and Pitt-Rivers, "Honour," 6: 503-11; Alex Lichtenstein (1988) " 'The disposition of theft, with which they have been branded': moral economy, slave management and law," *Journal of Social History* 22: 413–40.

52 See Harry G. LeFever (1981) " 'Playing the dozens': a mechanism for social control," *Phylon* 42 (Spring): 77; also 73–85; Lawrence W. Levine (1977) *Black Culture and Black Consciousness: Afro–American Folk Thought from Slavery to Freedom* (New York), 358.

53 Riesman, *Freedom in Fulani Social Life*, 124; also 76–9, 198: John Dollard (1939) "The dozens: the dialect of insult," *American Imago* 1 (November): 3–25; Roger Abrahams (1962) "Playing the dozens," *Journal of American Folklore* 75 (July–September): 209–20, esp. 213; Donald C. Simmons (1963) "Possible West African sources for the American negro dozens," *Journal of American Folklore* 76 (October–December): 339–40; Millicent R. Ayoub and Stephen A. Barnett (1965) "Ritualized verbal insult in white high school culture," *Journal of American Folklore* 78 (October–December): 337–44; William Labov (1972) "Rules for ritual insults," in Thomas Kochman (ed.) *Rappin' and Stylin' Out* (Urbana, Ill.), 314; Amuzie Chimezie (1976) "The dozens: an African-heritage theory," *Journal of Black Studies* 6 (June): 401–20; Walter F. Edwards (1979) "Speech acts in Guyana: communicating ritual and personal insults," *Journal of Black Studies* 10 (September): 20–39.

54 South Carolina Sessional Papers, Minutes of Council, December

1748–December 1749. Journal 17, Part 1, Public Record Office, British Manuscripts Project, Reel 34. I.C.O. 5/457, microfilm, 27 January 1749, pp. 55–120, South Carolina Department of Archives and History, Columbia.

55 Ibid., 64. Sambo, a witness, declared that they had collected no arms, at once a signal that no plot was underway. The head of the conspiracy was supposedly an overseer named James Springer, who had left for a northern colony long before the hearings and therefore could not be made a material witness. See ibid., 73, 85. See also Philip D. Morgan and George D. Terry (1982) "Slavery in microcosm: a conspiracy scare in colonial South Carolina," *Southern Studies* 21 (Summer): 122.

56 See, for instance, the story of Essex in John George Clinkscales (1916) *On the Plantation: Reminiscences of His Childhood* (reprinted New York, 1969), 12–36, a runaway slave who exhibited all these reactions in the course of a lifetime.

57 Katherine Du Pre Lumpkin (1948) *The Making of a Southerner* (reprinted Athens, Ga., 1974), 80; also 32.

58 Konstantin Stanislavsky (1949) *Building a Character*, trans. by Elizabeth Reynolds Hapgood (New York), 167.

59 Erik H. Erikson (1950) *Childhood and Society* (reprinted New York, 1963), 252–3. Whereas guilt involves transgression of one's own moral sense, shame arises from loss of pride, fear of ridicule, and anxiety of failure to achieve self-set, often unrealistic, goals. See Helen B. Lewis (1971) *Shame and Guilt in Neurosis* (New York) 18–23.

60 Ball quoted in Peter Kolchin (1987) *Unfree Labor: American Slavery and Russian Serfdom* (Cambridge, Mass.), 242.

61 Richard Wright (1945) *Black Boy: A Record of Childhood and Youth* (reprinted New York, 1966), 250.

62 Erikson, *Childhood and Society*, 253.

63 Charles Ball (1858) *Fifty Years in Chains* (reprinted New York, 1971?), 12; also 12–13.

64 Robert Staples (1982) *Black Masculinity: The Black Male's Role in American Society* (San Francisco), 62–71; Ronald L. Braithwaite (1981) "Interpersonal relations between black males and black females," in Lawrence E. Gary (ed.) *Black Men* (Beverly Hills, Calif.), 83–97.

65 Ralph Ellison (1947) *Invisible Man* (New York); Richard Wright (1940) *Native Son* (New York); Alice Walker (1970) *The Third Life of Grange Copeland* (New York) and (1982) *The Color Purple* (New York); Ernest J. Gaines (1964) *Bloodline* (New York) to name a few.

66 Karen Horney (1950) *Neurosis and Human Growth: The Struggle toward Self-Realization* (New York).

67 William Styron (1967) *The Confessions of Nat Turner* (New York); John Henrik Clarke (ed.) (1968) *William Styron's "Nat Turner": Ten Black Writers Respond* (Boston); but see James R. Huffman (1981) "A psychological redefinition of William Styron's *The Confessions of Nat Turner*," *Literary Review* 24 (Winter): 279–307.

68 James B. Stewart (1983) "Psychic duality of Afro–Americans in the

novels of W. E. B. Du Bois," *Phylon* 44 (June): 99. Du Bois expanded on this theme in *Dark Princess*, explaining that "the white always felt a Negro was watching him and he acted his assumed part . . . of strutting walk, loud talk, and swagger . . . accordingly. And the Negroes did watch from behind another veil. This was the veil of amusement or feigned, impudent humility" (Stewart, "Psychic duality of Afro–Americans," 102).

69 Stewart, "Psychic duality of Afro–Americans," 101. For a study of an analogous situation under colonial rule, see Leroy Vail and Landeg White (1983) "Forms of resistance: songs and perceptions of power in colonial Mozambique," *AHR* 88 (October): 883–919.

70 See, for instance, Walter L. Williams (1978) "The 'Sambo' deception: the experience of John McElory in Andersonville prison." *Phylon* 39 (Fall): 261–3.

71 Herbert G. Gutman (1976) *The Black Family in Slavery and Freedom 1750–1925* (New York); and Mitchell A. Green (1975) "Impact of slavery on the black family: social, political, and economic," *Journal of Afro–American Issues* 3 (Summer–Fall): 343–56. On Afro–American family interconnections, see Raymond T. Smith (1970) "The nuclear family in Afro–American kinship," *Journal of Comparative Family Studies* 1 (Autumn): 55–70; Niara Sudarkasa (1980) "African and Afro–American family structure: a comparison," *Black Scholar* 11 (November–December): 37–60; and Herbert J. Foster (1983) "African patterns in the Afro–American family," *Journal of Black Studies* 14 (December): 201–31, both of which essays argue for Afro–American extended kinship patterns.

72 Jean Lee argued that, at least until the 1780s in the Chesapeake, "no group of enslaved Afro–Americans was ever free from the threat of disruption," a circumstance that severely limited slave community development. Jean Butenhoff Lee (1986), "The problem of slave community in the eighteenth-century Chesapeake," *William and Mary Quarterly* 43, 3rd ser. (July): 341; also 333–61. Peter Kolchin found problems of instability in community life for antebellum slaves on small holdings; see his (1983) "Reevaluating the antebellum slave community: a comparative perspective," *Journal of American History* 70 (December): 584; W. E. B. Du Bois (1903) *The Souls of Black Folk* (reprinted New York, 1961), 16–17. On the internalization of the deferential mode, see John Dollard (1937) *Caste and Class in a Southern Town* (reprinted New York, 1949), 175–87, 286–313, pointing to a diversity of reactions, including degrees of deference and hostility.

73 Herbert G. Gutman (1975) *Slavery and the Numbers Game: A Critique of "Time on the Cross"* (Urbana, Ill.).

74 See Pearce Gervis (1963) *Of Emirs and Pagans: A View of Northern Nigeria* (London), 183–4. Corydon Fuller Diary, 21 June 1858, in William L. Clements Library, University of Michigan, Ann Arbor.

75 See, for instance, *State v. Dan* [Mrs Letty Barrett's], 22 September 1862, *State v. Sam* [Robert H. Todd's], 14 November 1863, Magistrates and Freedholders Court, Anderson County, South Carolina

Department of Archives and History, Columbia; Lawrence T. McDonnell, "The Whipping Post: Politics and Psychology of Punishment in the Slave South," unpublished paper, Social Science History Association, Toronto, 26 October 1984.

76 Blyden quoted in Wilson Jeremiah Moses (1982) *Black Messiahs and Uncle Toms: Social and Literary Manipulations of a Religious Myth* (University Park, Pa.), 51.

77 Edwin Adams Davis (ed.) (1945) *Plantation Life in the Florida Parishes of Louisiana, 1836–1846, as Reflected in the Diary of Bennet H. Barrow* (New York), entry for 24 December 1869, 175; pumpkin story told in Botkin, *Lay My Burden Down*, 6. For a similar acceptance of white perceptions in labeling of deviant slaves, see Bessie Hough Williams, "Memoir of the King Family," William Rufus King Family Papers, Alabama State Department of Archives and History, Montgomery.

78 See John W. Cell (1982) *The Highest Stage of White Supremacy: The Origins of Segregation in South Africa and the American South* (Cambridge), 241–3. Some planters were determined to insist on dependence for food, denying their slaves garden plots for fear of encouraging self-reliance, confidence, and laxity when working for their master. See "Governor [James H.] Hammond's instructions to his overseer," in Willie Lee Rose (ed.) (1976) *A Documentary History of Slavery in North America* (New York), 348; Botkin, *Lay My Burden Down*, 25, 35, 93; W. J. Cash (1941) *The Mind of the South* (New York), 319.

79 Nash quoted in Genovese, *Roll, Jordan, Roll*, 630; Lockhart quoted in Drew, *The Refugee*, 31.

80 James Redpath (1859) *The Roving Editor: or, Talks with Slaves in the Southern States* (reprinted New York, 1968), 241; Frederick Law Olmsted (1856) *A Journey in the Seaboard Slave States, with Remarks on their Economy* (reprinted New York, 1968), 47; see also Raymond A. Bauer and Alice H. Bauer (1942) "Day to day resistance to slavery," *Journal of Negro History* 27 (October): 388–419.

81 Wright, *Black Boy*, 94, and *passim*.

82 Genovese, "Toward a psychology of slavery," 33.

83 Baldus, "Responses to dependence," 450–8; Clyde W. Franklin II (1984) "Black male–black female conflict individually caused and culturally nurtured," *Journal of Black Studies* 15 (December): 139–54; Richard Staples (1979) "The myth of black macho: a response to angry black feminists," *Black Scholar* 10 (March–April): 24–32.

84 See Bertram Wyatt-Brown, review of O. Patterson, *Slavery and Social Death*, in *Society* 21 (March–April 1983): 92–4; Kolchin, "Reevaluating the antebellum slave community," 579–601. See also Lawrence T. McDonnell, "Slave against slave: dynamics of violence within the American slave community," unpublished paper, American Historical Association Convention, 28 December, 1983; and "Whipping Post," kindly loaned to me by their author.

85 Styron, *Confessions of Nat Turner*, 3–5.

86 Alford, *Prince among Slaves*, 180–3.

6

THE BLACK FAMILY AS A MECHANISM OF PLANTER CONTROL

Norrece T. Jones, Jr.

Norrece T. Jones's book, Born a Child of Freedom, Yet a Slave, *focuses on the "mechanisms of control and strategies of resistance in antebellum South Carolina." In the excerpt from Chapter 2 reprinted here, Jones argues that planter manipulation of slaves' family ties, and especially the threat of sale, was the most powerful of these mechanisms.*

While Jones acknowledges that planters often portrayed themselves as paternalists, his picture is one of unending conflict between master and slave, rather than accommodation. If the paternalist interpretation invokes a metaphor of the slave plantation as a family, however distorted and at times tyrannical, Jones's analysis invokes the metaphor of war, however muted or at times in a state of truce. Of course, Genovese has been at pains to insist that a paternalist master was not the same thing as a kind master. Nevertheless, the term paternalism carries with it the notion of a relationship based ultimately on moral force. Students should consider whether the evidence cited here by Jones is compatible with the idea that paternalism is at the heart of the master–slave relationship.

The fundamental principles upon which the system is based, are simply these: that all living on the plantation, whether colored or not, are members of the same family, and to be treated as such – that they all have their respective duties to perform, and that the happiness and prosperity of all will be in proportion to the fidelity with which each member discharges his part. I take occasion to inculcate repeatedly that, as the patriarch (not tyrant) of the family, my laws when clearly promulgated, must

162

be obeyed – that, as patriarch, it is my duty to protect their rights, to feed, clothe and house them properly – to attend to them carefully when sick – to provide for all their proper wants – to promote peace, harmony and good feeling, as so far as practicable, their individual comfort. *On the other hand, the servants are distinctly informed that they have to work and obey my laws, or suffer the penalty.* [Emphasis added.]

Southern planter, 1853[1]

Mother, is Massa gwine to sell us tomorrow?

Slave folksong[2]

The plantocracy of South Carolina attempted various methods of pacification and repression to cow African–American slaves into submission, but the most effective long-term mechanism of control was the threat of sale. Blacks feared the realization of that portentous suggestion more than any other mode of punishment, for while they could endure the pain of chastisement through whipping, it was more difficult to suffer the grave psychological injuries that stemmed from the severance of familiar bonds through sale. Memories of that traumatic experience would linger long after the wounds of a sadistic beating had healed. Parents who were sold would worry about the welfare of children growing up without a mother and a father. Slave men and women heard frightening tales from masters about the dangers of life in other states or in other parts of the same state where they might be sold.[3] Charles Ball, for instance, who was sold more than once before he was transported from Maryland to a South Carolina plantation in 1805, recalled:

I shall never forget the sensations which I experienced this evening on finding myself in chains, in the state of South Carolina. From my earliest recollections, the name of South Carolina had been little less terrible to me than that of the bottomless pit. In Maryland, it had always been the practice of masters and mistresses, who wished to terrify their slaves, to threaten to sell them to South Carolina; where it was represented that their condition would be a hundred fold worse than it was in Maryland.[4]

163

The removal of recalcitrant and incorrigible bondsmen was a time-tested and widespread custom. As one judge said in 1833,

The owners of slaves frequently send them off from amongst their kindred and associates as a punishment, and it is frequently resorted to, as the means of separating a vicious negro from amongst others exposed to be influenced and corrupted by his example.[5]

One planter who owned about 135 slaves was so pleased with this method of chastening blacks that he urged his heirs to continue the practice. He left instructions in an 1855 will that the "young negroes be kept on one of his plantations, and . . . to sell any of them that are turbulent or otherwise troublesome."[6]

Reliance on punitive sales had long been a tactic used by masters to rid themselves of non-compliant slaves. In 1740 the wealthy South Carolinian Robert Pringle sold "a Very Likely Young Wench" to Portugal for the sole reason that "she had a practice of going frequently to her Father and Mother, who Live at a Plantation I am Concern'd in about Twenty Miles from Town from whence there was no Restraining her from Running away there & Staying every now & then."[7] This savage and brutal mode of disciplining "execrable," "indifferent," or simply "bad" slaves was employed throughout the antebellum period and was even quite common during the Civil War.[8] Such sales were sanctioned by almost all in the white community and received particular approval from the religious sector.[9] With the exception of the Society of Friends, every denomination in the South had compromised with slavery until by midway in the nineteenth century religious leaders were either silent or offered divine justification for the traffic in human chattels.[10] One prominent Presbyterian preacher and slaveowner in South Carolina argued that nothing human was being sold, only the right to "labor and service." "When we buy and sell them," he declared, "it is not *human flesh and blood* that we buy and sell, but we buy and sell a *right*, established by Providence, and sanctioned by Scripture, to *their labor and service for life*."[11] [Emphasis in the original.]

Slaves knew that much more at stake than the sale of labor. Susan Hamlin, who was born in 1833, recounted after she was freed the heartrending sorrows and screams of slaves who were torn from loved ones and of others who had discovered that a sale was coming. Hamlin, who had been a house servant at the Charleston home of Edward Fuller, told of a couple who were married one night and learned the next morning that the wife had been sold: "De gal ma got in de street an' cursed de [owner] fur all she could find. . . . De police took her to de Work House . . . an' what become of 'er, I never hear."[12]

It is crucial to note that not only familiar ties but also the land on which black men and women had toiled, loved, borne children and buried their dead acted as a powerful centripetal force that made the prospect of sale all the more horrifying. Many observers, both before and during the war, remarked about the magnetism of African–American birth and burying places.[13] Charles Nordhoff, for example, said that ex-slaves displayed "the same strong local attachment . . . characteristic of the black freedmen in the British West Indies."[14] When Union forces evacuated Edisto Island, just off the coast of South Carolina, in 1862, Laura Towne, the northern schoolteacher who had come to teach liberated blacks, recorded: "A few old people had determined not to leave the home they loved so much, and they waited on shore till the last moment and then came hurrying down."[15] It is understandable, therefore, that most newly freed slaves returned to the area they had lived in while in bondage.[16] Funeral rites and burial grounds hold great importance in African–American culture. As late as the 1950s, some descendants of slaves arranged to have their remains interred on the plantations where their forebears rested.[17] Referring to blacks who had been slaves held by her relative R. F. W. Allston, Patience Pennington commented:

> Every year more hands leave the plantation [at Chicora Wood] and flock to the town, and every year more funerals wend their slow way from the town to the country; for though they all want to live in town, none is so poor but his ashes must be taken "home"; that is, to the old plantation where his parents and grandparents lived and died and lie waiting the final summons. . . . The whole family unite and "trow een" to make up the

165

sum necessary to bring the wanderer home; and even the most careless and indifferent of the former owners respect the feeling and consent to have those who have been working elsewhere for years, and who perhaps left them in the lurch on some trying occasion, laid to rest in the vine-covered graveyard on the old plantation.[18]

Such attachments were in all likelihood stronger before emancipation. An individual sold might be separated not only from the birthplace and burial grounds so important to black Carolinians, but removed perhaps forever from parents, cousins, aunts, uncles, grandparents, siblings, and friends. Bitter memories of such separations remained for years. The pain could still be seen in the tears of ageing men and women who recalled lost kin and in the invectives expressed by ex-slaves and their descendants about the whites who commanded the inhuman domestic and international slave trade.[19] At least for slaves, their disdain of masters as a whole often inspired a blanket distrust of whites in general.[20] A slave whose master or mistress did everything possible to prevent sales and to minimize lashings was still a slave. Resentment of this reality contributed to the steady flow of errant slaves streaming into distant states. So extensive was the influx of "undesirable" slaves into the Palmetto State that in 1847 a group of citizens from Charleston appealed to the legislature to limit admission of "vicious slaves." Their petition demonstrates how widespread that market had become as well as how prevalent the belief that "docile" local slaves were prodded to mischief by recalcitrant outsiders. Their appeal stated in part:

> Your petitioners . . . shew That the persevering efforts, in some parts of our Union, to intermeddle injuriously with our slave population furnish increased motives for vigilance on our part, not only in repelling interference from abroad, but in a stricter government of our slaves at home is liable to mischievous disturbance from the importation of vicious or criminal slaves from other states. That as laws have been passed by the states South West of us prohibiting the importation of slaves into those states merely for Sale and not the property of residents or immigrants passing through them [sic].
>
> This State and the City of Charleston in particular, have

become the common place of meeting between the slave dealer from places north of us and the purchaser South West of us. That the motive of the Slave dealer is not only to approach as near as he can to his buyer, but to remove the slave as far from his old range and from notorious bad character, as possible. That while on sale here many vicious slaves are palmed upon careless or confiding citizens among us, and their mixture with our own has had a sensible influence upon the docility and usefulness of our slaves. That your petitioners are not to be confounded with those inimical to Southern interests who oppose the removal of slaves from state to state under any circumstances. *We propose* to confine the admission of Slaves into this State, to those brought here by their owners, residents in this State and those the property of emigrants passing into or through this State and we propose to prohibit under proper sanctions the introduction of slaves into this state *merely for sale*. . . . [Emphasis in the original.][21]

Most masters chose not to accept the fact that blacks who were native-born and free from "outside forces" could be refractory. They continued to delude themselves that they could preserve the purity and peacefulness of their slaves by keeping out all troublemakers. Slaveholders continued exercising, therefore, the powerful lever of deportation not only to accomplish this objective, but to warn bondsmen that they were not the subjects of idle threats.[22] To be sure, the mere presence of non-South Carolinian slaves proved the seriousness of remote planters, but the departure of local, native-born neighbors who failed to heed their owners' warnings was evidence of the sudden uprooting *all* slaves could face. The consequences of R. F. W. Allston's orders, for instance, would not have missed the attention of blacks:

Appropos of sales you enquire what Brass is to do. I sent him up to split Rails, and told him upon his repeated failure that he must go to the vendue table [auction block], whenever he could not do this. Now if any one about you is going to Charleston, give Brass a new shirt and send to Robertson Blacklock and Co. to be turn'd into money, forthwith. It is the best thing to be done with Brass. There must be no fuss about it, or noise, or notice.[23]

Needless to say, sales, either effected or threatened, would have been less meaningful to someone who lacked the bonds of friendship and family. South Carolinian enslavers learned this lesson early when, as a cost-saving measure in 1714, they experimented with deportations instead of their traditional solution of executions of slaves who committed crimes. Within three years, slaveholders revoked the law establishing the policy of deportations after they discovered that it prompted slaves "to commit great numbers of robberies, burglaries and other felonies, well knowing they were to suffer no other punishment for their crimes, but transportation, which to them was rather an encouragement to pursue their villainies."[24] In a black population largely male and single, planters during the first quarter of the eighteenth century had to find other methods of control.[25] The next century, however, brought new life to an old experiment.

By 1800 Africans and African–Americans generally had enmeshed themselves in an intricate and extensive network of kinship ties that commanded a loyalty so powerful that the atmosphere was ripe for masters to impose more successfully a compliance based on slave fears of banishment. Indeed, until the Confederacy lost its war, the prospect of being sold, whether for profit or punishment, hovered over all those in chains. This most-feared possibility was made real in innumerable ways. Not only did planters threaten to sell slaves who persistently refused to comply, but they saw to it that insubordinate slaves, as well as other bond people, constantly witnessed auctions and the endless processions of human chattels driven by diverse whites to distant destinies in captivity.[26] While one could choose not to watch such scenes, there very likely were black neighbors who had traveled on and remembered well each step of that route.

Jacob, a slave who belonged to Charles Manigault, would not have taken lightly the message from his master delivered to him after he had spent three weeks in solitary confinement while in jail and received a whipping for being "a bad disposed Nigger." Manigault's "compliments" were to be given to Jacob with notice that if he did not change for the better, New

Orleans would be his destination – a marketplace, Jacob was reminded, where "several of the gang" had already been sent for "their misconduct, or their running away for no cause."[27] Although it is not possible to determine the exact number of punitive sales, virtually all sources indicate that the communication network among blacks was so efficient and extensive that most slaves were probably aware of those that did occur. As former slave Isaiah Butler declared, everyone knew the meaning of "I'll put you in my pocket, sir!"[28] . . .

Sidney Mintz and Richard Price suggest in their brilliant anthropological study that "certain widespread fundamental ideas and assumptions about kinship in West Africa" may have been retained and shared by enslaved Africans landing in the Americas. The two scholars noted also that "the aggregate of newly-arrived slaves, torn from their own local kinship networks, would have continued to view kinship as the normal idiom of social relations."[29] Such beliefs could have been passed on easily to the descendants of indigenous Africans held captive in South Carolina, for on many plantations generations of particular slave families lived and flourished.[30] This was especially true in the district of Georgetown because after the 1780s "very few slaves [were] brought in from outside" its borders and apparently fewer were exported to foreign parts than in other areas.[31] Numerous sources indicate that native-born Africans were often the transmitters of social norms and history both to their progeny and to members of the broader society.[32]

One such African evidently so inspired his daughter, for many years later her young mistress remembered,

> Often we children would . . . listen with rapt absorption to Maum Hetty's tales of the Guinea Negroes of whom her father was one before he was brought as a slave to Carolina. Sometimes she taught us scraps of native African songs, and when we were able to count to ten in African we concluded that our education was complete indeed.[33]

What the Maum Hettys of the South added to their lessons to blacks in private, however, was a different story. Collectively, they instilled in black children and young adults familiar obligations that reached far beyond the typical white American

169

nuclear family. These and other norms – particularly those dictating what were acceptable marital bonds – distinguished slaves from members of the planter class. In his massive study of the black family, Herbert Gutman found that slaves adhered to rigid rules of exogamy in their selection of mates, while the men and women of the slaveholding elite often married first cousins. Because he found similar patterns, mores, and norms among slaves on quite disparate plantations, Gutman concluded that those patterns were influenced neither by slaves' occupation nor by the type of planter on the estate. He therefore discarded the ever-popular "mimetic theories of Afro–American culture."[34] It is my belief that because of the strength of the black family, sale and the threat of sale acted as a major determinant of slave behavior. Sold slaves not only disseminated and unified slave culture, but graphically demonstrated the reality behind each threat of sale.

Sidney Mintz was correct in arguing that "within the structure of a slave society the slaves were required to engineer styles of life that might be preserved in the face of terrible outrage."[35] The black family did engineer such survival strategies. It was an extremely cohesive and resilient unit that demanded from its members numerous obligations and infinite devotion. Slave parents, for example, played certain economic roles, such as vegetable gardening and hunting, that were essential to the procurement of adequate food for their offspring. Moreover, although other relatives gave some assistance, fathers and mothers were responsible for the bulk of their children's socialization. So intense was loyalty to one's family that Union officers found it difficult initially to recruit blacks into the army because they feared to leave loved ones unprotected. Once freedmen did enlist, it was difficult sometimes to retain them because, as one observer noted, "A negro thinks to go and see his family the height of happiness."[36] Thus, the magnetism of African–American kinship ties sometimes irritated the self-proclaimed friends of the slave, just as it infuriated his adversaries almost perennially.

The family was, ironically, not only at the base of masters' most effective control mechanism, it was the source also of their most persistent aggravation, the runaway. Contemporary publications and correspondence are replete with cases of absconding blacks who were thought to have deserted in order to reunite with relatives.[37] Such knowledge must have simply added to the frustration of many masters, for it did not always help in retrieving their property. "A black fellow named Ned," for instance, was still evading capture almost a year later despite his master's careful listing in a runaway advertisement of "relations" that the 32-year-old plowman and wagoner had living "at Mrs Bird's, at the Rocks, at Dr Wilson's, on the State Road, and at Moorer's in St Mathews Parish."[38] Half a century earlier, John Davis recalled about his travels in South Carolina:

> The Charleston papers abound with advertisements for fugitive slaves. I have a curious advertisement now before me. – "Stop the runaway! Fifty dollars reward! Whereas my waiting fellow, Will having eloped from me last Saturday, *without any provocation*, (it being known that I am a *humane master*) . . . *Will may be known by the incisions of the whip on his back*; and I suspect has taken the road to *Coosohatchie*, where he has a wife and five children, whom I sold last week to Mr Gillespie."[39] [Emphases in the original.]

Analogous suspicions about why and where bondsmen ran were expressed throughout the antebellum period. In 1829 monetary compensation was offered for the apprehension of "George, Celia, and Sarah." Their owner declared that

> there is every reason to suppose the wenches are harboured on John's Island, from whence they came, and where they have connexions . . . and that the fellow George, who has runaway since has joined them, the whole being of one family.[40]

There was, of course, no single reason for slave desertions, but it is interesting that members of the immediate family often escaped together.[41]

Enslaved husbands, wives, daughters, and sons shipped great distances from each other rarely forgot those left behind and frequently pursued every method of ending the separation. In an effort to join family members in South Carolina a Samuel Tayler wrote the following letter to his former mistress:

> My Dear Mistress I have been in this City about three years and belong at present to Mr Sam'l Jerques, mer-

chant. I was sold for $1,900. He is remarkably kind and gives me a fair opportunity of making pocket money. But still my mind is always dwelling on home, relations, & friends which I would give the world to see. As times now are, I suppose I may be purchased for about 10 or $11 hundred dollars. If you my Dear Mistress, can buy me, how happy I would be to serve you and your heirs; I beg you will write me how *all* my relations are, and inform them that I have enjoyed uninterrupted health since I came here. Remember me also to Sarah, my ma ma, and Charlotte my old fellow servant & Amy Tayler.

I would be glad to belong to my young mistress, Mrs Parker in case you should not feel disposed to take me.[42]

Some slaves never gave up the hope of reuniting with loved ones many miles away. Pitiful efforts were still being made long after Emancipation. Black newspapers well into the 1870s and 1880s were filled with "Information Wanted" sections carrying appeals from mothers, fathers, sisters, brothers, and children who refused to abandon the glimmer of hope that they might yet find family members who had been torn from them in bondage.[43] Charles Gatson pleaded for "information of his children, Sam and Betsy Gatson" in 1870. He wrote:

They formerly belonged to Washington Fripp, of Newhaw, South Carolina; were carried to Charleston and there sold by a trader to go far South, it is supposed to Mississippi or Louisiana. They are now about twenty-two to twenty-five years old, and were taken away in 1861.[44]

The role slave mothers and, particularly, slave fathers played in the acquisition of food for their families made the threat of sale all the more intimidating. While most scholars do stress the adequacy of slaves' diet, few note or address the significance of why and how it became so sufficient.[45] . . . [A] plethora of evidence indicates that most slaves considered their food allotment insufficient and complained frequently about its quality and quantity – particularly the paucity of meat.[46] John Jackson, who was enslaved by Robert English in Sumter district, said he was fed "twice a day," but protested:

All we got to eat then was three corn cake dumplins and one plate of soup. No meat unless there happened to be a rotten piece in the smoke house. This would be given to us to make our soup. Why the dogs got better eating than we poor colored folks.[47]

Another former slave declared that the males on his plantation in Beaufort District "didn't have time to frolic 'cause they had to fin' food for the family; master never give 'nough to las' the whole week."[48] An awareness of these conditions enables one to understand why the struggle for food is such a consistent theme in African–American folklore. As Charles Joyner observed, blacks "like folk groups everywhere, remembered what they found memorable, used what they found usable, and forgot what they found forgettable."[49]

In order to make their daily fare adequate, American bondsmen demonstrated remarkable resourcefulness and industry. Slaves were the de facto owners of garden patches around their homes and/or on other parts of the plantation where a wide assortment of vegetables were grown. Planters sanctioned and encouraged this practice universally in South Carolina and even allowed men they did not own to keep and farm such land on their estates if their wives were there.[50] Others foraged for wild greens. And many raised poultry, or sometimes hogs, which they either saved for family consumption or sold in order to procure certain luxury food items. But the principal method of obtaining the much-coveted meat and fish in their diet was by hunting and fishing by which the men procured rabbits, raccoons, oysters, shad, trout, and clams. Both males and females appropriated foodstuffs from their masters, but they also acquired delicacies through "legal" pursuits, such as the manufacture and sale of baskets, bowls, ladles, and the like, and through paid labor during free time which enabled them to purchase many of the desired articles not furnished by slaveholders.[51] Charles Pinckney was not far from correct when he said of the enslaved worker: "When his owner is barbarian enough to withhold the necessary food, he has always intellect, and generally opportunity to supply the deficiency."[52]

It is clear that slave parents supplied a large percentage, if not the bulk, of their families' food. The fulfilment of this vital function explains why mothers and fathers were particularly apprehensive about threatened sale. They would have been

173

tempted inevitably to ask, "Will our children be provided for as well if either of us is sold?" In view of the dreaded day that they might be separated, parents began instructing children early in certain techniques and stratagems of survival. The first lessons taught to young bondsmen were strict obedience to elders and silence unless spoken to or addressed in some manner. Laura Towne did not think blacks were "harsh" to their offspring, but commented that, "They have a rough way of ordering them that sounds savage. When you speak to a child who does not answer, the others say, 'Talk, talk. Why you not talk?' – in the most ordersome tone to the silent one."[53] Growing accustomed to imperious commands was part and parcel of being a slave. Moreover, it was imperative that each child learn how to hold his or her tongue, for a careless slip could bring down the wrath of masters on all. This was probably the reason bondsmen did not "allow their children under certain ages to enter into conversations with them."[54] In the eyes of the enslaved, the home was the safest training ground for teaching these modes of combating white repression.

There is some evidence that slaves instructed their youngest progeny to view masters as evil and powerful adversaries with whom they should have as little contact as possible. In reference to his former owner, John Collins recalled,

> De slaves whisper his name in fear and terror to de chillun when they want to hush them up. They just say to a crying child: "Shet up or old Nick will ketch you!" Dat child sniffle but shet up pretty quick.[55]

Contemporary travelers observed frequently that slave children were afraid of whites and would run away at their approach.[56] A native South Carolinian, fearful about how outsiders might view this, suggested that

> Young servants should not be suffered to run off and hide when the master comes up, or any other white person; they should be taught to stand their ground and speak when spoken to, in a polite manner; have them well clothed and this thing is more easily accomplished. A lot of ragged little negroes always gives a bad impression to strangers, and is often the cause of their

174

running away and being hard to manage when grown. Talk to them; take notice of them; it soon gives them confidence and adds greatly to their value.[57]

As young laborers grew older, their parents entrusted them with the more difficult and dangerous lessons of prevarication and appropriation. Juvenile blacks were such good students that one of the major impetuses among planters for the religious proselytizing of young slaves was the hope that it would neutralize their "negative" home influences. The ruling class was not very successful, however, for the descendants of slaves continued to internalize antiservile characteristics. To inculcate various stratagems, mores, and values, African–American slaves relied heavily on a didactic, as well as an entertaining, folklore.[58] In this regard things do not appear to have changed greatly when Julia Peterkin early in the twentieth century became mistress of an Orangeburg District plantation once owned by Langdon Cheves. She observed:

The training of children is concerned chiefly with self-preservation in this world and preparation for the life to come. They are taught to provide for the needs of their bodies, to save their souls and to abide by the ancient customs, beliefs and rules of conduct handed down from generation to generation by word of mouth. In the hot summer evenings when they sit on cabin doorsteps with their parents, or in the winter time around fires that burn in the wide chimneys, time not whiled away with singing is often spent listening to the old folk tales which are rich in negro philosophy, and sparkle with negro ideas of wit and repartee. Many of these tales teach some simple moral lesson. The people who treasure these stories have no books, have never seen a play or moving picture, have never read a newspaper; but whether the stories are of men or of beasts, they invariably portray the same human traits and problems that make worth-while literature and plays and moving pictures.[59]

In much the same fashion, slave children learned not only how to "lib on de fat uv de land," but how to share with fellow blacks. They were instilled with principles of cooperation and assistance, illustrated most dramatically during the Civil War when, as a result of the benevolence of blacks, few orphans went uncared for. In addition, slaves generally were taught to treat elders with great reverence and to address them with honorific titles such as "Daddy" and "Maumer." Blacks of the same age group referred to each other as "Bro" (brother), "Titty" (sister), or "Co" (cousin), which caused northerners trying to discern actual blood ties no small confusion. These traditions and mores stemmed most likely from the efforts of African–Americans to assure the well-being of children who might be separated from *real* parents.[60] Gutman states that "fictive, or quasi, kin" bound

> *unrelated adults to one another* and thereby [infused] enlarged slave communities with conceptions of obligation that had flowed initially from kin obligations rooted in blood and marriage. The obligations to a brother or a niece were transformed into the obligations toward a fellow slave or a fellow slave's child, and behavior first determined by familiar and kin obligation became enlarged social obligation. Just as the fictive aunts and uncles may have bound children to quasi kin, so, too, the ties between a child and its fictive adult kin may have bound children's parents to their fictive aunts and uncles.[61] [Emphasis in the original.]

Such attitudes and beliefs undoubtedly helped more than anything else to preclude the divisive tendencies inherent in an excessive loyalty to *particular* families, especially when one's own might be sold.

Obviously, young slaves were learning more than simply what adults demanded of them: they also began to perceive what adults expected of each other. It would have been difficult to miss the great importance older blacks placed on inquiries about one's family as part of all greetings. Similarly, children gradually would have learned that those who best provided for their families, and who verbally thrashed and even physically assaulted a mysterious and amorphous group known simply as "buckra" or "whites," were for some as yet undetermined reason considered pillars of the community.[62] To be sure, much was unclear to the young, but these early messages no doubt had an impact.[63] So, too, must the names and titles slaves gave one another, for once entering interracial settings the pervasive "Sirs," "Madames," "Mrs," and "Mr's," whom black youth both knew and admired, were reduced – despite age and status – to "boy," "girl," or a generic "nigger."[64] The psychic damage done could not be erased, but in a multitude of ways prior to this awakening, young blacks had been subtly, explicitly, and continuously taught that, regardless of their status in the broader society, there would be dignity and respect among themselves. . . .

These unlettered but driven educators hoped that this spirit and the various techniques of survival they taught would one day congeal among the young into a base from which yet another generation could launch their people's seemingly endless struggle for freedom. In their thinking, the key prerequisite for that legacy was knowledge. As a result, they labored continually to learn as much about the world around and beyond them as possible. The postwar mania of freedmen for learning was no less real during slavery. Those responsible for the control of slaves were confronted too often with slaves who could read, decipher, and convey craftily their findings. Southern controllers watched closely any setting in which a dangerous "progress and diffusion of knowledge" might occur.[65]

In 1838 more than three hundred South Carolinians from the districts of Abbeville and Edgefield lashed out against the proposal of a missionary to preach to blacks. They argued:

> Some of the negroes will attend your meetings for religious improvement; others from idle curiosity; and a few of the more daring and intelligent, with restless spirits, to impart to each other every whisper that reaches them of the progress of Abolition, and the glowing prospect of their liberation. . . . When the last census was taken, the black population exceeded the white upwards of sixty-one thousand five hundred. We consider the common adage true, that "knowledge is power." . . . Intelligence and slavery have no affinity for each other.[66]

With the last view in mind, lawmakers repeatedly passed legislation prohibiting the written instruction of slaves. The recurrence of such laws and the uncovering recently of extensive correspondence by ex-slaves fighting in the Civil War make it clear that neither threats of maimings nor severe beatings prevented some slaves from becoming literate.[67] Most, of course, never did, but masters feared those who succeeded because they sometimes aided escapes and other illegal travels by forging passes and obtaining information belying planter myths about the impossibility of blacks surviving as free men and women. That slaves could escape, survive, and overcome a hostile white world were insights not a few black adults had acquired. Young blacks were both the beneficiaries of this knowledge and the ones who could make the most troublesome use of it. The enslaved thus taught their owners a bitter lesson: while they with relative ease could maintain a predominantly illiterate mass beneath them, it was far more difficult to keep an ignorant one.

Although slave elders succeeded in capturing some autonomous space and the minds of most among them, they did so under a complex system of controls that made each unservile move a serious risk. In such a setting, they could ill afford to shield their children indefinitely from the looming dangers. Consequently, children received many perplexing, contradictory, and paradoxical messages. Two family histories provide stark insights on the contradictions in slave responses to danger. George Cato, the great-great-grandson of Cato, leader of the Stono Rebellion of 1739, described the risks his ancestor had been willing to take:

> As it come down to me I thinks de first Cato take a darin' chance on losin' his life, not so much for his own benefit as it was to help others. . . . Long befo' dis uprisin, de Cato wrote passes for slaves and do all he can to send them to freedom. He die but he die for doin' de right, as he see it.[68]

But the descendants of Robert Nesbit, who had been acquitted of insurrection charges during the Denmark Vesey conspiracy of 1822, learned why their forebear failed to help Vesey, though he was his friend and fellow "property-owner." Israel Nesbit wrote:

> My great-granddaddy never take no part in de plannin, 'cause he tried all de time to show Vesey he was headin' to a fall and was playin' wid dynamite. . . . Granddaddy say dat de loyalty of de slave to his master was so deep

under de skin of de slave, dat it was even stronger than de long dream of freedom.[69]

Obviously, young slaves in the transition from childhood to adolescence had much to question and to resolve. How, for example, would they have reconciled tales of their people's courage and strength with the lacerated backs of so many among them? Some explanation, too, had to be forthcoming when loved ones were sold, slave rebels killed, or everyone in the quarters punished. Was it worth emulating slave and free black heroes if it meant death or shipment to worse circumstances? The discord and ambiguity such questions raised is reflected in the testimony of ex-slaves who were still children at the outbreak of the Civil War. Reuben Rosborough said, "My marster was a kind and tender man to slaves. You see a man love hosses and animals? Well, dat's de way he love us, though maybe in bigger portion." Still, he had to concede that his master "was good enough to buy my old gran' mammy Mary, though she never could do much work."[70] With similar reasoning, Ellen Renwick concluded her owner was "good": he "didn't whip . . . much."[71]

While distinguishing between "good" and "bad" masters implicitly seems to legitimize planter rule, most slaves never sanctioned the authority of slaveownership. They lived and usually died, however, in a war zone that made accurate comparative assessments of their oppressors vital. An owner who fed more, parted family members less, and left wider channels open for autonomy had to be preferred over one who often did the opposite. Differences were always on the minds of those in chains, yet despite variations in treatment, a slave was a slave. This was the crucial constant. Through their words and actions, the unfree consistently brought that point home. Rarely did they allow any kindness or humoring to blur the reality that the principal objective and motive of planters was the enrichment of their pockets and their power. Nor is it coincidental that ex-slaves so often referred to themselves as beasts of burden when they described their former owners' behavior. One former slave could not resist adding a pungent note to her recollections of slave food: "Us had all us need to eat. . . . Marse like to see his slaves fat and shiny, just like he want to see de carriage hosses slick and spanky when he ride out to preachin' at Ainswell."[72]

However ignorant planters might be of such sentiments in the slave community, they were keenly aware of slaves' devotion to their families and cognizant of how effectively that affinity could be exploited. Adele Petigru Allston settled on the following plan to control workers after three children of "a highly favoured servant"[73] had absconded toward the end of the Civil War.

I think Mary and James should be taken up and sent to some secure jail in the interior and held as hostages for the conduct of their children. And they should understand that this is done by the police of the country, who require that the older negroes should endeavour to influence the younger ones to order and subordination while this war lasts, and that they will be held responsible for the behavior of their children. For this course to have the best effect it ought to be universal, and ought to be required by the police of the country. I wish you to show this letter to Col. Francis Heriot and consult him as to what course he thinks best. If he thinks it best to make an example among the old people whose children have deserted, then let a cart or wagon be ready as soon as the search of the houses is over, and Mary and James sent off. Some place of confinement would be the best . . . letting them understand they would have to remain there until the end of the war, and desertion or rebellion in any of their children would be laid at their door. If this is done let them not have a day or an hour on the place after it is fixed on. Let them have no communication with any of their family except in presence of a white person, and put their children who have never learnt to work at once to learn. It does not seem to me reasonable or right to leave negroes in the enjoyment of privileges and ease and comfort, whose children go off in this way. I am persuaded it is done with their knowledge and connivance."[74]

Members of the plantocracy realized also the conservative effect of marriage and, for the most part, encouraged such unions.[75] Holland McTyeire, a Baptist minister who supported this policy, observed that

> Local as well as family associations . . . are strong yet pleasing cords binding him to his master. His welfare is so involved in the order of things that he would not for any consideration have it disturbed. He is made happier and safe; put beyond discontent, or temptations to rebellion and abduction; for he gains nothing in comparison with what he loses. His comforts cannot be removed with him and he will stay with them.[76]

The gravitational pull of the connubial relations of slaves was revealed most vividly to Captain and Mrs Basil Hall while traveling through South Carolina in 1828. They witnessed a slave coffle of about twenty-five individuals, two of whom were "bolted together." When one of the men was asked the reason for the chains, he replied quite happily, "Oh sir, they are the best things in the world to travel with." His companion said nothing. Upon further inquiries, Captain Hall learned that the silent bondsman had a wife on a neighboring plantation whose owner refused to sell her and, thereby, caused their separation. To prevent desertion, "the wretched husband was . . . shackled to a young unmarried man, who, having no such tie to draw him back, might be more safely trusted on the journey."[77] If the single male were to wed, he would undoubtedly remember the distraught partner en route to his new home and very likely behave without misconduct so as to avoid following in those shackled footsteps. . . .

Although the black family was the source of the planters' most effective control mechanism, it was also, for slaves, the greatest mitigation of the harshness and severity of bondage. John Jackson spoke angrily of the many sadistic and humiliating beatings he received as a slave, but stressed the following turning point during "those horrible times": "I growed up and married when I was very young, and I loved my little girl wife. Life was not a burden then. I never minded the whippings I got. I was happy."[78] The kinship networks created by African–Americans helped shield bondsmen from the dehumanization inevitable in any slave society. Slaves could depend on familiar relations – both real and fictive – when in need, and however futile it may have been, protection sometimes from white oppressors.[79] Yet the family served as a pacifying institution as well. Gutman suggests that slave women bore children in part because they were aware that evidence of their fertility might persuade masters not to exchange them for more "profitable" servants.[80] Because a slave, once informed of the owner's decision to sell, could do little to alter the decision other than to appeal to the owner or practice self-mutilation,[81] many slaves sought to prevent separation from loved ones by abiding by the rules of the plantation. Not a few slaves regarded obedience as a fair price to pay for keeping their families intact.

Some slave elders, without any direct external pressure, taught their progeny lessons that can be classified as "internal controls," in the sense that they kept community members "out of trouble" and "peaceful."[82] Aaron Ford, a former slave, recalled these guidelines and instructions he received from his grandfather throughout his sixteen years of servitude:

> I remember my grandfather all right. He de one told me how to catch otters. Told me how to set traps. I heard my grandfather tell bout whippin slaves for stealin. Grandfather told me not to take things dat were not mine. If a pile of corn was left at night, I was told not to bother it. In breakin corn, sometimes people would make a pile of corn in de grass en leave it en den come back en get it in de night. Grandfather told me not to never bother nothing bout people's things.[83]

One slaveholder, David Golightly Harris, received help from his slaves when he "had difficulty with Matt," one of his slaves.

> I tied him [Matt] up and gave him a gentle admonition in the shape of a good whipping. I intended to put him in jail and keep him there until I sold him but he seemed so penitent & promised so fairly & *the other negroes promising to see that he would behave himself in future* that I concluded that I would try him once more.[84] [Emphasis added.]

For exactly two months, Matt's neighbors, some of whom were certainly his relatives, were able apparently to constrain him, but, finally, he was converted into cash. Harris noted that Matt himself "was willing to be sold."[85]

Perhaps the most telling statement on the role of the family came in 1863 from Jim, a slave captured by Union forces with his master on Bailey's Island in South Carolina. Laura Towne described Jim as "sad" and recorded his declaration that "he would not give up the wife and children now on the Main for all the freedom in the world."[86] Familiar bonds militated against and sometimes prevented revolutionary fervor. The difference in the number of men and women who ran away reflects this phenomenon indirectly. According to one scholar, at least 80 per cent of all runaways were males between the ages of 16 and 35. He posited that mothers were more unwilling to defect because of their stronger attachment to children, whereas many young men had yet to assume the responsibilities of marriage and fatherhood and therefore felt less obligated to stay.[87] Although some bondsmen fled to the North, the majority simply remained "out" near their homes and often for remarkably long periods of time through the assistance of their families and friends.[88] While this was a constant annoyance to planters, it did not hurt their pockets as much as the loss of captive laborers who obtained permanent freedom above the Mason–Dixon line. Again, African–Americans' family ties guaranteed and protected the property interests of the ruling class.

It is not difficult to imagine the influence masters had over slaves with mates and kin on other plantations: they had the power to withhold the passes that bondsmen were required to carry when absent from the estates of their owners. Although most blacks probably did not wait for such "permission," they still would have needed, on occasion, the sanction of planters, and good behavior was undoubtedly a major criterion.[89] Mrs Benjamin Perry, for example, promised the visiting mother of Delia, a 15-year-old servant, that Delia could visit her at Christmas "if" she was "a good girl."[90] Members of the plantocracy did help slaves sometimes to see relatives and to keep their families together,[91] and it is highly unlikely that such aid was unappreciated or forgotten by blacks. In the eyes of the enslaved, kinship ties were of paramount importance and worthy of infinite sacrifice. In this lay the force of masters' threats to sell. Not surprisingly, those slaveholders who made it a habit of "transporting" unruly and incorrigible blacks were known to have "well-ordered people" who gave "little trouble."[92] The threat of sale was the most effective long-term mechanism of control.

NOTES

The Editor gratefully acknowledges permission to reprint material from chap. 2, "The threat of sale: the black family as a mechanism of control," of *Born a Child of Freedom, Yet a Slave: Mechanisms of Control and Strategies of Resistance in Antebellum South Carolina*, by Norrece T. Jones, Jr., Wesleyan University Press. Copyright © 1990 by Norrece T, Jones, Jr. By permission of University Press of New England.

1 Foby (1853) "Management of servants," *Southern Cultivator* XI (August): 226.

2 George P. Rawick (ed.) (1977) *The American Slave: A Composite Autobiography*, Supplement Ser. I (Westport, Conn.), 11, 283.

3 Bobby Frank Jones, "A cultural middle passage: slave marriage and family in the ante-bellum South" (Ph.D. diss., University of North Carolina, 1965): 6–7. . . .

4 Charles Ball (1837) *Fifty Years in Chains*, introduction by Phillip Foner (reprinted New York, 1970).

5 Helen T. Cattarall (ed.) (1929) *Judicial Cases Concerning American Slavery and the Negro* (Washington, D.C.), II, 352.

6 Ibid., 477.

7 Robert Pringle to Edward and John Mayne & Co., in Walter B. Edgar (ed.) (1972) *The Letterbook of Robert Pringle* (Columbia, S.C.).

8 Plantation Book of Charles Cotesworth Pinckney and Successors, 1812–1861, "Slave list," 1–11, Pinckney Family Papers, Library of Congress. . . .

9 Charles C. Jones (1842) *The Religious Instruction of the Negroes* (reprinted New York, 1969), 133. . . .

10 H. Shelton Smith (1972) *In His Image, But . . . Racism in Southern Religion, 1780–1910* (Durham, N.C.), 43–7, 53–5, 59–60, 69, 138.

11 John B. Adger (1849) *The Christian Doctrine of Human Rights and Slavery* (Columbia, S.C.), quoted in ibid., 138.

12 Rawick, *American Slave*, II, ii. 234–5.

13 Una Pope-Hennessey, *The Aristocratic Journey: Being the Outspoken Letters of Mrs Basil Hall Written During a Fourteen Months' Sojourn in America, 1827–1828* (reprinted New York, 1931), 210. . . .

14 Charles Nordhoff (1863) "The freedmen of South-Carolina," in Frank Moore (ed.) *Papers of the Day* (New York), 11.

15 Rupert Sargent Holland (ed.) (1912) *Letters and Diary of Laura M. Towne* . . . (Cambridge, Mass.), 74–5.

16 Joel Williamson (1965) *After Slavery: The Negro in South Carolina During Reconstruction, 1861–1877* (Chapel Hill, N.C.), 39–44. . . .

17 Elsie Clews Parsons (1923) *Folklore of the Sea Islands, South Carolina* (Cambridge, Mass.), 213–16. . . .
18 Quoted in Leon Stone Bryan, Jr., "Slavery on a Peedee River rice plantation, 1825–1865" (M.A. thesis, Johns Hopkins University, 1963), 186.
19 George Rogers, Jr. (1970) *The History of Georgetown County, South Carolina* (Columbia, S.C.), 328. . . .
20 Thomas Wentworth Higginson (1869) *Army Life in a Black Regiment* (reprinted Boston, 1962), 52–3.
21 "Petition of certain citizens of Charleston . . . ," 1847 (Folder 64), Slavery Files, SCA.
22 "Memoirs of S. W. Ferguson," 3, Heyward and Ferguson Family Papers, Southern Historical Collection, University of North Carolina (SHC). . . .
23 J. H. Easterby (ed.) (1945) *The South Carolina Rice Plantation as Revealed in the Papers of Robert F. W. Allston* (Chicago), 184.
24 Peter Wood (1974) *Black Majority: Negroes in Colonial South Carolina From 1670 Through the Stono Rebellion* (New York), 280.
25 Ibid., 25–6, 140, 159–60.
26 Rawick, *American Slave*, sup., II, 132–3. . . .
27 Charles Izard Manigault to Mr Haynes, 1 March 1847, Manigault Letter Book, Charles Manigault Papers, South Caroliniana Library, University of South Carolina (SCL).
28 Rawick, *American Slave*, II, i, 159.
29 Sidney Mintz and Richard Price (1976) *An Anthropological Approach to the Afro–American Past: A Caribbean Perspective* (Philadelphia), 34.
30 Arney Robinson Childs (ed.) (1947) *The Private Journal of Henry William Ravenel, 1859–1887* (Columbia, S.C.), 240. . . .
31 Rogers, *History of Georgetown County*, 328, 343. . . .
32 Rawick, *American Slave*, III, iii, 14. . . .
33 Anne Sinkler Fishburne (1949) *Belvidere: A Plantation Memory* (Columbia, S.C.), 25.
34 Herbert G. Gutman (1976) *The Black Family in Slavery and Freedom, 1750–1925* (New York), 36–220, passim.
35 Sidney Mintz (1974) *Caribbean Transformations* (Chicago), 77.
36 Elizabeth Ware Pearson (ed.) (1906) *Letters From Port Royal, 1862–1868* (reprinted New York, 1969), 97.
37 "150 Reward," Charleston *Mercury*, 6 January 1829. . . .
38 Charleston *Courier*, 17 February 1849.
39 John Davis (1803) *Travels of Four Years and a Half in the United States of America: During 1798, 1799, 1800, 1801, and 1802* (London), 92–3.
40 "John's island," Charleston *Mercury*, 1 July 1829.
41 Frances Lance, "Ranaway on the 29th," *The Southern Patriot*, 18 April 1829. . . .
42 Samuel Tayler to Mrs Elizabeth Blythe, 2 September 1838, R. F. W. Allston Papers, South Carolina Historical Society.
43 "Information wanted," *South Carolina Leader*, 12 May 1866.
44 "Information wanted," *New Era*, 28 July 1870. . . .
45 Ulrich B. Phillips (1919) *American Negro Slavery: A Survey of the*

Supply, Employment and Control of Negro Labor as Determined by the Plantation Regime (reprinted Baton Rouge, La., 1966), 265–8. . . .

46 Ball, *Fifty Years in Chains*, 54, 207, 262–3, 323. . . .

47 John Blassingame (ed.) (1977) *Slave Testimony: Two Centuries of Letters, Speeches, Interviews and Autobiographies* (Baton Rouge, La.), 511–12.

48 Rawick, *American Slave*, II, i, 125.

49 Charles W. Joyner, "Slave folklife of the Waccamaw Neck: antebellum black culture in the South Carolina lowcountry," (Ph.D. diss., University of Pennsylvania, 1977), 158–9, 162–4, 321.

50 Ball, *Fifty Years in Chains*, 194. . . .

51 Charles Joyner (1984) *Down By the Riverside: A South Carolina Slave Community* (Urbana, Ill.), 99. . . .

52 Charles Cotesworth Pinckney (1829) *An Address Delivered . . . The 18th August, 1829*, (Charleston, S.C.), 4.

53 Holland, *Letters of Laura M. Towne*, 25.

54 Jacob Stroyer (1885) *My Life in the South* (Salem, Mass.), 23–4. . . .

55 Rawick, *American Slave*, II, i, 224–5.

56 Ibid., III, iii, 261–2. . . .

57 W. W. Gilmer (1852) "Management of servants," *FP*, III (July): 110.

58 "Report on management of slaves, duty of overseers, and employers to Darlington County Agricultural Society," August 1852, Thomas Cassels Law papers, SCL. . . .

59 Julia Peterkin (1933) *Roll, Jordan, Roll. Photographic Studies by Doris Ulmann* (New York), 231. . . .

60 Rawick, *American Slave*, II, i, 220. . . .

61 Gutman, *Black Family*, 220.

62 Joyner, "Slave folklife," 169. . . .

63 See Thomas Webber (1978) *Deep Like the Rivers: Education in the Slave Quarter Community, 1831–1865* (New York), 261.

64 Alice R. Huger Smith (1936) *A Carolina Rice Plantation of the Fifties . . . With Chapters From the Unpublished Memoirs of D. E. Huger Smith* (New York), 71. . . .

65 Stroyer, *My Life in the South*, 33–4. . . .

66 "Remonstrance," Greenville, *Mountaineer*, 2 November 1838. . . .

67 *The Suppressed Book About Slavery!* (New York, 1864), 245. . . .

68 Rawick, *American Slave*, sup., II, 98, 100.

69 Ibid., 261–2.

70 Ibid., III, iv, 45.

71 Ibid., 9.

72 Ibid., II, i, 235.

73 Easterby, *South Carolina Rice Plantation*, 199–200.

74 Ibid., 292.

75 Jones, "A cultural middle passage," 76–8.

76 Quoted in Gutman, *Black Family*, 79–80.

77 Basil Hall (1829) *Travels in North America, in the Years 1827 and 1828* (Edinburgh), III, 128–9.

78 Blassingame, *Slave Testimony*, 512.

79 Catterall, *Judicial Cases*, 315. . . .
80 Gutman, *Black Family*, 75–6.
81 Ibid., II, 387. . . .
82 Jones, "Cultural middle passage," 211–18. . . .
83 Rawick, *American Slave*, II, ii, 75–6.
84 Harris Farm Journals, 6 January 1858, SHC.
85 Ibid., 6 March 1858.
86 Holland, *Letters and Diary of Laura M. Towne*, 109–10.
87 Eugene Genovese (1974) *Roll, Jordan, Roll: The World The Slaves Made* (New York), 648–9.
88 Peter Lewis, "50 dollars reward," Georgetown *Gazette*, 19 November 1800. . . .
89 Jones, "Cultural middle passage," 52. . . .
90 E. Perry to B. F. Perry, 29 November 1843, Benjamin Perry Papers, SCL.
91 William Jones to Langdon Cheves, 18 June 1830, Cheves Family Papers, South Carolina Historical Society. . . .
92 *Proceedings of the Meeting in Charleston, S. C., May 13–15, 1845, on the Religious Instruction of the Negroes* . . . (Charleston, S.C., 1845), 53–5. . . .

Part III

WOMEN AND MEN

7

LOVE AND BIOGRAPHY
Three courtships
Steven M. Stowe

Steven M. Stowe's Intimacy and Power in the Old South: Ritual in the Lives of the Planters, *(Baltimore) is a study "of the interior lives of certain planter families." Based primarily on diaries and letters, this book focuses on family life and social rituals – duels, courtship, and "coming of age". Stowe's goal was to understand the perceptions that planters had of themselves and their culture and thereby discover how the "intimate understandings" of planters "reappeared in the public rituals that proclaimed their social power" (ix–x).*

In the excerpt reprinted here, from his Chapter 2, Stowe examines courtship – first placing his work in the context of other historians' studies, then focusing closely on three courtships. His purpose is to illustrate in the particular southern world certain themes of courtship – the ideals of love and the rituals through which love was expressed and intimacy created between young men and women in planter families. As he puts it below, this examination of courtships is in effect a study of the way young men and women came to understand their separate "spheres" in life. As was pointed out in the introduction to Elizabeth Fox-Genovese's essay above, in the North at this time middle-class Americans were developing the idea that men and women properly belonged to different spheres, each with its own special roles and obligations – the male as breadwinner, the female as the center of domestic life. At the same time, the idea of separate spheres assumed that marriages should be based primarily on mutual love between partners who had freely chosen one another, rather than on economic motives or because of parental choices. Here, Stowe is examining the southern versions of these ideas about the proper roles of men and women and the proper relationships between husbands and wives. While his book is not explicitly a North–South comparison, he does write that planter families can be distinguished from northern upper-

class families in two ways: the former understood "family and gender duties" as well as intimacy in ways that "more sharply divided, even alienated, female from male;" and they celebrated more clearly a "hierarchal scheme of value and belief in family life" (Intimacy and Power, *xvii–xviii). Such an argument is compatible with Genovese's argument for a distinct southern world-view based on plantation slavery. Stowe, however, asserts that his evidence does not "argue for a separate southern culture," although it does "support a thesis of significant southern emphasis in certain key aspects of upper-class American life" (ibid., xvii).*

Changes in the significance of emotion in courtship and marriage are a key to courtship's pivotal role in the making of new families. By the early nineteenth century, some recent histories have shown, the desires of courting couples began to take precedence over parental judgment. As marriage was increasingly seen as a field for personal happiness, the argument goes, courtship became a mirror for youth's sexual expression and ideals. Romantic love appeared in place of the ribaldry and blunt, material calculation of the eighteenth century, casting both into relative disuse. Simultaneously, the means for distributing property between the generations in the planter class became more regular (partible inheritance among sons, and for daughters a trend toward giving slaves as dowry). Courtship itself thus had less to do with opportunities for windfall gains in wealth. In this view, nineteenth-century courtship ritual became more "modern" and more superfluous at the same time. That is, as the transference of property became differently rationalized, and as the provenance of marriage became more tied to youthful sentiment, courtship became decorative and relatively removed from the seat of elite power.[1]

The tack taken in this [essay] is quite different, though it generally confirms the change in parental decisionmaking, the more orderly means for transferring property, and the rise of personal happiness as a reason for marriage. But courtship did not therefore become less significant. In fact, the shift in courtship's social importance is not best described in quantitative terms at all, but in terms of the kind of social expectations it embodied. In the early nineteenth century, the ritual of courtship in the planter class became flooded with a vocabulary of personal wish, romantic choice, profound contrast between the sexes, emotional crisis, and transcendent pleasure which reveals what women and men hoped to experience in relation to each other. Far from becoming superficial to class and society, and scarcely peculiar only to youth, the change in the ritual reveals a profound shift in the culture of family and sexuality. This [essay] explores this changed context and clarifies how courtship impressed men and women not only with the power of personal affinities but also with love's reach into the social order.[2]. . .

Each couple had to sort out the [courtship] ritual's feelings and consequences in their own lives, and it is the personal texture of obligation and desire fashioned from courtship that deepens our understanding of the unique importance accorded to gender in the planter class. This [essay] concludes, therefore, with three courtships shaped by the questions of identity and intimacy raised by the ritual. In the first, a young man claims his sphere; in the second a young woman encounters hers; and in the last, a South Carolina couple move beyond theirs.

On its surface, the Georgia courtship of Henry Harford Cumming in 1823–4 appears uncomplicated and quite successful. It resulted in a marriage that lasted for forty years, producing eight living children and a helpmeet relationship. But a closer look at Cumming's courtship letters reveals him discovering some unexpected things. Working to win his lady, Cumming found himself learning about being a man. Intending to write courtship letters for his sweetheart, he found himself writing about himself. Neither outcome was necessary to the success of his suit, perhaps, but both taught him indelible lessons about the strategies of the heart. In his letters to Julia A. Bryan, Henry Cumming displayed his accomplishments in fine style. He made puns and presented elegant compliments in the best oblique, powerful manner. He addressed her in the third person, and made certain to ornament feeling with general observation and literary allusion. He bent his every effort to "occupy an important place in her esteem." And although Julia responded (sometimes, however, permitting a line or two to do the work of a letter), Henry began to feel thwarted. Julia avoided setting a wedding date even after they had declared their love for each other and secured family approval. She was nineteen years old, he twenty-four; what reason was there to hurry? Marrying too hastily, she said, would be "consenting to make [my] self miserable." She even referred to the wedding day as the "day that is to bring evil" upon her. Henry was first puzzled, then annoyed; it seemed, he told her, "that while you are increasing my happiness, you seem to yourself . . . to be in danger of diminishing your own."[3] He kept up the pressure of his campaign, determined to create love out of opposition. His letters to Julia began to repeat conversations they had had, going back over ground that he refused to concede. As a wedding day, he recalled suggesting " 'some day in the last week of January [and] to this you replied 'No.' 'The first week in February?' 'No.' 'The Second.' 'I don't know.' 'The fifteenth of February?' 'No.' 'The sixteenth?' 'No.' 'The seventeenth?' 'Oh, I don't know.' 'Shall it take place between the 15th and the 18th?' To this you replied 'Yes' – 'Well' – 'If you please.' "[4]

Along with attempts to lock Julia into her own words, Henry continued to persuade her by writing eagerly of the love they would share. Although his letters were within proper bounds, Henry encountered resistance here as well. As the months passed, he perceived Julia shrinking from an intimacy that was not only a "necessary" part of his happiness but of hers as well. She, however, continued to remind him of her worry over "some things that must necessarily occur in the untried situation" of marriage. At times Henry tried to make light of sexual fears by joking, for example, that

> we might occupy adjoining houses arranged so that we might just see each other all the livelong day and then sigh away the night. . . . For tho' young Leander did nightly cross the raging Hellespont to reach his dear Hero . . .'twas surely only that he might see her.

At other times, however, Henry was greatly distressed over what he felt was her lack of interest in his feeling and all that it implied. She was altogether wrapped up in her own world with its own images, he complained, scorning "such a *milk and honey* thing as a *love-letter*" though continuing to accept his. "I will not, for a moment, allow myself to believe that it will not give you pleasure to [write]," he told her. To believe otherwise would leave him "on a sea of anxieties and doubts."[5]

Neither Julia nor Henry considered these exchanges as a prelude to ending their courtship. Letters continued to be exchanged, occasional meetings brought them together, and friends and family went on supporting the match. But the struggle between them, however much a part of their love affair, began to influence the way Henry wrote to her and perceived himself. The more he fell into love and the more he encountered the strangeness of her likes and aversions, the more Henry felt himself drifting apart from his accustomed life. She made him feel, he told her, "the necessity of appearing in a borrowed character." He was sure neither what this character represented nor, indeed, what it had to do with the man he thought himself to be. His "extravagant protestations of affection" to her began to frighten himself as well, and he resolved to control his "unmanly bursts of feeling." He believed that this behavior is what she wished and promised. "I will not again play the Baby as it seems I did." He placed the whole affair into her care, asking her to give him the "means for making me more like the ideal personage you prefer. . . . I am still young and flexible." But at the same time, Henry wrote of his manliness in a surer way, telling her that perhaps she already had an ideal lover: "a venerable but still vivacious old gentleman" who would be sexually unthreatening and content "to permit you to rule." Gradually Henry's letters shifted to a discourse on manhood, especially his own. Did she think him too sensitive? Well, perhaps he was. On the other hand, "Perhaps you are afraid of *touching* a *heart* already too tender. If this be the case you mistake me much – I have far more of the 'sterner stuff' in my nature than you are inclined to think." Pursuing an ideal Julia, Henry ran up against the real one and encountered, to his surprise, vexed questions about his own nature. What ought a man to want, and what sort of heart ought he to have?[6]

In the fashion of most courtships, clear answers were not forthcoming. Nevertheless, Julia Bryan and Henry Cumming were married on 24 February, 1824, at Rotherwood plantation near Mount Zion, Georgia. What did Henry Cumming believe his new wife had shown him? What did his courtship finally contribute to what he once called the "love-policy" behind his desires? It had to do with power and its uses in love – the mythic power of romance and the quite worldly powers of the sexes. In looking at the quality of his manliness Henry Cumming claimed a married man's sphere. It was a territory of compromise but also of sure identity. He wished to please Julia and "I submit myself to your guidance," he wrote her; but only "so far as a man can submit." Their contest had not drained away affection and sexuality (he still warmed to "a 'sidelong glance' from an eye like Yours"), but Henry came to perceive that their love was in fact founded in a "singular union of opposing feelings" which mystified him as it drew him on. Though sometimes he regretted the conflict of their temperaments, when one or the other of them had to play the "base strings of Humility," he also confessed to a "thrilling sense of delight" in those differences. He was describing the male sphere from within, defining it by its collision with the female. As he adjusted his own needs to fit the new "untried situation," Henry created a new self-image as well. Opposites and oppositions of all kinds which clarified his manhood would not have happened without her. "It must be admitted," he told Julia, "that you have managed me admirably well." He became dependent on her "mingling the moral sweets and acids" in their relation "as to produce by their union a very 'delectable' kind of beverage." Henry Cumming drank deeply, and friends agreed on his wedding day that the young man, soon to become a successful lawyer, planter, and politician in Augusta, had chosen wisely and courted well.[7]

The courtship of Penelope Skinner shows how personal meanings agitated by the ritual lay beneath the calm, social surface of a companionate marriage. When Penelope wrote her older brother Tristrim in the early spring of 1840 to tell him that she was to be married and that her fiancé "is devotedly attached to me and I to him so we can get along," she seems to have been about to embark on a mature, sensible union.[8] Yet a closer look at her courtship suggests much more about the emotional underpinnings of such marriages at a particular point in a woman's life. Penelope's romantic alternatives were channeled by both Tristrim and their father Joseph Blount Skinner, and her situation as a recently "finished," 19-year-old woman isolated in her father's house contributed to the meaning marriage came to have for her. In courtship Penelope

196

like many women first gazed upon the limits of feminine influence.

Joseph Skinner had established himself as an important planter near Edenton, North Carolina, before the birth of his only son Tristrim Lowther in 1820. Skinner emerges from his letters as a blunt, outspoken paterfamilias of the old style, and in the older fashion he sent Tristrim to school in Philadelphia at age 14. Penelope was not sent North to be "finished" but was enrolled in a much-admired female seminary in Hillsboro, North Carolina. She returned from her schooling to the plantation where she became mistress of her father's house. Indeed, it was a household, not a family that she had a sense of mastering; her father was often absent on planting business, as was Tristrim. In some ways, Penelope was satisfied to return home, relieved that she no longer had to write her brother in academic French or stare at the Hillsboro countryside. In other ways, however, she longed for her seminary friends. She missed the female intimacy punctuated by the excitement of shared activities and hopes. Romance and love were frequent topics in her letters to Tristrim. Even before leaving Hillsboro, she wrote to him about marriage and about the courtships of her friends. She was straightforward and not shy. She was looking for a lover, and she felt she could choose. "I cannot see anyone to suit my fancy and beaux are not *very* scarce with me," she wrote Tristrim. "Do not tell if I tell you something. I refused three or four a week before last. So you see your little sister is not forgotten in the crowd." Success for Penelope was success in love, obvious social success "in the crowd," and her last weeks in the academy were keyed to a high pitch of romantic anticipation. She and her friends were preparing to leave the world of school, and marriage and men were thick in the air. "A lady told me the other day she expected I had had more offers than any other Lady in the state," Penelope told Tristrim. "I said nothing but thought it very probable."[9]

Once home in Edenton, however, Penelope could write of little else than pacing around the empty house and of happy times recalled and wished for. She made sly, sometimes cutting remarks about her father who had become a surprisingly watchful gatekeeper despite his frequent absences. The young woman was wistful in her letters to her brother, and maternal.

She advised him on his social contacts, told him to study diligently, and remember her to his male friends "when you go to see the girls." When a former beau turned up in Williamsburg, Penelope urged Tristrim to meet him: "I know you would like him he is such a favorite of mine. Notice if you see him if he has my ring on. I fear he has forgotten me by this time."[10] By the autumn of 1838, now nine months home, Penelope spent entire days in melancholy dreaming, broken only, it seemed, by letters from women friends engaged to be married. Her discontent peaked in the winter of 1838 when, alone in the house for hours, she wrote Tristrim:

> I really feel so wretched that I know not what to do. Father is so strict and particular that the young men will I fear soon begin not to come here at all. I do my best to make them spend their time pleasantly but he is as cross and crabbing [sic] as it is possible for any one to be and insists on my being so – but no, the crosser he is the more agreeable I shall be. He even says that they ought to entertain me and that I must sit still and listen to them but it has ever been customary in my day for persons to entertain their visitors and I shall do it to the best of my abilities in spite of all he can say or do – for at times he is unreasonable and that every one knows. But I suppose I must not complain – the next eligible offer I have I am gone, for anything would be better than this dull gloomy place.[11]

Quite unlike her father, and stifled by him, Penelope believed that courtship was a matter for her own abilities and feelings. Courtship "in my day" should offer more than an opportunity to sit by passively and hope for the best. Penelope's struggle to control her own affairs was joined in the winter of 1838 when she allowed James French to ask her father for permission to court her. She probably saw the contest ahead; in any event, she knew enough to try to enlist Tristrim's support. She wrote him in confidence that "I am partially engaged to James French – papa seems quite pleased with the match – he is a fine fellow [and] you would like him." She cautiously added, "If we are married at all I think it will be in February, provided Pa is willing." And, ever the excited purveyor of family romance, she asked her brother to "find out from

Cousin Barbara how she would like to have me marry Mr. F." The engagement was "partial," of course, because Joseph Skinner's approval had not been obtained, and had Penelope known of her father's letter to Tristrim four days earlier she would not have been so sanguine. Writing "in strictest confidence," the elder Skinner observed that French ("whom you saw at the Springs") had "paid a visit to your sister, and had mentioned to me his intention to propose himself to her." Joseph wished to keep a short rein on the affair, and asked his son to make inquiries into French's reputation. His instructions were model lessons in male duty, combining paternal watchfulness with a delicacy always present when one man probed the character of another. "[Y]ou can inquire . . . by merely observing that you have *heard* he had been at my house and there would be no impropriety in asking about him," Skinner wrote his son.

> Maybe some of your young acquaintances in college may have heard or know something about him. . . . [N]obody shall know what you write to me, not even your sister. I must make up my mind, and you must be *free*, frank, and *full* in all you know or can hear.[12]

Penelope challenged her father for Tristrim's support in the ensuing investigation of James French's character. The men spared no effort to obtain estimates of French's morals and prospects. A few face-to-face meetings between the suitor and the father evidently produced more tension than clear air, however, and by late January 1839, Penelope no longer supposed her father pleased by French. "Poor man," she wrote of her suitor, "if he ever gets me he will be worthy of me for he has suffered enough for my sake." Sometimes Penelope seemed on the verge of resigning herself to her father's control, as when she told Tristrim to "not let my wishes prevent you from saying all you know [to father], I know there is nothing but disappointment in this world." Forced to await the outcome of the men's negotiations, she nevertheless tried to ease some of the pressure on Tristrim and assured him, "You are a good fellow Brother." But Penelope also fought for French, faulting her father for caring too much for "what the world has to say about me or my affairs. I cannot please the world, nor do I care to do so." Her courtship, she insisted, should be ruled not by opinion but by her personal happiness. She told her father as much, and took every chance she could to counter his opinions. When Joseph wrote Tristrim that French seemed "too much pleased with himself, to please others," for example, adding that the suitor "has given a very flattering account of himself," Penelope caught her father's letter before it was posted and wrote in the margin: "[French] has also told his faults – which he has of course as well as others."[13]

But despite Penelope's efforts, and despite French's own marshaling of friends and references, Joseph Skinner stayed against the courtship. It is not clear why. Nothing that Tristrim discovered yielded any sure reason to reject the man. In fact, several friends touted French's "integrity and honor," and even Tristrim ventured once that Penelope "loves him very much." It seems that Joseph, and ultimately Tristrim as well, were put off by what they took to be French's vanity and his "not . . . having more than his share" of intellect. In any case, when Penelope wrote her brother dejectedly in March, "Well, I have discarded Mr French," both Tristrim and their father approved. "Pa is delighted at the news," she confirmed bitterly. For his part, Tristrim wrote Joseph that he was "very glad to hear" of Penelope's rejection and that "all her friends here expressed their satisfaction as soon as they heard it." Penelope herself had to act to end the suit, but it is clear that she was hustled toward her decision by family and friends.[14]

From here on, Penelope's courtship story was shaped by her disappointment in the French affair, her nearly frantic efforts to be rid of her father's house, and her increasingly critical observations about men in general. Together these mapped the remainder of Penelope's life as a single woman. Even as she mourned the loss of French she cast about for someone else, and her conflation of romantic love and a desire for freedom from her father remained at the center of courtship's meaning for her. Even though Tristrim had come out against her wishes in the French affair, Penelope continued to enlist her brother's help. "Who is Judge Christian attentive to at present[?]" she asked him. "Do you think I stand any chance?" At this point, the spring of 1839, Thomas Warren, a medical doctor in Edenton, entered the picture. Warren was one of the men to whom James French had appealed as a character reference. Now Warren made his own case, cautiously at first, by spending more and more time in Joseph Skinner's house. In the midst of lamenting her isolation, Penelope observed in April that "Dr Warren is almost my only constant visitor. He enables me to spend many an hour agreeably which would otherwise hang very heavily upon my mind." The hours spent with Warren helped her to keep her promise to her father not to see French, though the latter attempted to call on her. "He could not believe it possible," Penelope remarked after one of French's letters, "that I should turn him off." Her resolve was as strong as her discontent, however, the struggle giving her a new strength of will. "Mr French has been here again," she wrote Tristrim. "But I sent him sailing and hope never to see him again."[15]

Throughout the summer and fall of 1839 Penelope continued to receive Warren but at some point also became interested in a Mr S., a man met at a resort and popular with her friends, who soon dominated her reveries. There were new difficulties, however. Penelope was kept waiting on more than one occasion for his letters. Joseph Skinner was skeptical of Mr S., and Penelope once again faced a courtship transformed into a test of wills and a possible break with her father. Disappointment layered disappointment, and by January 1840 Penelope was writing in a different tone of her love life: "I think it is time for me to take it in hand." When she once again did not receive an expected letter from Mr S., she reacted with wounded pride ("To think that I should have been disappointed") and a growing skepticism of men in general. Men probably were untrustworthy and love quite likely a chimera; yet perhaps marriage would put both in their place. Ending her uncertainty as an unmarried daughter became her first goal. "I declare I am pretty miserable and have a strong notion of marrying Dr T. W.," she told her brother. "What do you think of it[?] If I marry him I will go away from here to live and never come back again." Penelope wondered if her father would approve of Warren and believed that if she married against his wishes he might even cut her off from her inheritance. She kept her lines open with Tristrim, telling him that "I know, you would help me when you become master of Ceremonies here."[16]

By late January the "rascally" behavior of the silent Mr S. led Penelope to write him off and reflect on how in the past year Thomas Warren had "behaved so handsomely even when I had injured him so deeply." Looking back on her courtships over the past eighteen months, the young woman began to see her situation more clearly and pare down her romantic expectations until they became a quite manageable cluster of companionate qualities. "Indeed I love him more than ever," she wrote of Warren. "And if Father would give his consent I do not know what might happen." Warren, she continued,

> is not rich, nor of great birth, but he is my equal and my *superior* in some respects. Everybody loves him. I have been anxious to marry a great man, one who would be distinguished in the world, more to please my Father than myself. So I gave up on one whom I loved devotedly [i.e. French] for one whom I admired and who I knew would please my friends [i.e. Mr S.] and now see what it has all come to. The most distinguished men do not make the happiest husbands by a great deal, neither does wealth for I have that and am not happy.[17]

Penelope began to understand her story. Her quest for a lover had become a fruitless search for a great man, whether in her father's terms or love's. And however much she remained bound by the feelings of family and friends she strengthened her own critical perspective as well: Warren, after all, was her superior only in some respects. This constellation of impulse and intention was integral to her marriage to Warren in March 1840. Writing Tristrim that she had decided "to become Mrs Dr Warren," Penelope repeated that she was "heartily sick and tired of the life I lead, it is too dull and melancholy. Therefore I have come to the conclusion to be married and that speedily. Pa also seems quite up to it." The ambivalence of marriage and "greatness" was strong in this letter, too, as was her sense of being a lover on display. In her marriage, she admitted to Tristrim,

> I know I am going to do nothing brilliant or in any way calculated to make a show, but I hope to be happy and that is all I ask. . . . Dr. Warren is thought a very fine young man by everyone. . . . He is also one whom I know will put up with Pa's queer ways and that is a great matter. Everyone knows I have had greater offers

as it regards wealth and distinction, but that is not all in this world. He is devotedly attached to me and I to him so we can get along. I will leave you to make all the show that is required to keep up the *family greatness*.[18]

It turned out that love was not all. Her fiancé was a fine man with whom she could get along, but neither Penelope nor anyone else felt that love had triumphed. Her courtship had pushed love from the foreground of her life. Yet, if not bliss, did not Penelope achieve a "good" match? She seems filled, in the letters just quoted, with the wisdom of a sensible, companionate marriage. Attentive to family, cognizant of her social place, and aware that a man's social agreeableness outweighed intimate charm or greatness, Penelope doubtless would have had the approval of moralists Hester Chapone or Virginia Cary.* But such approval misses entirely the personal meaning of this sensible marriage. It misses the effort involved in carving a niche in the woman's sphere. Amid the push and pull of romantic love, the demands of father and brother, and the sense of being isolated on display before men and "every one," she made a decision that held all at bay while she changed the most pressing circumstance of her life. She was ready to give up girlhood and be a married woman not because she loved, but because the time had come to mark out the first circle in the woman's sphere.

This essay has argued that courtship, in bringing the sexes together, traced a distinctive, lasting pattern of attraction and alienation between them. Passing simultaneously, and with tension, through the social cycle of courtship and through an inward search for meaning, elite southerners built their personal sense of the sexual spheres. But it should not be concluded that intimate companionship – a trusting familiarity and delight in personal qualities – never happened in courtship. Some lovers (relatively few, it seems) shaped the conventions of love and gender to permit intimacy. Rothman, in her study of northern courtship, found that lovers greatly valued candor for "the counterweight it provided to the idealization inherent in romantic love. Openness would ensure that a lover was loved for himself or herself."[19] But among southerners openness not only threatened the shared sense of certainty found

---

* Authors of advice books for young women, previously discussed by Stowe.

in the sexual spheres, it threatened the social order founded on gender division. Candor in this society was far more problematic. It might pass too swiftly into confessions which would sweep away the social orderliness protected by ritual along with love's personal illusions. Courtships that took this risk, however, reveal something more about the personal course love might take. The 1859 courtship of James H. (Harry) Hammond, Jr., and Emily H. Cumming was one such courtship.

Although their families had been acquainted for many years, Harry and Emily did not begin their romance until the early spring of 1859 when Emily was twenty-four and Harry twenty-six. Emily was living with her parents in Augusta, Georgia, and Harry was about one hundred miles away in Athens, where he was a professor at Franklin College. Harry's early letters to Emily were careful second drafts, written in an unusually fine, spidery hand for a man, full of the suppressed emotion typical of a new courtship. But Harry possessed a literary sense which soon went beyond convention to an earthier, plainer style. A single example of an early letter manifests his romantic yet personal voice:

> Ever since coming back from Augusta, I have been taking all the holiday I could to think over and congratulate myself upon the pleasant hours which your charity allowed me to spend in your company while I was there. I have been eating your candy. And I have been reading the novel (Kingsley's) you lent me. . . . You will pardon me . . . for expressing the overflowingness of my gratitude to you. Indeed so much has this feeling taken possession of me that I more than once had a mind to turn down this page of my heart keeping there what was already written on it and filling the other side with altogether new characters.[20]

Alluding to "this feeling" is enough to announce his love, yet his indirection is not coy. He mixes the tropes of love (the "pleasant hours," the "pages of my heart," her "charity") with solid, direct images ("I have been eating your candy") in a way quite unusual in a budding courtship. He closes this letter by wondering whether Emily, like himself, had noticed two sorts of people in the world: the sort who busily "improve" everything and the sort who have a "buoyancy and cheerfulness" that make "your blood warmer, and your eye brighter." His wondering aloud, of course, is a variation on courtship's indirect form of address, for clearly he means to say that she is the second sort, buoyant and warm. Yet in this letter, the distance such rhetoric creates serves to sharpen the closeness he wishes her to feel rather than to alienate feeling altogether, as so often happened. Without being too familiar, his early letters prefigured intimacy by not confusing the rhetoric of love with whatever else love might promise.

This is not to say that Emily and Harry were not often caught up in conventional expressions and swept away by the possession-and-loss language of romance. Just before their formal engagement in July 1859 Harry in particular strayed from his plain style into florid pleas for her to command his life through love. The "fate of our love," he wrote, "is, happen what may, *wholly in your hands* and at our disposal alone." Sometimes he appointed her his queen, after the fashion, so he might tease her about the "severity you are pleased to treat your humble and much enduring subject." At times Emily answered in kind, flirting with him by describing belles of her acquaintance who might interest him and asking him whether he did not rather prefer a woman "so 'coquettish' and so graceful, and witty, too." And even his proposal of marriage can be seen as entirely, if movingly, conventional: "Emmy . . . let me give not only the next afternoon, but all the afternoons and days of my life to add what I could to your pleasure." Nor is it to say that the two of them did not find themselves in conflict over many of the same issues as other lovers. For a time, religion was a difficulty between them. Harry doubted that she found him religious enough and he pressed her to join the Episcopal church, saying only half-jokingly that "it would cause me more pain than you can imagine to hear of our being Baptized or any-thing like that." More frequently, they fell out over letters. The usually patient Harry, who began most of his letters with a scene or a story, opened one October 1859 letter with a slap: "your excuse for not finishing the last page of your letter astonishes me. I have written you every day until yesterday and then failing to hear from you I restrained myself." Emily became angry with him in turn, and did not write or else told him very little of what she was doing. Distance between them, and the words to span it, were central. He once despaired, for both of them, "Shall I ever learn to give myself such expression as will translate my feelings justly?"[21]

In this way they were, as much as any young couple in love, exploring courtship for its limits and bonds. But they achieved more. In style and in content, their letters consistently cleared new terrain, allowed them to keep what they had and to discover even more. It is finally impossible to say why they were able to do so, but certain conditions of their lives hold part of the answer. Unlike many elite southerners, Harry and Emily shared something of work. Both were teachers, and although her home tutoring of Augusta students was different from his academic career, their letters show that they had much in common by way of anecdote and observation. She could understand his accounts of student tricks and muddled lectures and he could appreciate her desire to turn her teaching into work as an "authoress." Both were offspring of harsh, self-made planter-class men. Long settled into his paternal sphere, Henry H. Cumming was a force in Augusta politics. Harry's father, James H. Hammond, was a formidable figure in South Carolina politics and planting, and a daunting figure at home. Perhaps Emily and Harry shared a sense of filial oppression that helped bridge the gap between the sexes. Harry was a quiet young man who walked with a slight limp and who considered himself a failure in planting (as his father did) and a nonentity in politics. Emily thought herself less than beautiful, physically frail, and constantly felt the strain of satisfying a stentorian father and a close, anxious mother. Raised to grasp greatness, both of them desired it very little.[22]

But their letters are the best evidence of their route to intimacy. Both used their letters to recall, in great detail, times spent together. Instead of waxing poetic or playing word games, they wrote of their walks, the Sunday visits, the evenings on the piazza of Emily's Augusta home where they watched the moon rise and talked about the deep heavens and the (perhaps) pointless strivings of mankind. They read the same things and read them to each other, and then they wrote both critically and personally about it. More than passing the time, their courtship reading became a threshold for their intellects and mutual tastes. "Read Paradise Lost if you have nothing to do," Harry wrote Emily in the summer of 1859, "and mark the best passages. I will get them by heart for you." She wrote back, "Aunt Sophia offered to lend me Mrs King's new book 'Sylvia's World.' But I would not take it." She did not approve of Susan Petigru King's "morale, as you put it," and decided that Harry would be better off to read "all the Carolina literature W. G. Simms and all." Harry was delighted to have her choose readings, and praised her for leading him back to Shakespeare.[23] Reading not only fueled their letters and kept a mutual project before them, it also reached deeper. Harry recalled Emily's "low sweet tones" as she read the Bible to him, and combined conventional images of love with personal memories to stitch past and future together:

> Do you recollect laying your hand on my hand as you [read], as that touch thrilled through me it carried me back through years of my life to when I used to sit by mother during the long Sunday afternoons, and listen for the first time to those old, an[d] never to be forgotten stories in the Bible, and when I would be lost in the pathos or the interest of the narrative . . . she would sometimes lay her hand upon my hand, I know not whether it was to give her authority to what she was reading, or an instinctive desire on her part, that I should realize that she under God was the source of those first impressions to me.[24]

Each wrote, too, about the emotional satisfactions of love letters. They wrote not to register letters sent and received, but of the tactile pleasure of correspondence. Emily wrote that her

> letters have two meanings to me and I can connect no other with them, first I write them because it is delightful to feel that the words which I am one day scratching away here, are the next to bring to you, if not much meaning, and interest, at least a faint idea of how constantly I think of you, and love you, but most of all they mean that you will with this idea fresh in your mind, after reading them, sit down and with a few touches of

that magic pen of yours, make me the most elated of little women.

In the same way, Harry enjoyed thinking that his letter

is mine now, in my hands, but day after tomorrow it will be yours, and will tremble and bend in those little fingers. . . . It is a friend passive, mute, but infinitely obliging, it carries the woof . . . that binds the warp of our thoughts and feelings to the texture of our lives.[25]

Nearly all of Harry's letters, and most of Emily's, rely on physical description as the heart of emotional expression. They rarely let stylized rhetoric inflate their solid imagery. After an evening spent with her, he would immediately write to her: "As I stand here with my pen in my hand," about the time just passed, about the "night, and those dark eyes, and that soft silken hair, and the white dress, and all that there is of such mysterious and thrilling pleasure." He brought these images to the sharp focus of the present, imagining her in her world. "And you Emmy," he wrote in a typical passage, "have you too slept well? and are you now walking in this bright fresh morning?" He imagined her by her window, "your elbow on your knee, your left hand supporting your cheek." He wanted, and often received, what he called her "I and me" letters strong with images from her life that anchored his own view of her. Her letters permitted him to see, and he took what he could from all of them. "I can just catch a glimpse of you standing by Maria," he wrote of one letter, "and opening that yellow envelope, then a moment more at your writing desk, and even there the representation becomes dim, for I have never seen that desk, and then a curtain a hundred miles thick falls between us."[26]

This kind of reflective detail saturates their correspondence. Though not consciously thematic, it nevertheless gave their relationship its intellectual shape. The early sympathy between them ripened into intimacy by the summer of 1859 as they both sought a personal closeness belied by courtship games and display. They used typical courtship rhetoric only so they might move beyond it. Both lovers, for example, tempered flights of romantic wishfulness with clear, even critical appreciations of its dangers. Harry knew how imagination and the

distance between them could easily lead him to an all-absorb-
ing desire for the magical feminine. But he assured Emily that
no matter how much he desired the femininity she represented, "I do not look upon you at all . . . as a mystery or
as a myth." He would struggle with all his might, he told her
on another occasion, against a time "when the object of our
love proves other than we thought it."[27]

Along with precautions of this sort, Emily and Harry were
often able to write lightly about the responsibility of being a
man or a woman. They were able to put into words the ways
in which their sex-bound obligations became misconstrued or
ridiculous. Harry lightly diffused Emily's anxiety early in their
courtship, for example, regarding the frequency of their letters.
He wrote,

> I never made a request that you would write to me once
> a week, did I? It seems to me the most improbable thing.
> I remember talking about it and saying something para-
> doxical. I don't believe I knew what [I meant] then, and
> I am sure I do not now . . . Write to me whenever you
> can and will – let them not only be free gifts but gifts
> willingly and heartily bestowed.[28]

As to the social duties that each met in their respective sphere,
they could be wry and sympathetic – and learned to expect
each other to be. She wrote of making the feminine rounds of
visiting with her mother in a humorous vein many women
would not have risked in a letter to a lover. "Pity me! Pity
me!' she wrote,

> I am just starting out on a visiting tour, with my inexor-
> able parent, who will hear of no delay, no reprieve, but
> moves sternly on. I have exhausted every argument that
> occurred to a distressed heart, suggested that every one
> would be at home [sic], that it was very warm, and very
> dusty, and finally entreated her at least to wait for one
> of my pretty days, but this she considered would be an
> indefinite postponement, and so it remains that I go.[29]

Returning that afternoon from her "martyrdom" of five visits,
she knew that Harry "would have been proud of me, could
you have witnessed my social achievements . . . so happy,
and successful was I in all my 'efforts' to be pleasing and

amiable." And looking forward to being his wife, she told him, "you know I can't talk and do not expect much from me, in that line." Harry, too, wrote of the "sacrifice" he made by attending gay season parties, forced to respond to the invitations of women of his acquaintance in Athens. The ladies took their daughters to some decorated home where

> young men in black coats droop into the small hot rooms after them. It is a piteous spectacle. . . . Fruit cake and roast pig . . . feed the fire of life and love and wit that sparkles in the young ladies eyes, and comes sighing like a furnace from the young men's lips. I decline as often as it is prudent.[30]

Along with sharing an ironic sense of their duties, Emily and Harry also spoke of their felt deficiencies of character in strikingly open ways. Instead of appearing always in control, Harry more than once wrote of burning a letter to her after he became fouled in literary attempts "which spoiled the good sense of my letter, just as effectually as it would have been obliterated by turning my inkstand over on it." They revealed to each other the times when they were exhausted or inept with family and friends, and frequently were candid about their self-doubts. Emily wondered, for example, if he did "not wish that I was better tempered, and slightly more equable? That I had the lovely angelic temperament and disposition with which it is polite and orthodox to suppose women gifted? Well – I heartily echo the wish."[31]

More seriously, they resolved their conflicts by seeing their own expectations relatively; that is, not as absolute demands they had a right to make in a courtship, but as matters of temperament they would work to understand or change. They conversed. After Harry expressed his astonishment at her silence on one occasion, she was able, near the end of her long letter, to reply, "You were *right cross* to me, Harry . . . and you know I am not prepared to make any sort of allowance for any such weakness from *you*." Harry responded with an apology and an admission of having lived "selfishly drawn up into myself for years" so that his fear of losing her caused him to strike out at her. As a man, he explained, he had been self-important and guarded, "a stone, a block, and now that you have told this stone to live" he still did not quite know how.

Emily's reply also centered on the content and conditions of their quarrel, rather than simply blaming or absolving, as many women felt entitled to do. Like Harry, she saw the dimension of gender and found herself also implicated. If he was a block or a stone, "You know . . . in the abstract how frail, and weak in mind, and purpose, women are, for the most part." She hoped he would be able, once married to her, to tolerate "the inconveniences of a particular daily exhibition" of feminine weakness. The theme of gender and temperament ran throughout their letters, moving past self-pity into conversation about their deepest doubts regarding the future. Emily, "so happy that I can venture to tell you what I have just written," confided her frequent "vexation" with her own life as a woman and admitted that on the "verge of a changed untried existence" of married life she was afraid. And Harry put into words his dislike of planting and indifference to politics, confessing in an extraordinary admission for a planter-class male, that "I look forward to no grand career. . . . In a word, neither my abilities, nor my taste, induce me to hope for anything but the most ordinary of lives."[32]

Harry Hammond and Emily Cumming achieved a rare view of themselves as embedded in their culture. Seeing the irony, humor, and struggle in the spheres of men and women, they arrived at an uncommon pass in courtship. They used the ritual to go beyond its divisiveness and alienation. He did not picture Emily apart in her sphere, but felt her within him as he taught his students, "looking at them," giving his own look a new authority. No epiphany, such times became part of his routine and his self-image. "I'm not over busy," he wrote one Tuesday morning, "and I feel solid, smooth and angular. I hope the boys will find me well defined." As marriage approached, they weighed the joint project of their life together, rare in courtship letters. They traded views "on the 'more prosaic side' of our lives" in matters of money, household, and obligations to family. They must demand equality from each other, Harry wrote her, and then backed away: "demand is not the word, I request it." They delighted in imagining life after marriage, in concrete images not abstract duties. Harry took note of her "complaint of the cold mornings; this is a point where we do not sympathize – they are new life to me." Their differences worked to mutual advantage, however she would get all of the blankets and "I shall have the pleasure of wrapping you up." The fires of romantic love were banked into the more tangible warmth of winter evenings when "I will have my studies, you will darn stockings, and correct french exercises, and read the newspapers and the reviews, and wind your watch up."[33]

Though idealized in its own way, Harry Hammond's vision of domestic happiness must be seen as rather subversive in its southern context. It is a vision from inside the woman's sphere. Embracing it, Harry tucked himself away from the gaze of kin, competitor, and slave. What he wanted – and here he was an exception that underscored the rule – was to have his personal tie to Emily cut across the usual way the planters divided up the social order. He described their relationship as blurring the essential line between the sexes, a division on which rested every level of the social hierarchy. And in freeing his personal wishes from the usual masculine effort to keep up appearances, he challenged a key expectation that his society held for young men: the expectation that they would move out into the world and shape it by shaping their honor. In seeking intimacy with his wife, Harry Hammond necessarily turned his back on this dominant vision of reality. Instead, his courtship helped him to decide that reality was at home, and that even though this meant facing domestic risks to his happiness, married life's unmet needs and unmade beds, at least they would be risks of his own choosing.

NOTES

The Editor gratefully acknowledges permission to reprint material from *Intimacy and Power in the Old South: Ritual in the Lives of the Planters*, by Steven M. Stowe. Copyright © 1987 by The John Hopkins University Press. Reprinted by permission of Johns Hopkins University Press and the author.

1 For a view of eighteenth-century courtship and marriage that heavily stresses kinship and property values, see Edmund S. Morgan (1952) *Virginians at Home: Family Life in Eighteenth Century Virginia* (Charlottesville, Va.), chap. 2. Daniel Blake Smith emphasizes individual feeling and choice; Smith (1980) *Inside the Great House: Planter Family Life in Eighteenth-Century Chesapeake Society* (Ithaca, N.Y.). Jan Lewis (1983) *The Pursuit of Happiness: Family and Values in Jefferson's Virginia* (New York), chap. 5, shows how love was a

predicament for Virginians. For the antebellum years, kinship and property figure heavily in Bertram Wyatt-Brown (1982) *Southern Honor: Ethics and Behavior in the Old South* (New York), esp. chap. 8.

2 . . . Though path breaking in its attention to the family, Edmund S. Morgan's view of eighteenth-century courtship is slanted rather briskly toward the "business" of getting married and does not attempt a thorough analysis of the place of emotion and impulse in formal ritual. For the same century, Daniel Blake Smith finds that the "obsession with a balance and a well-ordered family" in courtship "gradually gave way . . . to a view of family life that prized intimacy, affection, and even a measure of passion." . . . Jan Lewis, finding intimacy much more a problem, discusses love in general rather than the shape of its rituals. But she insightfully sees that Virginians' increasing reliance on love rather than material calculations did not "free" them from courtship's demands; it only changed the nature of the demands. See Morgan, *Virginians at Home*, 29–35; Smith, *Great House*, 141; Lewis, *Pursuit of Happiness*, 178–9. . . . Ellen K. Rothman excludes the South from her fine survey of courtship in America. Anne F. Scott has little to say about courting, and curiously concludes that "pragmatism or impulse or necessity for the most part outweighed romance in the marriage market." With a different but brief look at women's courting, Catherine Clinton describes it as a time "filled with fun and frivolity" in grim contrast to the subjection that followed. . . . Perhaps the most inclusive pictures of courtship are those of Bertram Wyatt-Brown and Jane Turner Censer. The former is concerned with the broad economic and kinship strategies, however. Censer orients her interpretation to feeling and sexuality . . . but emphasizes harmony and good feeling perhaps overmuch. See Ellen K. Rothman (1984) *Hands and Hearts: A History of Courtship in America* (New York); Scott (1970) *The Southern Lady: From Pedestal to Politics, 1830–1930* (Chicago), 25–6; Clinton (1982) *The Plantation Mistress: Woman's World in the Old South* (New York), 62; Wyatt-Brown, *Southern Honor*, chap. 8; Censer (1984) *North Carolina Planters and Their Children, 1800–1860* (Baton Rouge, La.), esp. chap. 4.

3 Henry Cumming to Julia Bryan, 7 March 1823, 15 January 1824, 4 August 1823, Hammond–Bryan–Cumming Papers, South Caroliniana Library; all citations for the Cumming–Bryan courtship are from this collection.

4 Ibid., 15 January 1824.

5 Ibid., 4 August 1823, 9 April 1823, 5 June 1823.

6 Ibid., 26 November 1822, 18 September 1823, 4 August 1823, 23 August 1823, 18 September 1823.

7 Ibid., 17 May 1823, 4 August 1823, 7 March 1823, 26 November 1822, 17 May 1823, 24 January 1824.

8 Penelope Skinner to Tristrim Skinner, 26 February 1840, Skinner Papers, Southern Historical Collection, University of North Carol-

ina; all citations for Penelope Skinner's courtship are from this collection.

9 Ibid., 4 September 1837.

10 Ibid., 21 October 1838.

11 Ibid., 5 November 1838.

12 Ibid., 8 December 1838; Joseph B. Skinner to Tristrim Skinner, 4 December 1838.

13 Penelope Skinner to Tristrim Skinner, 29 January 1839; Joseph B. Skinner to Tristrim Skinner, 30 January 1839.

14 Tristrim Skinner to Joseph B. Skinner, 22 February 1839, 8 February 1839; Penelope Skinner to Tristrim Skinner, 13 March 1839; Tristrim Skinner to Joseph B. Skinner, 7 April 1839. Tristrim thought that French's vanity was rooted in his being the author of a book. It made a man vain, Tristrim remarked, "to see a large quantity of type put together knowing that it was his own composition." Tristrim Skinner to Joseph B. Skinner, 8 February 1839.

15 Penelope Skinner to Tristrim Skinner, 13 March 1839, 5 April 1839.

16 Ibid., 15 January 1840.

17 Ibid., 31 January 1840.

18 Ibid., 26 February 1840. She added, "We are to have no wedding *at all* not *even our* relations. Pa says that he disapproves of weddings."

19 Rothman, *Hands and Hearts*, 109, 118.

20 Harry Hammond to Emily Cumming, 7 April 1859, Hammond–Bryan–Cumming Papers, SCL; all citations for the Hammond–Cumming courtship are from this collection. Neither Harry nor Emily was given to dating letters, but they often noted the day of the week. Most of the citations here follow their notations or whatever internal evidence helps distinguish one letter from another. A few of the letters have been included in Carol Bleser (ed.) (1981) *The Hammonds of Redcliffe* (New York), 71–83. Also of interest is an edited volume of writings by Emily Cumming's sister-in-law, W. Kirk Wood (ed) (1951) *A Northern Daughter and a Southern Wife: The Civil War Reminiscences and Letters of Katherine H. Cumming, 1860–1865* (Baton Rouge, La).

21 Harry Hammond to Emily Cumming, 15 July 1859 [*c.* July 1859] (see also "Sunday morning and Sunday afternoon" [1859] and "Friday morning [1859]); "Thursday night" [October 1859]; Emily Cumming to Harry Hammond [1859]; Harry Hammond to Emily Cumming, 21 May 1859 (see also 11 July 1859, "Saturday morning" [1859], "Tuesday morning" [1859]).

22 The definitive biography of James H. Hammond and his times is Drew Gilpin Faust (1982) *James Henry Hammond and the Old South: A Design for Mastery* (Baton Rouge, La.); see chap. 15 for Harry Hammond's relation with his father.

23 Harry Hammond to Emily Cumming, "Monday and Tuesday" [1859] and 5 July 1859; Emily Cumming to Harry Hammond [1859]; Harry Hammond to Emily Cumming, "Saturday night" [1859]. On

their meetings, see also Harry Hammond to Emily Cumming, "Friday morning" [1859].

24 Harry Hammond to Emily Cumming, "Monday and Tuesday" [1859].

25 Emily Cumming to Harry Hammond, 30 September 1859; Harry Hammond to Emily Cumming [1859].

26 Harry Hammond to Emily Cumming, "Madison C[ourt] H[ouse] Monday morning" [1859] [May 1859], "Thursday morning" [probably September 1859]; see also 21 May 1859.

27 Ibid., "Saturday night" [1859]; 5 July 1859.

28 Ibid., [1859].

29 Emily Cumming to Harry Hammond [probably October 1859].

30 Harry Hammond to Emily Cumming, "Wednesday morning" [probably October 1859].

31 Ibid., "Wednesday night" [1859]; see also Harry's account of his social awkwardness, 7 April 1859, and his irritation with his work, "Tuesday night" [1859]; Emily Cumming to Harry Hammond [1859]; Harry Hammond to Emily Cumming, "Friday morning" [1859].

32 Harry Hammond to Emily Cumming, "Saturday morning" [1859]; Emily Cumming to Harry Hammond [October 1859], Harry Hammond to Emily Cumming, "Wednesday morning" [October 1859]; Emily Cumming to Harry Hammond [October 1859] and 30 September 1859; Harry Hammond to Emily Cumming [probably September 1859], and 26 September 1859.

33 Harry Hammond to Emily Cumming, "Monday and Tuesday" [1859], "Tuesday morning" [1859] [c. October 1859] [September 1859] (see also 28 September 1859, "Friday morning" [1859], and Emily Cumming to Harry Hammond, 30 September 1859; Harry Hammond to Emily Cumming, "Wednesday night" [1859]. Five years after their marriage, Harry wrote to Emily from a Confederate army camp in Virginia about his "spells of hopeless weariness which . . . made me, you know, a most unhappy person before I knew you." See Harry Hammond to Emily Cumming, 30 June 1864.

8

WOMEN AND THE SEARCH FOR MANLY INDEPENDENCE

Joan E. Cashin

Joan E. Cashin's A Family Venture: Men and Women on the Southern Frontier *is the first book-length study of the important migration of slaveowners to the old Southwest. Her focus on the family dynamics of the migration opens many angles of vision on planter family life. In the excerpt reprinted here, Cashin discusses the conflicts that arose between men and women as the decision to migrate was reached. Earlier in the chapter, she argues that a major motivation behind migration was a "search for manly independence." Here she shows how most women – wives, sisters, mothers – opposed and dreaded migration. Their opposition generally carried no weight in the families she studies, and the picture that emerges of planter marriages is more one of conflict and unwelcome subordination for women than is evident in Fox-Genovese's interpretation.*

The differences between the sexes on the migration issue were even more pronounced than those between generations of men. Women, with few exceptions, feared and dreaded the possibility of moving to the Southwest. Migration could not represent independence for them, as it did for young men, because women spent their entire lives in a state of dependency. If it came during a woman's childbearing years, it would deprive her of the practical aid of relatives in running households, and it would deprive her offspring of relationships with kinfolk that were crucial to socializing children. If a woman had to migrate in her old age, she would spend her last years far from relatives who would care for her. Finally, it would separate all women from the female kin who gave

216

them love, companionship, and a sense of identity throughout their lives.

Women accepted the partial separations from relatives that happened when they married, but migration portended losses that were radical and permanent, because it could remove women so far from their kinfolk that those relationships might deteriorate and eventually collapse. The frequent visits that kept kinship ties alive in the seaboard would be improbable, maybe impossible, from a new home hundreds of miles away. Journeys over great distances were unsafe and could not be undertaken without the company of a man, and many women feared such journeys. For example, widow Patience Laye of South Carolina decided to visit her daughter and son-in-law in Florida only "if you was to come . . . and help me there."[1]

Ideally, many women wished that their relatives would remain close enough for daily contact. One North Carolinian objected when her brothers moved twenty miles from home, just beyond a day's ride on horseback, and she told her cousin that the separation "of course will render us somewhat gloomy every day." Migration beyond the boundaries of a state was troubling, but the distance from the seaboard to the Southwest seemed unsurpassable. When the cousins of Catherine R. Patterson left North Carolina for Mississippi, she believed that she would not see them again in this world and pinned her hopes on a reunion in heaven. A distance of two hundred miles, according to Caroline Gordon, made visits highly unlikely. If this distance was a threshold in the minds of women, then they would certainly be anxious about removal to the Southwest, since the average distance per migration [for the families studied] was approximately five hundred miles.[2]

Women commonly compared migration to death, as men almost never did. A North Carolinian walked out into her yard to take a long "final look" at her sister as she left with her husband for Missouri in 1835. Another woman ran after her daughter as she departed with her husband, embraced her one last time, and cried, "Oh, Mary, I will never see you again on earth." Women compared the two losses so frequently that it is sometimes impossible to tell if "departed" relatives had died or migrated. Louisa Cunningham mourned the loss of her beloved sister whom "providence has then seen fit to remove away from us." It was "a circumstance at all times melancholy and distressing – sundering apart those near and dear ties which so long has bound [us] together." To many women family relationships were little short of life itself. Perhaps it was no accident that the word "removal" was used for both migration and death.[3]

Planter women described the dispersal of their relatives as if it were unprecedented, as if these upheavals followed a long period of tranquility. While the southern white population as a whole was highly mobile throughout the antebellum era, the families of some planter women actually had not moved in many decades, and these women demonstrated an abiding love for their homes. The family of Ann Gordon Finley had lived in Wilkes County, North Carolina, from the time of the Revolution until the 1840s. She was born in 1826, the third child of Sarah Gwyn Gordon and Nathaniel Gordon, and her father died in 1829. After attending Salem Academy, she was married at age twenty to John T. Finley, a local slaveowner and merchant. She was a practical, down-to-earth woman, but she was also closely attached to her many kinfolk from the Gwyn, Gordon, and Lenoir families, perhaps more so than the typical planter woman.

Ann Finley was dismayed when her husband planned to move to Alabama in 1847 because, as her mother said later, "Ann was so fond of her relations." She also loved the hilly landscape of western North Carolina, especially her childhood home, the Oakland plantation located near Wilkesboro. Before her departure, Mrs Finley visited her mother there and was saddened by the air of desertion about the place. "Once the habitation of so large a family," it was now empty except for her mother and stepfather. It had been "so long the homestead of the Gordon name," but "there was not one to answer by that name."[4]

Many women did not want to move because they perceived the Southwest as a violent, dangerous, sickly place. Like men, they constructed their images of the frontier from their reading and from conversations with relatives and friends. A Virginian recounted the grisly deaths of a neighboring family who had gone to Texas only to be murdered by a gang of thieves. Olive Packard worried that the Southwestern climate would ruin the health of her brother and sister-in-law, and Rachel Townes feared for the health of her children, Samuel Townes and

Eliza Townes Blassingame, in Alabama. Furthermore, women believed that frontier life would promote "dissipation," meaning drinking, gambling, and miscegenation. Somewhat inconsistently, they also dreaded its isolation. Mary Boykin Chesnut's visits to the Southwest over several decades left her with an impression of dreary loneliness, which she recalled as "despairing" and "depressing."[5]

Some women even criticized the greed of men who went to the Southwest. Flinty, plain-spoken Anne Dent chastised her son for the avarice that drove him from South Carolina to Alabama in 1837. Had he been contented with "moderate gains," she scolded, "we might yet have been enjoying family union, instead of being so widely scattered and unavailingly lamenting our mistake." Frances Berkeley of Virginia remarked acidly that one of her neighbors was "much pleased at first at the prospect of making a handsome speculation," but the man instead died from fever in Tennessee far from his wife and children. After Lydia Riddick's neighbor moved to the Southwest despite his mother's protests, she told her own son, who had also migrated, that "'tis strange that the love of money is stronger than the love of a kind and affectionate mother whose heart yearned to look on him." These women spoke directly to the issue of what constituted acceptable sacrifices in the pursuit of wealth, and they believed that family life was more important than material gain. Women viewed migration primarily as a moral issue, unlike either the young men who saw it as an opportunity to fulfill individual goals, or older men who saw it as a challenge to their power.[6]

Women none the less played only a marginal role, at best, in decisionmaking. Men knew that they opposed migration (Willis Lea advised his brother to leave North Carolina although "all do not like that move to the west – especially ladies"), but men almost always discounted women's perspectives. James Lide moved from South Carolina to Alabama over the strong objections of his adult daughters. Israel Pickens realized that his wife, Martha, did not want to leave North Carolina for Alabama, but he decided to go anyway, teasing her about her fears of the wilderness.[7]

Most planter men did not consult their spouses, in either new or long-standing marriages. One man brought his bride to Alabama "away from her family and friends, to a land of strangers, where she finds much to regret." After seven years of marriage, Elizabeth B. Ambler, wife of John J. Ambler, Jr., tried to dissuade him from buying a plantation in Alabama. She begged him not to settle there – "heaven forbid," she exclaimed – but he chose none the less to relocate in the Southwest. After twenty-three years of married life, North Carolinian Sarah Gordon Brown was not included in her husband's deliberations. She told her son, "he sais [sic] he is going to move but makes no farthere [sic] preparation and none of us know what he is going to do."[8]

Mothers also spoke out against migration, but with little effect. Elizabeth Otey objected that her son's migration from Virginia to Tennessee was a source of "great grief" and urged him to return from the corruptions of the frontier. Two years later she wrote that his hopes for success had been unrealistic and it was time to come home. After Sarah Irby's son departed Virginia for Mississippi, she regretted it more each day; wailing, "Would to God you had never gone." When Mary Allen's son left home, she was hurt and dismayed, asking, "Why did you go to Texas?" The next year she wrote that she could never be reconciled to his absence. Yet none of these men returned to the seaboard.[9]

Sometimes women could convince men to postpone their departure if they had the backing of their male relatives. A former slave recalled that her mistress's relatives "riz up an' put forth mighty powerful objections," persuading her master to delay leaving South Carolina for the frontier. William Townes, an uncle of Samuel Townes, heeded the wishes of his wife and children who very much wanted to remain in their native Virginia and searched for a suitable purchase in the Old Dominion. When he could find no promising land in the state, he finally decided to leave for the Southwest. Husbands sometimes attempted to alter their wives' opinions of the region. Samuel Van Wyck tried to depict Huntsville, Alabama, as a place fit for "a lady and a Methodist" like his wife.[10]

A handful of women went willingly to the Southwest because they too wanted to escape home. The Townes family opposed Samuel's marriage to Joanna Hall, perhaps because her family was not wealthy; whatever the reason, she was relieved to escape their disapproval and, more generally, the intense family life of the seaboard. According to her husband, she was glad to have a home of her own in Alabama. Elizabeth Witherspoon DuBose, wife of Kimbrough DuBose and part of the enormous DuBose–Witherspoon–Miller clan, gave up her initial opposition to migration after living for ten years in a kinsman's home in Cheraw, South Carolina. Her son related that she too decided she wanted a home of her own.

At least two women migrated to escape unhappy marriages: a South Carolinian took refuge with her Alabama cousins, and a Virginian moved to Kentucky to live with her sons. But these were only temporary solutions to the problem of domestic infelicity, and both women eventually returned to their homes. Women, unlike men, could not escape the dilemmas of familiar obligation by settling alone on the frontier.[12]

Despite their general opposition to migration, most women struggled to accept the decisions of their male relatives. One mother wished her son would return from Texas, but if he chose to stay, then "of course I ought not to object." Samuel Townes predicted that his female relatives would soon reconcile themselves to his sister's and brother-in-law's departure for Alabama. Eight months later they were still trying to accept the separation, but none of them openly challenged the decision to leave Carolina. The dependence of women was the counterpart to the independence of men, and at some point most women had to at least feign agreement with the decisions of their male kinfolk. Bernard Carr summed up the expectations of many men when he announced his engagement to a woman who was "willing to do as I would have her do" – accompany him without complaint to the Southwest.[13]

NOTES

The Editor gratefully acknowledges permission to reprint material from *A Family Venture: Men and Women on the Southern Frontier*, by Joan E. Cashin. Copyright © 1991 by Joan E. Cashin. Reprinted by permission of Oxford University Press, Inc.

1 Patience Laye to Mr and Mrs J. Oates, 18 November 1858, Oates Papers, University of South Carolina (USC). See also Martha Pickens to Ann Lenoir, 28 October 1814, Chiliab Smith Howe Papers, Southern Historical Collection, University of North Carolina (UNC); Sarah H. Gayle Diary, 20 June 1830, Bayne and Gayle Family Papers, UNC. Annette Kolodny (1984) *The Land Before Her:*

Fantasy and Experience of the American Frontiers (Chapel Hill, N.C.), 93–4, notes that American women from all regions objected to migration because it separated them from kin and friends.

2 Catherine R. Patterson to Neill Kelly, 7 February 1840, John N. Kelly Papers, Duke University (DU) (first and second examples); Caroline Gordon to Allen Brown, n.d., 1854, Gordon and Hackett Family Papers, UNC.

3 Thomas Felix Hickerson (1940) *Happy Valley: History and Genealogy* (Chapel Hill, N.C.), 113; *Memoirs of Mary A. Maverick. arranged by Mary A. Maverick and her son George Madison Maverick, ed. Rena Maverick Green* (San Antonio, Tex., 1921), 12; Louisa Cunningham to Benjamin Yancey, 18 September 1839, Benjamin Cudworth Yancey Papers, UNC. Kolodny, *Land Before Her*, 94–5, and Julie Roy Jeffrey (1979) *Frontier Women: The Trans-Mississippi West, 1840–1880* (New York), 37, observe that women from the Northeast and Midwest compared migration to death.

4 Mrs W. O. Absher, *Land Entry Book, Wilkes County North Carolina 1778–1781* (n.d.), land deed 28; Hickerson, *Happy Valley*, 67, 194; Sarah Brown to her son, 22 February 1853, Hamilton Brown Papers, UNC; S. A. [for Sarah Ann, called "Ann"] Finley to Caroline Gordon, 30 December 1847, Gordon and Hackett Family Papers, DU.

5 Jane Dunn to William E. Jones, 19 December 1852, William Edmonson Jones Papers, Virginia Historical Society (VHS); Olive Packard to Chilion Packard, 10 December 1823, Packard Family Papers, South Carolina Historical Society (SCHS); H. H. Townes to Rachel Townes, 8 December 1833, Townes Family Papers, USC; Elisabeth Showalter Muhlenfeld, "Mary Boykin Chesnut: the writer and her work" (Ph.D. diss., University of South Carolina, 1978), Appendix C, 824. Women's apprehensions about the Southwestern climate resemble fears of Britons about the unhealthy climate of the southern colonies and the West Indies. See Karen Ordahl Kupperman (1984) "Fear of hot climates in the Anglo–American colonial experience," *William and Mary Quarterly* 3rd ser., 41 (April): 213–40.

6 Ray Mathis (1979) *John Horry Dent: South Carolina Aristocrat on the Alabama Frontier* (University, Ala.), 149; Frances C. Berkeley to Callender Noland, 24 September 1838, Noland Papers, University of Virginia (UVA); Lydia Riddick to Charles Riddick, 11 November 1852, Charles C. Riddick Papers, UNC. Martin E. Marty (1978) "Migration: the moral framework," in (1978) William H. McNeill and Ruth S. Adams (eds) *Human Migration: Patterns and Policies* (Bloomington, Ind.), 387–403, discusses migration as a moral issue but does not distinguish between the views of men and women. Other American women were skeptical about the riches to be found on the frontier; see Kolodny, *Land Before Her*, 105. George C. Rable (1989) *Civil Wars: Women and the Crisis of Southern Nationalism* (Urbana, Ill.), 29–30, remarks that many white women adhered to "anticommercial values" in the late antebellum era, although he

argues that they none the less supported the slavery regime and the southern social system.

7 Willis Lea to William Lea, 11 January 1847, Lea Family Papers, UNC; Fletcher M. Green (ed.) (1952) *The Lides Go South . . . and West: The Records of a Planter Migration in 1835* (Columbia, S.C.), 15; Israel Pickens to Martha Pickens, 18 March 1816, Israel Pickens Papers, ALA. I have found no evidence that the moral authority of the southern "lady" enhanced women's actual influence in families considering migration. Nor did women's "separate sphere" or their allegedly more spiritual nature give them an effective voice in family discussions of migration; neither did the large amount of work plantation mistresses performed in raising children and running households. See William R. Taylor (1957) *Cavalier and Yankee: The Old South and American National Character* (New York), 146–76; Catherine Clinton (1982) *The Plantation Mistress: Woman's World in the Old South* (New York), 16–35; Anne Firor Scott (1970) *The Southern Lady: From Pedestal to Politics, 1830–1930* (Chicago), 4–21, 27–37. Cf. Jan Lewis (1983) *The Pursuit of Happiness: Family and Values in Jefferson's Virginia* (New York), 211, and Carl N. Degler (1980) *At Odds: Women and the Family in America from the Revolution to the Present* (New York), 30, 42, 50, who argue that separate spheres gave women genuine moral authority in the family. Suzanne Lebsock (1984) *The Free Women of Petersburg: Status and Culture in a Southern Town, 1784–1860* (New York), xv–xvi, 232–6, argues that the so-called cult of womanhood and its "separate spheres" constituted a backlash against women's increasing autonomy.

Most scholars of southern families agree that women were excluded from the decision to migrate; see Lewis, *Pursuit*, 144–5; Clinton, *Plantation Mistress*, 166–7; and James Oakes (1982) *The Ruling Race: A History of American Slaveholders* (New York), 87–8. Cf. Jane Censer (1984) *North Carolina Planters and Their Children 1800–1860* (Baton Rouge, La.), 132, who stresses women's influence over their husbands. Historians of migration to other American frontiers disagree on women's exclusion from decisionmaking. Kolodny, *Land Before Her*, 31–4; Lillian Schlissel (1982) *Women's Diaries of the Western Journey* (New York), 28, 31, 14; and John Mack Faragher (1979) *Women and Men on the Overland Trail* (New Haven, Conn.), 67, 163, argue that women were excluded, while Sandra Myres (1982) *Westering Women and the Frontier Experience, 1800–1915* (Albuquerque, N.M.), 9–11, 16–36; Joanna L. Stratton (1981) *Pioneer Women: Voices from the Kansas Frontier* (New York), 44–5; Glenda Riley (1981) *Frontierswomen: The Iowa Experience* (Ames, Iowa), 5–11, 26; and Jeffrey, *Frontier Women*, 30–3, argue that women were involved in decisionmaking or approved the decision once it was made.

8 Gayle Diary, 26 October 1827, Bayne and Gayle Family Papers, UNC; Elizabeth B. Ambler to John J. Ambler, Jr., 25 September 1835, Ambler and Barbour Family Papers, UVA; Sarah Brown to

Allen Brown, 22 February 1853, Hamilton Brown Papers, UNC. On the inequities of planter marriages, see Jean E. Friedman (1985) *The Enclosed Garden: Women and Community in the Evangelical South. 1830–1900* (Chapel Hill, N.C.), 21–38; Bertram Wyatt-Brown (1982) *Southern Honor: Ethic and Behavior in the Old South* (New York), 254–71; Clinton, *Plantation Mistress*, 68–85; Eugene Genovese (1974) *Roll, Jordan Roll: The World the Slaves Made* (New York), 74; Anne Firor Scott (1974) "Women's perspective on the patriarchy in the 1850s," *Journal of American History* 61 (June): 55–64; Scott, *Southern Lady*, 46–66. Cf. Censer, *Planters and Children*, 65–95, who emphasizes parity and companionship in planter marriages.

9 Elizabeth M. Otey to James Otey, 23 February 1823, 21 September 1825, James Hervey Otey Papers, UNC; Sarah W. Irby to John W. Irby, 18 April 1849, Neblett and Irby Family Papers, UVA; Mary E. P. Allen to John J. Allen, Jr., 28 December 1854, 6 March 1855, Allen Family Papers, UVA.

10 George P. Rawick (ed.) (1972) *The American Slave: A Composite Autobiography*, Contributions in Afro–American and African Studies, No. 11, Westport, Conn.: Greenwood Publishing Company, South Carolina, 3: part 3, 74; William Townes to S. A. Townes, 1 May 1824, Townes Family Papers, USC; Samuel Van Wyck to Margaret Van Wyck, 28 March 1860, Maverick and Van Wyck Family Papers, USC. See also Joseph H. Parks (1962) *Leonidas Polk C.S.A., The Fighting Bishop* (Baton Rouge, La.), 63–4.

11 S. A. Townes to G. F. Townes, 18 July 1833, 22 June 1834, H. H. Townes to G. F. Townes, 16 January 1834, Townes Family Papers, USC; John W. DuBose, "Memoir of four families," John Witherspoon Dubose Papers, Alabama Archives, 2: 191.

12 Gayle Diary, 11 May 1830, 9 May 1830 or 9 June 1830, Bayne and Gayle Family Papers, UNC; Elizabeth Blaetterman to "Mrs Michie," 26 December 1845, 8 July 1846, n.d., George Carr Papers, UVA. The dates and pagination in the Gayle Diary are inconsistent.

13 Mary E. P. Allen to John J. Allen, Jr., 6 March 1855, Allen Family Papers, UVA; S. A. Townes to G. F. Townes, 18 July 1833, G. F. Townes to J. A. Townes, 4 February 1834, Townes Family Papers, USC; Bernard Carr to Mead Carr, 8 April 1829, George Carr Papers, UVA. Widows could have given property to their sons to help them migrate, depending upon restrictions on the disposition of property in their husbands' wills, but I have found no record of these kinds of transactions.

9

FEMALE SLAVES

Sex roles and status in the antebellum plantation South

Deborah G. White

The final essay is Deborah White's article on female slaves. White makes good use of now-standard primary sources on slavery, but with an eye on what they can tell us specifically about female roles. Using these sources, as well as anthropological studies of the family in Africa and elsewhere, White argues that slave families were, "matrifocal," in the sense that the mother–child relationship was the most important one in the slave family and that women performed vital economic roles on the plantation. She later expanded on her argument in a book, Ar'n't I a Woman? Female Slaves in the Plantation South *(1985).*

One of the most striking things about White's presentation is that women are seen as relatively independent not only of male slaves, but, by implication, of the cultural influences of the masters. Female slaves appear here as affected in important ways by the organization of work on the plantation, but there is no hint of the kind of reciprocal cultural influence that is at the heart of the Genovese interpretation of the Old South.

In his 1939 study of the black family in America, sociologist E. Franklin Frazier theorized that in slave family and marriage relations, women played the dominant role. Specifically, Frazier wrote that "the Negro woman as wife or mother was the mistress of her cabin, and, save for the interference of master and overseer, her wishes in regard to mating and family matters were paramount." He also insisted that slavery had schooled the black woman in self-reliance and self-sufficiency and that "neither economic necessity nor tradition had instilled in her the spirit of subordination to masculine authority."[1] The

Frazier thesis received support from other social scientists, including historians Kenneth Stampp and Stanley Elkins, both of whom held that slave men had been emasculated and stripped of their paternity rights by slave masters who left control of slave households to slave women.[2] In his infamous 1965 national report, Daniel Patrick Moynihan lent further confirmation to the Frazier thesis when he alleged that the fundamental problem with the modern black family was the "often reversed roles of husband and wife," and then traced the origin of the "problem" back to slavery.[3]

Partly in response to the criticism spawned by the Moynihan Report, historians reanalyzed antebellum source material, and the matriarchy thesis was debunked. For better or worse, said historians Robert Fogel and Stanley Engerman, the "dominant" role in slave society was played by men. Men were dominant, they said, because men occupied all managerial and artisan slots, and because masters recognized the male head of the family group. From historian John Blassingame we learned that by building furnishings and providing extra food for their families, men found indirect ways of gaining status. If a garden plot was to be cultivated, the husband "led" his wife in the family undertaking.[4] After a very thoughtful appraisal of male slave activities, historian Eugene Genovese concluded that "slaves from their own experience had come to value a two-parent, male-centered household, no matter how much difficulty they had in realizing the ideal."[5] Further tipping the scales toward patriarchal slave households, historian Herbert Gutman argued that the belief that matrifocal households prevailed among slaves was a misconception. He demonstrated that children were more likely to be named after their fathers than mothers, and that during the Civil War slave men acted like fathers and husbands by fighting for their freedom and by protecting their wives and children when they were threatened by Union troops or angry slaveholders.[6]

With the reinterpretation of male roles came a revision of female roles. Once considered dominant, slave women were now characterized as subordinated and sometimes submissive. Fogel and Engerman found proof of their subordinated status in the fact that they were excluded from working in plow gangs and did all of the household chores.[7] Genovese maintained that slave women's "attitude toward housework, especially cooking, and toward their own femininity," belied the conventional wisdom "according to which women unwittingly helped ruin their men by asserting themselves in the home, protecting their children, and assuming other normally masculine responsibilities."[8] Gutman found one Sea Island slave community where the black church imposed a submissive role upon married slave women.[9]

In current interpretations of the contemporary black family the woman's role has not been "feminized" as much as it has been "deemphasized." The stress in studies like those done by Carol Stack and Theodore Kennedy is not on roles per se but on the black family's ability to survive in flexible kinship networks that are viable bulwarks against discrimination and racism. These interpretations also make the point that black kinship patterns are not based exclusively on consanguineous relationships but are also determined by social contacts that sometimes have their basis in economic support.[10]

Clearly, then, the pendulum has swung away from the idea that women ruled slave households, and that their dominance during the slave era formed the foundation of the modern day matriarchal black family. But how far should that pendulum swing? This essay suggests that we should tread the road that leads to the patriarchal slave household and the contemporary amorphous black family with great caution. It suggests that, at least in relation to the slave family, too much emphasis has been placed on what men could not do rather than on what women could do and did. What follows is not a comprehensive study of female slavery, but an attempt to reassess Frazier's claim that slave women were self-reliant and self-sufficient through an examination of some of their activities, specifically their work, their control of particular resources, their contribution to their households and their ability to cooperate with each other on a daily basis. Further, this essay will examine some of the implications of these activities, and their probable impact on the slave woman's status in slave society, and the black family.

At the outset a few points must be made about the subject matter and the source material used to research it. Obviously, a study that concentrates solely on females runs the risk of overstating woman's roles and their importance in society. One must therefore keep in mind that this is only one aspect, although a very critical one, of slave family and community life. In addition, what follows is a synthesis of the probable sex role of the average slave woman on plantations with at least twenty slaves.[11] In the process of constructing this synthesis I have taken into account such variables as plantation size, crop, region of the South, and the personal idiosyncrasies of slave masters. Finally, in drawing conclusions about the sex role and status of slave women, I have detailed their activities and analyzed them in terms of what anthropologists know about women who do similar things in analogous settings. I took this approach for two reasons. First, information about female slaves cannot be garnered from sources left by slave women because they left few narratives, diaries, or letters. The dearth of source material makes it impossible to draw conclusions about the slave woman's feelings. Second, even given the ex-slave interviews, a rich source material for this subject, it is almost impossible to draw conclusions about female slave status from an analysis of their individual personalities. Comments such as that made by the slave woman, Fannie, to her husband Bob, "I don't want no sorry nigger around me," perhaps says something about Fannie, but not about all slave women.[12] Similarly, for every mother who grieved over the sale of her children there was probably a father whose heart was also broken. Here, only the activities of the slave woman will be examined in an effort to discern her status in black society.

Turning first to the work done by slave women, it appears that they did a variety of heavy and dirty labor, work which was also done by men. In 1853, Frederick Olmsted saw South Carolina slaves of both sexes carting manure on their heads to the cotton field where they spread it with their hands between the ridges in which cotton was planted. In Fayetteville, North Carolina, he noticed that women not only hoed and shovelled but they also cut down trees and drew wood.[13] The use of women as lumberjacks occurred quite frequently, especially in the lower South and Southwest, areas which retained a frontier quality during the antebellum era. Solomon Northrup, a kidnapped slave, knew women who wielded the axe so perfectly that the largest oak or sycamore fell before their well-directed blows. An Arkansas ex-slave remembered that her mother use to carry logs. On Southwestern plantations women did all kinds of work. In the region of the Bayou Boeuf women were expected to "plough, drag, drive team, clear wild lands, work on the highway," and do any other type of work required of them. In short, full female hands frequently did the same kind of work as male hands.[14]

It is difficult, however, to say how often they did the same kind of field work, and it would be a mistake to say that there was no differentiation of field labor on southern farms and plantations. The most common form of differentiation was that women hoed while men plowed. Yet, the exceptions to the rule were so numerous as to make a mockery of it. Many men hoed on a regular basis. Similarly, if a field had to be plowed and there were not enough male hands to do it, then it was not unusual for an overseer to command a strong woman to plow. This could happen on a plantation of twenty slaves or a farm of five.

It is likely, however, that women were more often called to do the heavy labor usually assigned to men after their child-bearing years. Pregnant women, and sometimes women breastfeeding infants, were usually given less physically demanding work.[15] If, as recent studies indicate, slave women began childbearing when about twenty years of age and had children at approximately two-and-a-half year intervals, at least until age thirty-five, slave women probably spent a considerable amount of time doing tasks which men did not do.[16] Pregnant and nursing women were classified as half-hands or three-quarter hands and such workers did only some of the work that was also done by full hands. For instance, it was not unusual for them to pick cotton or even hoe, work done on a regular basis by both sexes. But frequently, they were assigned to "light work" like raking stubble or pulling weeds, which was often given to children and the elderly.[17]

Slave women might have preferred to be exempt from such labor, but they might also have gained some intangibles from doing the same work as men. Anthropologists have demonstrated that in societies where men and women are engaged in the production of the same kinds of goods and where widespread private property is not a factor, participation in production gives women freedom and independence.[18] Since neither slave men nor women had access to, or control over, the products of their labor, parity in the field may have encouraged

229

equalitarianism in the slave quarters. In Southern Togo, for instance, where women work alongside their husbands in the fields because men do not alone produce goods which are highly valued, democracy prevails in relationships between men and women.[19]

But bondswomen did do a lot of traditional "female work" and one has to wonder whether this work, as well as the work done as a "half-hand", tallied on the side of female subordination. In the case of the female slave, domestic work was not always confined to the home, and often "woman's work" required skills that were highly valued and even coveted because of the place it could purchase in the higher social echelons of the slave world. For example, cooking was definitely "female work" but it was also a skilled occupation. Good cooks were highly respected by both blacks and whites, and their occupation was raised in status because the masses of slave women did not cook on a regular basis. Since field work occupied the time of most women, meals were often served communally. Female slaves therefore, for the most part, were relieved of this traditional chore, and the occupation of "cook" became specialized.[20]

Sewing too was often raised above the level of inferior "woman's work." All females at one time or another had to spin and weave. Occasionally each woman was given cloth and told to make her family's clothes, but this was unusual and more likely to happen on small farms than on plantations. During slack seasons women probably did more sewing than during planting and harvesting seasons, and pregnant women were often put to work spinning, weaving, and sewing. Nevertheless, sewing could be raised to the level of a skilled art, especially if a woman sewed well enough to make the white family's clothes. Such women were sometimes hired out and allowed to keep a portion of the profit they brought their master and mistress.[21]

Other occupations which were solidly anchored in the female domain, and which increased a woman's prestige, were midwifery and doctoring. The length of time and extent of training it took to become a midwife is indicated by the testimony of Clara Walker, a former slave interviewed in Arkansas, who remembered that she trained for five years under a doctor who became so lazy after she had mastered the job that he would sit down and let her do all the work. After her "apprenticeship" ended she delivered babies for both slave and free, black and white.[22] Other midwives learned the trade from a female relative, often their mother, and they in turn passed the skill on to another female relative.

A midwife's duty often extended beyond delivering babies, and they sometimes became known as "doctor women." In this capacity they cared for men, women, and children. Old women, some with a history of midwifery and some without, also gained respect as "doctor women." They "knowed a heap about yarbs [herbs]," recalled a Georgia ex-slave.[23] Old women had innumerable cures, especially for children's diseases, and since plantation "nurseries" were usually under their supervision, they had ample opportunity to practice their art. In sum, a good portion of the slaves' medical care, particularly that of women and children, was supervised by slave women.

Of course, not all women were hired-out seamstresses, cooks, or midwives; a good deal of "female work" was laborious and mundane. An important aspect of this work, as well as of the field work done by women, was that it was frequently done in female groups. As previously noted, women often hoed while men plowed. In addition, when women sewed they usually did so with other women. Quilts were made by women at gatherings called, naturally enough, "quiltins." Such gatherings were attended only by women and many former slaves had vivid recollections of them. The "quiltin's and spinnin' frolics dat de women folks had" were the most outstanding remembrances of Hattie Anne Nettles, an Alabama exslave.[24] Women also gathered, independent of male slaves, on Saturday afternoons to do washing. Said one ex-slave, "they all had a regular picnic of it as they would work and spread the clothes on the bushes and low branches of the tree to dry. They would get to spend the day together."[25]

In addition, when pregnant women did field work they sometimes did it together. On large plantations the group they worked in was sometimes known as the "trash gang." This gang, made up of pregnant women, women with nursing infants, children and old slaves, was primarily a female work gang.[26] Since it was the group that young girls worked with when just being initiated into the work world of the plantation, one must assume that it served some kind of socialization function. Most likely, many lessons about life were learned by 12-year-old girls from this group of women who were either pregnant or breastfeeding, or who were grandmothers many times over.

It has been noted that women frequently depended on slave midwives to bring children into the world; their dependence on other slave women did not end with childbirth but continued through the early life of their children. Sometimes women with infants took their children to the fields with them. Some worked with their children wrapped to their backs, others laid them under a tree. Frequently, however, an elderly woman watched slave children during the day while their mothers worked in the field. Sometimes the cook supervised young children at the master's house.[27] Mothers who were absent from their children most of the day, indeed most of the week, depended on these surrogate mothers to assist them in child socialization. Many ex-slaves remember these women affectionately. Said one South Carolinian: "De old lady, she looked after every blessed thing for us all day long en cooked for us right along wid de mindin'."[28]

Looking at the work done by female slaves in the antebellum South, therefore, we find that sex role differentiation in field labor was not absolute but that there was differentiation in other kinds of work. Domestic chores were usually done exclusively by women, and certain "professional" occupations were reserved for females. It would be a mistake to infer from this differentiation that it was the basis of male dominance. A less culturally biased conclusion would be that women's roles were different or complementary. For example, in her overview of African societies, Denise Paulme notes that in almost all African societies, women do most of the domestic chores, yet they lead lives that are quite independent of men. Indeed, according to Paulme, in Africa, "a wife's contribution to the needs of the household is direct and indispensable, and her husband is just as much in need of her as she of him."[29] Other anthropologists have suggested that we should not evaluate women's roles in terms of men's roles because in a given society, women may not perceive the world in the same way that men do.[30] In other words, men and women may share a common culture but on different terms, and when this is the case, questions of dominance and subservience are irrelevant.

The degree to which male and female ideologies are different is often suggested by the degree to which men and women are independently able to rank and order themselves and cooperate with members of their sex in the performance of their duties. In societies where women are not isolated from one another and placed under man's authority, where women cooperate in the performance of household tasks, where women form groups or associations, women's roles are usually complementary to those of men, and the female world exists independently of the male world. Because women control what goes on in their world, they rank and order themselves vis-à-vis other women, not men, and they are able to influence decisions made by their society because they exert pressure as a group. Ethnographic studies of the Igbo women of eastern Nigeria, the Ga women of central Accra in Ghana, and the Patani of southern Nigeria confirm these generalizations.[31] Elements of female slave society – the chores done by groups, the intrasex cooperation and dependency in the areas of child care and medical care, the existence of high echelon female slave occupations – may be an indication, not that slave women were inferior to slave men, but that the roles were complementary and that the female slave world allowed women the opportunity to rank and order themselves and obtain a sense of self which was quite apart from the men of their race and even the men of the master class.

That bondswomen were able to rank and order themselves is further suggested by evidence indicating that in the community of the slave quarters certain women were looked to for leadership. Leadership was based on either one or a combination of factors, including occupation, association with the master class, age, or number of children. It was manifested in all aspects of female slave life. For instance, Louis Hughes, an escaped slave, noted that each plantation had a "forewoman who . . . had charge of the female slaves and also the boys and girls from twelve to sixteen years of age, and all the old people that were feeble." Bennet H. Barrow repeatedly lamented the fact that Big Lucy, one of his oldest slaves, had more control over his female slaves than he did: "Anica, Center, Cook Jane, the better you treat them the worse they are. Big Lucy, the leader, corrupts every young negro in her power."[32] When Elizabeth Botume went to the Sea Islands after the Civil War, she had as house servant a young woman named Amy who performed her tasks slowly and sullenly until Aunt Mary arrived from Beaufort. In Aunt Mary's presence the obstreperous Amy was "quiet, orderly, helpful and painstaking."[33]

Another important feature of female life, bearing on the ability of women to rank and order themselves independently of men, was the control women exercised over each other by quarreling. In all kinds of sources there are indications that women were given to fighting and irritating each other. From Jesse Belflowers, the overseer of the Allston rice plantation in South Carolina, Adele Petigru Allston learned that "mostly mongst the Woman," there was "goodeal of quarling and disputing and telling lies."[34] Harriet Ware, a northern missionary, writing from the Sea Islands in 1863 blamed the turmoil she found in black community life on the "tongues of the women."[35] The evidence of excessive quarreling among women hints at the existence of a gossip network among female slaves. Anthropologists have found gossip to be a principal strategy used by women to control other women as well as men. Significantly, the female gossip network, the means by which community members are praised, shamed, and coerced, is usually found in societies where women are highly dependent on each other and where women work in groups or form female associations.[36]

In summary, when the activities of female slaves are compared to those of women in other societies a clearer picture of the female slave sex role emerges. It seems that slave women were schooled in self-reliance and self-sufficiency but the "self" was more likely the female slave collective than the individual slave woman. On the other hand, if the female world was highly stratified and if women cooperated with each other to a great extent, odds are that the same can be said of men, in which case neither sex can be said to have been dominant or subordinate.

There are other aspects of the female slave's life that suggest that her world was independent of the male slave's and that slave women were rather self-reliant. It has long been recognized that slave women did not derive traditional benefits from the marriage relationship, that there was no property to share and essential needs like food, clothing, and shelter were not provided by slave men. Since in almost all societies where men consistently control women, that control is based on male ownership and distribution of certain culturally valued subsistence goods, these realities of slave life had to contribute to female slave self-sufficiency and independence from slave men. The practice of "marrying abroad," having a spouse on a different plantation, could only have reinforced this tendency, for as ethnographers have found, when men live apart from women, they cannot control them.[37] We have yet to learn what kind of obligations brothers, uncles, and male cousins fulfilled for their female kin, but it is improbable that wives were controlled by husbands whom they saw only once or twice a week. Indeed, "abroad marriages" may have intensified female intradependency.

The fact that marriage did not yield traditional benefits for women, and that "abroad marriages" existed, does not mean that women did not depend on slave men for foodstuffs beyond the weekly rations, but since additional food was not guaranteed, it probably meant that women along with men had to take initiatives in supplementing slave diets. So much has been made of the activities of slave men in this sphere that the role of slave women has been overlooked.[38] Female house slaves, in particular, were especially able to supplement their family's diet. Mary Chesnut's maid, Molly, made no secret of the fact that she fed her offspring and other slave children in the Confederate politician's house. "Dey gets a little of all day's going," she once told Chesnut.[39] Frederick Douglass remembered that his grandmother was not only a good nurse but a "capital hand at catching fish and making the nets she caught them in."[40] Eliza Overton, an ex-slave, remembered how her mother stole, slaughtered, and cooked one of her master's hogs. Another ex-slave was not too bashful to admit that her mother "could hunt good ez any man."[41] Women, as well as men, were sometimes given the opportunity to earn money. Women often sold baskets they had woven, but they also earned money by burning charcoal for blacksmiths and cutting cordwood.[42] Thus, procuring extra provisions for the family was sometimes a male and sometimes a female responsibility, one that probably fostered a self-reliant and independent spirit.

The high degree of female cooperation, the ability of slave

women to rank and order themselves, the independence women derived from the absence of property considerations in the conjugal relationship, "abroad marriages," and the female slave's ability to provide supplementary foodstuffs are factors which should not be ignored in considerations of the character of the slave family. In fact, they conform to the criteria most anthropologists list for that most misunderstood concept – matrifocality.[43] Matrifocality is a term used to convey the fact that women *in their role as mothers* are the focus of familiar relationships. It does not mean that fathers are absent; indeed two-parent households can be matrifocal. Nor does it stress a power relationship where women rule men. When *mothers* become the focal point of family activity, they are just more central than are fathers to a family's continuity and survival as a unit. While there is no set model for matrifocality, Smith has noted that in societies as diverse as Java, Jamaica, and the Igbo of eastern Nigeria, societies recognized as matrifocal, certain elements are constant. Among these elements are female solidarity, particularly in regard to their cooperation within the domestic sphere. Another factor is the economic activity of women which enables them to support their children independent of fathers *if they desire to do so or are forced to do so*. The most important factor is the supremacy of the mother–child bond over all other relationships.[44]

Female solidarity and the "economic" contribution of bonds-women in the form of medical care, foodstuffs, and money has already been discussed; what can be said of the mother–child bond? We know from previous works on slavery that certain slaveholder practices encouraged the primacy of the mother–child relationship.[45] These included the tendency to sell mothers and small children as family units, and to accord special treatment to pregnant and nursing women and women who were exceptionally prolific. We also know that a husband and wife secured themselves somewhat from sale and separation when they had children.[46] Perhaps what has not been emphasized enough is the fact that it was the wife's childbearing and her ability to keep a child alive that were the crucial factors in the security achieved in this way. As such, the insurance against sale which husbands and wives received once women had borne and nurtured children heads the list of female contributions to slave households.

236

In addition to slaveowner encouragement of close mother–child bonds there are indications that slave women themselves considered this their most important relationship.[47] Much has been made of the fact that slave women were not ostracized by slave society when they had children out of "wedlock."[48] Historians have usually explained this aspect of slave life in the context of slave sexual norms which allowed a good deal of freedom to young unmarried slave women. However, the slave attitude concerning "illegitimacy" might also reveal the importance that women, and slave society as a whole, placed on the mother role and the mother–child dyad. For instance, in the Alabama community studied by Charles S. Johnson in the 1930s, most black women felt no guilt and suffered no loss of status when they bore children out of wedlock. This was also a community in which, according to Johnson, the role of the mother was "of much greater importance than in the more familiar American family group."[49] Similarly, in his 1956 study of Guiana, Smith found the mother–child bond to be the strongest in the whole matrix of social relationships, and it was manifested in a lack of condemnation of women who bore children out of legal marriage.[50]

The mystique which shrouded conception and childbirth is perhaps another indication of the high value slave women placed on motherhood and childbirth. Many female slaves claimed that they were kept ignorant of the details of conception and childbirth. For instance, a female slave interviewed in Nashville noted that at age 12 or 13, she and an older girl went around to parsley beds and hollow logs looking for newborn babies. "They didn't tell you a thing," she said. Another ex-slave testified that her mother told her that doctors brought babies, and another Virginia ex-slave remembered that "people was very particular in them days. They wouldn't let children know anything."[51] This alleged naiveté can perhaps be understood if examined in the context of motherhood as a *rite de passage*. Sociologist Joyce Ladner found that many black girls growing up in a ghetto area of St Louis in the late 1960s were equally ignorant of the facts concerning conception and childbirth. Their mothers had related only "old wives' tales" about sex and childbirth even though the community was one where the mother–child bond took precedence over both the husband–wife bond and the father–child bond. In this St Louis area, having a child was considered the most important turning point in a black girl's life, a more important *rite de passage* than marriage.[52] Once a female had a child all sorts of privileges were bestowed upon her. That conception and childbirth were cloaked in mystery is perhaps an indication of the sacredness of motherhood. When considered in tandem with the slave attitude toward "illegitimacy," the mother–child relationship emerges as the most important familiar relationship in the slave family.

Finally, any consideration of the slave's attitude about motherhood and the expectations which the slave community had of childbearing women must consider the African slave's African heritage. In many West African tribes the mother–child relationship is and has always been the most important of all human relationships.[53] To cite one of many possible examples, while studying the role of women in Ibo society, Sylvia Leith-Ross asked an Ibo woman how many of ten husbands would love their wives and how many of ten sons would love their mothers. The answer she received demonstrated the precedence which the mother–child tie took: "Three husbands would love their wives but seven sons would love their mothers."[54]

When E. Franklin Frazier wrote that slave women were self-reliant and that they were strangers to male slave authority he evoked an image of an overbearing, even brawny woman. In all probability visions of Sapphire danced in our heads as we learned from Frazier that the female slave played the dominant role in courtship, marriage, and family relationships, and later from Elkins that male slaves were reduced to childlike dependency on the slave master. Both the Frazier and Elkins theses have been overturned by historians who have found that male slaves were more than just visitors to their wives' cabins, and women something other than unwitting allies in the degradation of their men. Sambo and Sapphire may continue to find refuge in American folklore but they will never again be legitimized by social scientists.

However, beyond the image evoked by Frazier is the stark reality that slave women did not play the traditional female role as it was defined in nineteenth-century America, and regardless of how hard we try to cast her in a subordinate or submissive role in relation to slave men, we will have difficulty reconciling that role with the plantation realities. When we consider the work done by women in groups, the existence of upper echelon female slave jobs, the intradependence of women in childcare and medical care; if we presume that the quarreling or "fighting and disputing" among slave women is evidence of a gossip network and that certain women were elevated by their peers to positions of respect, then what we are confronted with are slave women who are able, within the limits set by slaveowners, to rank and order their female world, women who identified and cooperated more with other slave women than with slave men. There is nothing abnormal about this. It is a feature of many societies around the world, especially where strict sex role differentiation is the rule.

Added to these elements of female interdependence and cooperation were the realities of chattel slavery that decreased the bondsman's leverage over the bondswoman, made female self-reliance a necessity, and encouraged the retention of the African tradition which made the mother–child bond more sacred than the husband–wife bond. To say that this amounted to a matrifocal family is not to say a bad word. It is not to say that it precluded male–female cooperation, or mutual respect, or traditional romance and courtship. It does, however, help to explain how African–American men and women survived chattel slavery.

NOTES

The Editor gratefully acknowledges permission to reprint material from "Female slaves: sex roles and status in the antebellum plantation South," by Deborah G. White. *Journal of Family History* Fall (1983): 248–60. Copyright © 1983. Used by permission of JAI Press, Inc.

1 E. Franklin Frazier (1939) *The Negro Family in the United States* (Chicago), 125.
2 Kenneth Stampp (1956) *The Peculiar Institution: Slavery in the Ante-Bellum South* (New York), 344; Stanley Elkins (1959) *Slavery: A Problem in American Institutional and Intellectual Life* (Chicago), 130.
3 Daniel Patrick Moynihan (1965) *The Negro Family: The Case for National Action* (Washington, D.C.), 31.
4 John Blassingame (1972) *The Slave Community: Plantation Life in the Antebellum South* (New York), 92.
5 Eugene Genovese (1974) *Roll, Jordan, Roll: The World the Slaves Made* (New York), 491–2.

6 Herbert Gutman (1976) *The Black Family in Slavery and Freedom, 1750–1925* (New York), 188–91, 369–86.
7 Robert William Fogel and Stanley Engerman (1974), *Time on the Cross: The Economics of American Negro Slavery* (Boston), 141–2.
8 Genovese, *Roll, Jordan, Roll*, 500.
9 Gutman, *Black Family*, 72.
10 Carol Stack (1974) *All Our Kin* (New York), Theodore Kennedy (1980) *You Gotta Deal With It: Black Family Relations in a Southern Community* (New York).
11 The majority of the available source material seems to be from plantations or farms with more than one or two slave families. Relatively few ex-slave interviewees admit to being one of only three or four slaves. If Genovese is right and at least half of the slaves in the South lived on units of twenty slaves or more, this synthesis probably describes the life of a majority of slave women. Genovese, *Roll, Jordan, Roll*, 7.
12 Ophelia S. Egypt, J. Masuoka, and Charles S. Johnson (eds) (1945) *Unwritten History of Slavery: Autobiographical Accounts of Negro Ex-Slaves* (Nashville, Tenn.), 184.
13 Frederick L. Olmsted (1971) *The Cotton Kingdom*, ed. David Freeman Hawke (New York), 67, 81.
14 Gilbert Osofsky (ed.) (1969) *Puttin' On Ole Massa* (New York) 308–9, 313; George Rawick (ed.) (1972) *The American Slave: A Composite Autobiography*, 19 vols (Westport, Conn.), vol. 10, pt 5, 54 . . . [Further citations on women doing "men's" work omitted here.]
15 See Rawick, *American Slave*, vol. 4, pt 3, 160; Louis Hughes (1987) *Thirty Years a Slave* (Milwaukee, Wisc.), 22, 41; Frederick L. Olmsted (1856) *A Journey in the Seaboard Slave States* (New York), 430 . . .
16 Although Fogel and Engerman cite the slave woman's age at first birth as 22.5, other historians, including Gutman and Dunn, found that age to be substantially lower – Gutman a range from 17 to 19, and Dunn (average age at first birth on the Mount Airy, Virginia plantation) 19.22 years. More recently, economists Trussel and Steckel have found the age to be 20.6 years. See Fogel and Engerman, *Time on the Cross*, 137–8; Richard Dunn (1977) "The tale of two plantations: slave life at Mesopotamia in Jamaica and Mount Airy in Virginia, 1799–1828," *William and Mary Quarterly* 34: 58; Gutman, *Black Family*, 50, 74, 124, 171; James Trussel and Richard Steckel (1974) "The age of slaves at menarche and first birth," *Journal of Interdisciplinary History* 8: 504.
17 For examples, see n. 15.
18 Leith Mullings (1976) "Women and economic change in Africa," in Nancy J. Hakfin and Edna G. Bay (eds) (1976) *Women in Africa: Studies in Social and Economic Change* (Stanford, Cal.), 243–4; Karen Sacks (1974) "Engels revisited: women, the organization of production, and private property," in Michelle Rosaldo and Louise Lamphere (eds) *Women, Culture, and Society* (Stanford, Cal.), 213–22.

19 Guy Rocher, R. Clignet, and F. N. N'sougan (1962) "Three preliminary studies: Canada, Ivory Coast, Togo," *International Social Science Journal* 14: 151–2.

20 For an example of the privileges this occupation *could* involve, see Mary Boykin Chesnut (1905) *A Diary from Dixie* (New York), 24.

21 Rawick, *American Slave*, vol. 17, 158, vol. 2, pt 2, 114; White Hill Plantation Books, Southern Historical Collection, University of North Carolina, 13.

22 Rawick, *American Slave*, vol. 10, pt 5, 21; see also ibid., vol 6, 256, 318. . . .

23 Ibid., vol. 2, pt 2, 112; see also ibid., vol 2, pt 2, 55. . . .

24 Rawick, *American Slave*, vol. 6, 297, 360.

25 Ibid., vol. 7, 315.

26 Sometimes pregnant women were made to weave, spin, or sew, in which case they usually did it with other women. The term "trash gang" was probably used only on very large plantations, but units of pregnant women, girls, elderly females, as well as boys and elderly men, probably worked together on a farm with twenty slaves. See n. 14.

27 See, for instance, Olmsted, *Seaboard Slave States*, 423, and Ulrich B. Phillips (ed.), (1909) *Plantation and Frontier Documents* (Cleveland, Ohio), 127.

28 Rawick, *American Slave*, vol. 2, pt 1, 99.

29 Denise Paulme (ed.) (1963) *Women of Tropical Africa* (Berkeley, Cal.), 4.

30 Susan Carol Rogers (1978) "Women's place: a critical review of anthropological theory," *Comparative Studies in Society and History* 20: 152–62.

31 Nancy Tanner (1974) "Matrifocality in Indonesia and Africa and among black Americans," in Rosaldo and Lamphere, *Women, Culture, and Society*, 146–50; Nancy B. Leis, "Women in groups: Ijaw women's associations," in ibid., 221–42; Claire Robertson (1976) "Ga women and socioeconomic change in Accra, Ghana," in Hakfin and Bay, *Women in Africa*, 115–32.

32 Hughes, *Thirty Years a Slave*, 22; [Edwin] Adams Davis (1943) *Plantation Life in the Florida Parishes of Louisiana 1836–1846 as Reflected in the Diary of Bennet H. Barrow* (New York), 191. Big Lucy thwarted all of Barrow's instructions and her influence extended to the men also; see Davis, 168, 173.

33 Elizabeth Hyde Botume (1893) *First Days Amongst the Contrabands* (Boston), 132. On a given plantation there could be a number of slave women recognized by other slave women as leaders. For instance, when Frances Kemble first toured Butler Island she found that the cook's position went to the oldest wife in the settlement.

34 J. E. Easterby (ed.) (1945) *The South Carolina Rice Plantations as Revealed in the Papers of Robert W. Allston*, 291.

35 Elizabeth Ware Pearson (ed.) (1906) *Letters From Port Royal Written at the Time of the Civil War* (Boston), 210. Additional evidence that

women quarreled can be found in a pamphlet stating the terms of an overseer's contract: "Fighting, particularly amongst the women . . . is to be always rigorously punished." Similarly, an ex-slave interviewed in Georgia noted that "sometimes de women uster git whuppins for fightin." See John Spencer Basset (1925) *The Southern Plantation Overseer, As Revealed in His Letters* (Northampton, Mass.), 32, and Rawick, *American Slave*, vol. 12, pt 2, 57.

36 Gossip is one of many means by which women influence political decisions and interpersonal relationships. In Taiwan, for instance, women gather in the village square and whisper to each other. In other places, such as among the Marina of Madagascar, women gather and shout loud insults at men or other women. In still other societies, such as the black ghetto area studied by Carol Stack, the gossip network takes the form of a grapevine. See Michelle Rosaldo (1974) "Woman, culture and society: a theoretical overview," in Rosaldo and Lamphere (eds) *Woman, Culture and Society*, 10–11, Margery Wolf, "Chineses women: old skill in a new context," in ibid., 162, and Stack, *All Our Kin*, 109–15.

37 For instance, it is thought that Iroquois women obtained a high degree of political and economic power partly because of the prolonged absences of the males due to trading and warfare: John A. Noon (1949) *Law and Government of the Grand River Iroquois* (New York), 30–1. See also Rosaldo, *Woman, Culture and Society*, 36, 39.

38 Of male slaves who provided extra food, John Blassingame wrote: "The slave who did such things for his family gained not only the approbation of his wife, but he also gained status in the quarters." According to Genovese, "the slaves would have suffered much more than many in fact did from malnutrition and the hidden hungers of nutritional deficiencies if men had not taken the initiative to hunt and trap animals." See Blassingame, *Slave Community*, 92; Genovese, *Roll, Jordan, Roll*, 486.

39 Chesnut, *Diary From Dixie*, 348.

40 Frederick Douglass (1855) *My Bondage and My Freedom* (New York), 27.

41 Rawick, *American Slave*, vol. 11, 53, 267.

42 Olmsted, *The Cotton Kingdom*, 26; Rawick, *American Slave*, vol. 7, 23.

43 Nancie Gonzalez (1970) "Toward a definition of matrifocality," in Norman E. Whitten, Jr. and John F. Szwed (eds) *Afro–American Anthropology: Contemporary Perspectives* (New York), 31–43; Raymond T. Smith (1956) *The Negro Family in British Guiana: Family Structure and Social Status in the Villages* (London), 257–60; Tanner, "Matrifocality," 129–56.

44 Raymond T. Smith (1973) "The matrifocal family," in Jack Goody (ed.) *The Character of Kinship* (London), 125, 139–42.

45 Bassett, *Plantation Overseer*, 31, 139, 141; Frances Anne Kemble (1961) *Journal of a Residence on a Georgian Plantation*, ed. by John

A. Scott (New York), 95, 127, 179; Phillips, *Plantation and Frontier Documents*, I, 109, 312.

46 Gutman, *Black Family*, 76.

47 Gutman suggests that the husband-wife and father-child dyads were as strong as the mother–child bond. I think not. It has been demonstrated that in most Western Hemisphere black societies as well as in Africa, the mother–child bond is the strongest and most enduring bond. This does not mean that fathers have no relationship with their children or that they are absent. The father–child relationship is of a more formal nature than the mother–child relationship. Moreover, the conjugal relationship appears, on the surface, to be similar to the western norm in that two-parent households prevail, but, when competing with consanguineous relationships, conjugal affiliations usually lose. See Gutman, *Black Family*, 79; Raymond T. Smith (1970) "The nuclear family in Afro–American kinship," *Journal of Comparative Family Studies*, 1: 62–70; Smith, "Matrifocal family," 129; Stack, *All Our Kin*, 102–5.

48 Genovese, *Roll, Jordan, Roll*, 465–6; Gutman, *Black Family*, 117–18.

49 Charles S. Johnson (1934) *Shadow of the Plantation* (Chicago), 29, 66–70.

50 Smith, *Negro Family in British Guiana*, 109, 158, 250–1.

51 Egypt, *Unwritten History of Slavery*, 8, 10; Rawick, *American Slave*, vol. 16, 15, 25; vol. 7, 3–24; vol. 2, 51–2.

52 Joyce Ladner (1971) *Tomorrow's Tomorrow: The Black Woman* (New York), 177–263.

53 Paulme, *Women of Tropical Africa*, 14; Tanner, "Matrifocality," 147; Mayer Fortes (1939) "Kinship and marriage among the Ashanti," in A. R. Radcliffe-Brown and Daryll Forde (eds) *African Systems of Kinship and Marriage* (London), 127.

54 Sylvia Leith-Ross (1939) *African Women: A Study of the Ibo of Nigeria* (London), 127.

FURTHER READING

For bibliographical guidance on the slave South, students can turn to several of the essays in John B. Boles and Evelyn Thomas Nolen (eds) (1987) *Interpreting Southern History: Historiographical Essays in Honor of Sanford W. Higginbotham* (Baton Rouge, La.). Peter J. Parish (1989) *Slavery: History and Historians* (New York), also offers an excellent guide to the literature on slavery in the American South, including those important areas, such as slavery in the colonial period of US history, neglected in the present volume.

The Introduction and the notes for each essay, as well as the full volumes of the authors excerpted here, are places to begin for students who wish to pursue the themes highlighted in this volume. Other important works to consult are Willie Lee Rose (1982) *Slavery and Freedom*, ed. by William W. Freehling (New York); Kenneth S. Greenberg (1985) *Masters and Statesmen: The Political Culture of American Slavery* (Baltimore), and (1990) "The nose, the lie, and the duel in the antebellum South," *American Historical Review* 95: 57–74; James Oakes (1982) *The Ruling Race: A History of American Slaveholders* (New York); Lawrence Shore (1986) *Southern Capitalists: The Ideological Leadership of an Elite* (Chapel Hill, N.C.); Suzanne Lebsock (1984), *The Free Women of Petersburg: Status and Culture in a Southern Town, 1784–1860* (New York); Jean E. Friedman (1985) *The Enclosed Garden: Women and Community in the Evangelical South, 1830–1900* (Chapel Hill, N.C.); Jane Turner Censer (1984) *North Carolina Planters and Their Children, 1800–1860* (Baton Rouge, La.); Jacqueline Jones (1982) "My mother was much of a woman: black women, work, and the family under slavery," *Feminist Studies* 8: 235–70; Orville Vernon Burton (1985) *In My*

Father's House Are Many Mansions: Family and Community in Edgefield, South Carolina (Chapel Hill, N.C.); and Charles Joyner (1984) *Down by the Riverside: A South Carolina Slave Community* (Urbana, Ill.).

One important direction for recent scholarship, not represented here, has been studies of the place of the white non-slaveholding majority and of small slaveowners in the South's society and culture. An overview is offered in Bruce Collins (1985) *White Society in the Antebellum South* (London). Local and state studies, often the best way to investigate this aspect of southern society, include Barbara J. Fields (1985) *Slavery and Freedom on the Middle Ground: Maryland During the Nineteenth Century* (New Haven, Conn.); the first part of Steven Hahn (1983) *The Roots of Southern Populism: Yeoman Farmers and the Transformation of the Georgia Upcountry, 1850–1890* (New York); Robert C. Kenzer (1987) *Kinship and Neighborhood in a Southern Community: Orange County, North Carolina, 1849–1881* (Knoxville, Tenn.); Randolph B. Campbell (1983) *A Southern Community in Crisis: Harrison County, Texas, 1850–1880* (Austin, Tex.); John C. Inscoe (1989) *Mountain Masters, Slavery, and the Sectional Crisis in Western North Carolina* (Knoxville, Tenn.); and my own (1985) *Plain Folk and Gentry in a Slave Society: White Liberty and Black Slavery in Augusta's Hinterlands* (Middletown, Conn.).

Comparative studies are also important in current scholarship on the Old South. See especially Peter Kolchin (1987) *Unfree Labor: American Slavery and Russian Serfdom* (Cambridge, Mass.); Shearer Davis Bowman (1980) "Antebellum planters and Vormarz Junkers in comparative perspective," *American Historical Review* 85: 779–808; Stuart B. Schwartz (1982) "Patterns of slaveholdings in the Americas," *American Historical Review* 87; and the recent synthesis of scholarship by Herbert S. Klein (1989) *African Slavery in Latin America and the Caribbean* (New York).